AGAIN

If Christ Came Again

By

Lee Roy Neal

© 2002 by Lee Roy Neal. All rights reserved.

No part of this book may be reproduced, stored in a retrieval system, or transmitted by any means, electronic, mechanical, photocopying, recording, or otherwise, without written permission from the author.

ISBN: 1-4033-2561-8 (e-book)
ISBN: 1-4033-2562-6 (Paperback)
ISBN: 1-4033-2563-4 (Hardcover)

Library of Congress Control Number: 2002091600

This book is printed on acid free paper.

Printed in the United States of America
Bloomington, IN

1stBooks - rev. 08/07/02

DEDICATION

To my son, Lee Roy Neal II
For all the times when we have not been on the same beam, my love
for you has remained steadfast, unmovable and everlasting

AMOR VINCIT OMNIA

FOREWORD

We live in a time of turmoil, uncertainty and complication; a world so filled with selfishness and disappointments; a world rife with riots and violence that I sometimes wonder how anyone could face a single new day without a sure knowledge that he does not have to travel alone: that somewhere, out there, was help. Someone who was as near as breathing who was as close as a heart beat in case of a crisis or who could lend a hand when one's own resources were expended.

This is not a new feeling for it has ever been so, and God knew this, for over 2000 years ago, He sent His Son to come into the world, to be born as a tiny baby to be born in a small country held captive by the Godless Roman Empire. The babe was to grow up and live among the poorest of the poor.

He came and He lived among man as the very Son of God, and His only crime during that life time was to get in the way of some church officials who had political ambitions. It mattered not that this Man had the power to heal the sick, even the power to raise the dead back to life. Yes, it mattered not that Jesus did only good during his 33 years of existence on earth. He was persecuted, arrested, illegally tried and was executed in a horrible manner by the officials of the traditional church. The very people who were supposed to lead the people to a higher ground.

I often hear people lament the Crucifixion of Jesus saying that they would have liked to have been living then so that they could have done something in an effort to prevent this tragedy., this evil perpetrated by the then existing church leaders.

I began to wonder, and after several years, I came to the conclusion that if Jesus had come to earth in the twentieth century instead of the first century, the same fate would befall him.. The same group of people would instigate the tragedy a second time.

With this in mind, I have written AGAIN. It is hoped that in the reading of it you might once again fall in love with the Savior.

Lee Roy Neal
Athens, Texas, 2000

Again
If Christ Came Again

PART ONE

Lee Roy Neal

CHAPTER ONE

"It's time, Joe, I know it's time." The young girl tried hard not to scream as the pain wrapped itself across her body once again. Her dark eyes reflected the rising fear in those of her husband despite his efforts to show a calmness he did not feel. He tried to show a man in control as he slowly walked to the small gas heater to turn it higher, but he found that it was as high as it would go. The little stove, made to heat a small bath room, was fighting a losing battle against the cold air creeping into the room. Joe's dark hair fell over his eyes as he stood. Fighting his rising panic he tried to brush it back with a callused hand. He crossed the room to the bed and again tucked the covers about his wife. He saw a throw-rug on the floor and also placed this over her shaking body.

"I'll go find a doctor, sweetheart. Surely here in New York there must be one near here. I'll find one and convince him to come here and deliver the baby" He tried to show a bravado he did not feel. "You'll be all right, dear. I'll try not to be long." He pulled a ragged slipover sweater over his head and then donned an old coat. He kissed his wife on her damp forehead and whispered an endearment in her ear.

Joe raced down the tenement stairway, his feet adroitly missing beer cans and other debris scattered in the stairwell. Smells of offal assaulted his nostrils as he reached a landing where there was a communal bathroom. The smell of cooking cabbage mingled with the polluted air.

He brushed besides some teenagers just coming in the front door of the old brown stone building. A blast of frigid air assailed his body as he started down the steps to the front walk Before he could button the top of his coat, a blast raced down to his chest. He leaped down the last two steps to the street and almost tripped over a pile of plastic garbage bags covered with snow.. The storm was picking up speed. A savage blizzard had rolled in from Canada the day before and had grounded planes and delayed trains and had brought all sorts of traffic to a halt. The great city of New York lay almost helpless beneath the white blanket.

Now it began again falling before him steadily. The deserted side walks were white and the streets virgin with not a single track to disturb the purity. He heard the mournfully crying snow plows on Fifth Avenew, just a block away. They were illustrating a lesson in futility as the cotton stuff rapidly replaced itself as the plow moved slowly up the street. Parked cars and lamp posts were capped with a growing mound of crystal looking like giant sugar loaves in the growing darkness, He turned to his right and bent his head into the wind. His feet stirred up miniature cyclones as he walked. It was trying to snow again, and the sleet that was its companion stung his nose and ears with harsh stings.

The few trees growing in concrete tubs whipped and lashed as the wind blew them in different directions. The buildings seemed to huddle together as if they might join forces to beat the storm. Drifts of snow had already piled on steps and against buildings and even on the window sills. Chimneys belched black smoke and steam rose from almost every building forming white clouds that suddenly disappeared in the wind... Joe was conscious of the stinging and the burning of his face as the sleet attacked him in earnest. His ears were becoming numb.

Joe tried to think. He remembered seeing a doctor's sign somewhere along here. He cursed his neglect for not locating one before now., but the baby was not due for two weeks yet. The tiny radio in their apartment had warned anyone against venturing outside in weather like this storm. It had been predicted that this would be the coldest December seen in New York in many many years.

Few people could be seen as Joe plodded along. His eyes watered, and he tried to blink the water away so that he could see.. Joe felt that today was the dreariest day of his 26 years of life. Even the Christmas season did little to cheer him up. He supposed that his melancholy was blunted a bit because of the Christmas season. He bent his body almost double so as to give the wind less of a target. He lifted his head now and then to see where he was going. Snow came at him at an angle and some found its way down his collar in spite of his efforts to keep it out. He passed a Mom and Pop type store and saw that it was closed. The iron bars over the window and doors sported a new coat of sparkling white snow. A catenary of cardboard letters hung in the window saying MERRY CHRISTMAS. Now and then a snow slide fell from a roof, and once he barely escaped being buried. He passed one tenement and saw a pile of garbage bags covered with snow making them look like huge piles of cotton. He came to one corner where a group of buildings had been razed to make room for more and bigger slums. Drifts of snow several stories high were piled against one remaining building that had somehow escaped the wrecking ball.. Now the sky showed its self, and it was a winter pale and now and then the sun managed to get a ray in edge-wise. He passed more buildings with more embattled trees in concrete containers, each carrying a load of the white stuff causing the limbs to bend toward the earth. Joe's thrift-store shoes made squashing noises with each new step. He could feel the wetness between his toes. Steam from his breath rose in front of his face and as he lifted his head he saw a bright Neon sign on a bank building giving the time and the temperature. The large 10 made him feel even colder.

Somewhere an elevated train left Grand Central Station, and as it reached ground surface it seemed to scream as it was embraced by the frigid cold, its whistles making mournful lonesome sounds. As the train reached the East River bridge, it let forth another howl from its main whistle, full of lostness and despair reflecting, surely, the heartbreak of someone on board..

Joe hated trains for usually some traveler was enroute to sorrow or tragedy waiting at the end of the ride. At best someone aboard harbored the pain of separation from a loved one., He plodded on, passing steps after steps leading up to the front doors of the buildings. He looked in vain for a sign he remembered seeing somewhere around here. In his mind he remembered a small sign announcing the location of a doctor's office. He noticed people inside windows; children with wonder in their eyes, their faces showing the strain of being good just before Christmas. He saw happiness on faces that usually wore a frown of poverty sad futility in this part of the city.

Joe thought of his one room flat, a walk-up with a fifth-hand kerosene stove that was no match for weather under 50 degrees. he thought of sparse work, for December was a bad time for a cabinet maker to find work. Joe was tall and thin, his waist a bare 30 inches. His lithness could be attributed to hard work, even missed meals as a youth or a combination of the two. His dancing blue eyes had fluttered many a girl's heart. Usually his eyes were vivid and full of laughter, but of late worry had taken over. His cheekbones were high, and his nose had a slight hook above his mouth from which almost perfect white teeth were always visible.. He wore a small pointed beard that was so popular with most young men in the late 1950's. His lips matched his rosy cheeks, and now and then a pink tongue moistened his lips and darted back before the sleet could take a nip.. His brows above his eyes were thin as if shaped by a barber. His forehead was extra broad and his hair, almost black, framed an undeniably handsome face. He usually walked with a slight swagger, not from vanity, but from a self-confidence that would never allow defeat to enter his mind. To quit never occurred to Joe whatever the circumstances.

Joe bent even lower into the determined wind as the train let out a final wail as it headed for open country. He placed both hands over his now brittle ears. He began to realize the futility of the task before him: first, to find a doctor, and secondly, to find a doctor old-fashioned enough to make house calls, and thirdly, a doctor who would come before the color green was flashed in front of his eyes. Joe realized that he did not have even one dollar to offer on the altar of greed.

Mary, his precious wife of nine months, had began experiencing pains last night: pains that heralded the outset of birth. Just this morning she felt that time had run out. Just minutes ago, she was sure that the time of birth was at hand. His feet became frantic as he looked and looked..

The sun had given up the battle and was hiding above the storm. He turned into another street and met the world's biggest optimist: an old man pushing a fruit cart across the ice, the cart obviously nearing the end of its existence. "Fresh fruits" the feeble voice cried and the words fell on nonexistent ears. Joe could not help but feel sorry for one worse off than he was.

The wind caught the cuff of his trousers and he felt the icy fingers fondle his navel. He shuddered and stomped his feet for want of anything better to do. He saw a young girl about sixteen, coming toward him. He stepped off the curb to give her room to pass on the walk. As she passed she lifted bashful eyes to glance at him and then hurried on leaving a whiff of cheap perfume. He noticed that her reddish hair had a yellow scarf tied over it and tied beneath her chin. The scarf looked new, probably an early Christmas gift. She was likely a servant girl headed for the big houses over on Park Avenue.

Joe tried to focus his eyes. He knew the sign was somewhere around this area. He knew it. He plodded on. The wind became stronger and some lazy snow was flung in his face dashing his hopes and bruising his faith..

How was he going to be able to persuade a doctor, providing he ever found one, to come to Mary when he had no money.? He had sure hated to leave Mary, but what other choice was there? They had to have help. He knew he would be useless in helping her give birth. He had never lived on a farm where the opportunity to see animals give birth was common. O, sure, he and Mary knew the fundamentals, but nothing of the actual thing. Their parents had moved away soon after Joe and Mary married, and the few friends they had were about their own ages and were just as ignorant about birthing as were Joe and Mary.

Joe admitted that months ago he should have had Mary seeing a doctor, but there had been barely enough money for rent and food. Few people now days could afford custom made cabinet work and furniture in their homes, and in the mid-fifties, people had taken to the mass produced products, so Joe had been devoid of many customers. He knew he was a fine cabinet maker. All who had come in contact with his work were most lavish in their praise of his talents. He had learned his trade from his father and he would not turn out a shoddy piece of furniture, no matter what. Always it was money, money, money, or the lack of it had been formost in the young couple's minds.

He began to walk faster. Perhaps it was along here where he had noticed the location of the sign and the doctor's office. It could have been the next street over. He plodded up to the traffic light and turned to the right.. He saw the bright cherry red of the light reflected in the snow and the colored flakes looked like rays from a Buck Rogers episode.

Lee Roy Neal

As he turned into the next street, the snow fell more abundantly.. It was wetter and colder than before. He was conscious of a lump of fear forming in his chest.. A light from a large window lighted the walk a bright yellow as if to defy the hissing snow and battering wind.

This street sported better houses and Christmas decorations. Joe noticed that his tracks disappeared as soon as he lifted his foot, leaving no trace that he had ever been there or that he had ever existed in the world. He thought that this was a like many people who lived in this section of the city: they were born, grew up and died and there was nobody to take notice.

Now he saw that there were better Christmas decorations in the homes and businesses. Even though most of the houses were over 100 years old, some were quite nice, even beautiful in the snow.. Some houses had twisted marble colums at the top of the steps leading up from street level. Most of the steps here had been shoveled, and he saw no garbage bags piled anywhere.. From the top of each building, huge red brick chimneys belched black smoke. "Good for them," Joe muttered," at least they are warm.

He plodded on, his watery eyes darting from side to side. Suddenly his heart leaped. There was the sign! As he looked he remembered having seen it often. He chided himself for his faulty memory. It hung in a black twisted iron frame, and even though the sign waved violently in the wind, some snow managed to hang on for the free ride.. He saw part of the name and the letters 'M.D.' at the end.. He ran up the steps and slipped on a patch of ice and fell back down to the street.. He cried out as his ankle turned, sending sharp pains racing up his leg. He forgot the pain and managed to get up the steps again and pushed the bell button. As he waited, he noticed a small brass plaque beneath the button. It read **Homer Lacy, M.D.**

His ankle hurt badly as the door opened and a girl in a maid's uniform stood there.. She asked him to enter the foyer, closing the door quickly. A voice from the other room asked: "Who is it Jeannie?" Before she could answer, the doctor entered the room picking his teeth with a gold tooth pick. Joe looked at the man with the drooping jowls, the florid face, the gargantuan nose. He had small beady eyes, and his bald head shown as if someone had waxed and polished it.. His ears reminded Joe of those of a pig, they stuck out from his head and they were pointed and leaned slightly forward.. His thick lips were overly full as they ruled above his small mouth and double chin. Everything about the man reeked of the fact that he could not resist rich food and plenty of it. His eyebrows were jet black above icy blue eyes..

"What can I do for you, young man?" He belched. "It had better be really urgent to disturb me and my family at Christmas time."

"Oh, sir," Joe licked his lips, his heart pounding. He rebelled at even the thought of this man touching Mary. "My wife is about to have a baby."

"What business is that of mine. It's not my fault." He tried to get a stubborn piece of meat from a tooth. "Go to your own doctor and don't bother me about it." He belched. "If you poor chaps spent more time working instead of in bed, there would be less demand for us doctors."

"We don't have a doctor." Pleading colored Joe's words. "She's in labor now. We live just two blocks away. Please hurry, sir. I'll carry your bag."

"I don't want to go out in this storm," he smiled, "but as a doctor, I must remember my oath. I will do it this once as a favor to you." Joe's heart leaped in gratitude as the doctor continued speaking. "I will have to have $100 now and you can pay the remaining $900 a payment each week."

"But, doctor," Joe gasped, "I don't have $100!"

"How much do you have?"

"I don't have any money at all, but I'll pay you every cent. I will do any kind of work. Please, doctor."

"Take her to the charity ward at Belleview."

"I can't do that sir," Joe cried. "It's over a mile away and it's still snowing. She would freeze to death before we got halfway."

"I can't help you." The fat man turned and left the hallway and slammed the door, The maid reappeared and showed Joe out and Joe found himself out on the walk again.

It was doubtful if even Joe could explain his inner feelings at this point as he stood in the blowing snow at the foot of the steps. The wind was at his back now, and he felt the ice blades piercing through his worn coat. He kicked at the snow, he hit the palm of his hand with his fist, he wished the fat doctor would drop dead.. His heart raced in panic as he thought of Mary. It was dark now. All the street lights had come on. He could barely see the snow dunes looking not unlike the work of some talented sculptor. The clouds hugging the tops of the buildings pulsed as if they were alive.. His thoughts of his beloved wife ran over his mind like ripples over a sand dune. He had to have help, but where? Where? Where? He knew that should he find another doctor, the end result would be the same.

He rubbed his fingers together in a vain effort to get the blood moving faster. A purple specter loomed over the street, and a white tree rose pitifully in a vain effort to shake off the deadly snow that threatened its branches. He began to retrace his steps, leaning into the wind. He drew the thin coat closer about his throat. He notice that some of the apartments now had no lights, and the windows were bleak and sad. A draft of wind blew a mouthful of smoke down to street level and right into Joe's nostrils. He expelled the acrid taste.

He had to return to Mary at once. Together they could face the ordeal better than alone.. He stumbled and almost fell as he tried to make his icy feet move faster.. Even as he knew he would be useless to Mary, he nevertheless would rush to her side. What could they do? He knew that the baby would not wait. Mary might even die. How could that blamed doctor be so heartless?

"God help us!" He spoke the words aloud. Then, for no reason he could fathom, he said the words again. "God help us!". It was at that instant that an awful idea seared his brain. Is there really a God? Out there, up there, some place, was there really a Being, a Presence, who really was concerned with what was happening on this little speck of a planet? How was it possible for such a Being to be aware of..of, for example, of Mary's predicament and at this instant? Was it all a farce? Was it a 'gimmick' that preachers used to make a living on the gullibility and the superstitions of a gullible public?

Was there really anything to this so called worship, to prayer, to service to others? Was all this in fact a door to the ear of some alturistic Person who had power to come to the aid of any believer who happened to call on His name? Come on, he thought, how could there be a Something up there or out there..Something to worship and to say a prayer to, a Mastermind who knew even the thoughts, unspoken or not.

Take for example that woman in Texas, named O'Hare, the woman who had launched a successful effort to ban prayer from the public schools of America. A woman who had founded the Atheist church. Was she right and Joe and others like him all fools? In reality, Joe's thoughts sped on, in reality was she right? Was there in fact nothing out there, no one to call on, no one to put hope in, nothing to pray to? Nothing or no one to hear and have mercy? Joe's thoughts troubled him as he plodded on, now on the street where he lived. His thoughts did not make pleasant company.

What about all the people in the world who are born in dire poverty and who have a constant need each day of their miserable lives and they die, and their remains are in a cardboard coffin and placed in an unmarked grave to quickly turn into dust? What about their prayers uttered all the days of their lives, prayers uttered or shouted in the deepest of despair, calls for help to a God who perhaps was nonexistent. If he was indeed out there, how could He be so heartless? What about all those little children in Africa, shows on the TV screens of the world, those poor little kids with their protruding bellies, the flies crawling on their faces, their gaunt eyes crying for food. Did this so call God send an angel to feed them as a result of much prayer?

All of a sudden, Joe felt like a fool, a most ignorant fool at that, for having nurtured a belief in that so called God, a God not seen and a God not heard. He felt a slight panic as he felt his faith slipping away. *"You irrational idiot!"* He muttered to himself as hate moved in to keep his faltering faith company. He loathed that fat doctor. He viciously kicked a snow covered beer can high into the air.. He began trying to run. He vowed he would kill that fat slob if Mary died. He wished that the man would drop dead in his tracks at this moment. Thousands of innocents die daily and no god seems to notice or to care and no god helps.. For the first time in his life, Joe felt a deep and unending dispair. He muttered to himself so loudly that a couple he met gave him a wide space, certain that he was on some drug trip.

By the time Joe reached the steps of his tenement building, he had regained control of himself. He realized that Satan was ever ready to tarnish a man's faith when he was at his lowest emotional point. He raced up the tenement steps ignoring the ache in his leg from the fall at the doctor's place. He flung the door open and started quickly up the stairs yelling: "I'm coming,, Mary, I'm coming. Hold on!, I'm coming!" As he raced up the stairs, the snow on his shoes was letting go and magically changing to water on each stairstep., By the time he reached his floor, he had been climbing the steps two at a time.

As he entered his flat, he saw his modonna-like wife trying unsuccessfully to hide the panic and fear and anxiety filling every nerve. When she saw that Joe was alone, her eyes asked the question.

"No, Little One," he licked his now thawed lips, as he removed his wet coat. "The doctor refused to come. It's snowing harder now than when I left and I don't dare risk trying to get you to the hospital."

"It's all right, Joe, really it is." Her hair was matted to her forehead. She winced as another labor pain came. "We will have to go it alone" The next pain showed plainly on her face. She moved slightly trying to find some place to ease the pains., any ease.

"But darling," he knelt beside the bed and took her hand in his. He pulled the covers up higher beneath her chin. "I would be of no help whatever. Very likely I would faint when I was needed most."

"Let's trust in God. I am sure He will help us" She tried to smile as Joe prayed silently for forgiveness of his thoughts so short a time ago, "It's about time, Joe. In fact it is now." She couldn't stop the scream as the sharpest pain yet raced throughout her body. Her hands reach down to hold her groin.

"Put a pot of water on the stove to boil. Get that ball of twine you found the other day and get my scissors. Cut two pieces of string about six inches long and put them and my scissors in the water and let it boil. Joe's hands shook and he was barely able to cut the twine. Later he wondered how he had managed to cut three pieces of string. He turned to his wife and at that time the worst pain ever assailed her body.. Joe never felt so helpless in his life.

++++++++++

Joe and Mary had known each other since first grade. When he had first seen her on on the playground, he felt that she was the

Again
If Christ Came Again

prettiest girl in all the world. At that age, he did not know why he felt like that, but he really felt that way. If another boy was foolish enough to pull her hair, he would feel the wrath of Joe. Once when it had happened, Joe knocked the offender down and then told him what it was for. When Mary was hardly fourteen, she and Joe vowed to each other that someday they would get married to each other.. Joe found it harder to stay in school, for he was the sole support of his widowed mother. Joe did odd jobs while his mother took in washings and she also went to the big houses to clean and cook. He dropped out one year in ninth grade, but his mother insisted that he go back to school. He was intelligent enough to make up the lost year, and soon he was even once again with his peers. in school.

Joe and Mary loved to climb to the top of her tenement building just be alone and to look at the stars. They managed to find time to go to the museums and other cultural things which were free.. They had agreed to get married when Joe finished school, one year away. Joe hoped by then to have a steady job. He had been taking manual arts since tenth grade, and he soon found that he had a knack for working in woods. He soon was the best cabinet maker in the school.

When Joe had graduated he was disappointed in that he could not find a regular steady job. He did the only thing he could do, he began to free-lance. He would find a job and when it was finished, the owner was so pleased that he recomended him to friends. In the early 1950's, money was tight and not many people could afford to buy custom made cabinets and furniture.. Jobs became fewer and fewer, and in between, Joe, with disgust, found himself in an unemployment or food stamp line. Sometimes, there was no other choice. He felt that if a person was able to work it was a sin to accept charity.

On Mary's fifteenth birthday, she noticed that a change had been happening to her body.. Yes, her body was definitely changing. Her breasts had grown fuller, and her hair had a luster it had not had before. Her waist began to expand, and she became alarmed when her monthly cycles had ceased.. Since the death of her mother, she had lived with her maiden aunt, and she had no other woman to confide in. The very subject of such things sent the aunt running red-faced from the room. She was wondering what was happening to her.. She was afraid to talk to the school counselor, for all the kids knew she thought all teenager were like dirt, utterly worthless.

One night, in early Spring, she and Joe were at their favorite place on the roof.. They sat on a box that Joe had found and holding hands watched the sun as it dipped behind the buildings in the west.. The blue sky had been clear when they sat down, but now, fleecy clouds were dancing in the western sky.. The western sky began to blush as the sun threaded the fleecy clouds. A slight breeze ruffled Mary's hair. The sounds of the traffic below was almost pleasant, and they felt the building give a slight tremble as a subway train roared beneath the streets.

"Joe," Mary snuggled closer to his chest. She loved being near this man whom she loved, She loved the faint masculine smell when she was near him. "Joe," she went on, "I've got to talk to you about something. I haven't the faintest notion on how to begin, but I have no one to talk about it but you."

"You should know by now, sweetheart, that you can talk to me about anything." He drew her closer and kissed her softly.

"Nevertheless, I still feel that you will not understand. I know I don't understand it." She dropped her head and shuddered slightly.

"Mary," Joe pushed her at arm's length so he could look into her eyes.. "Surely you should know by now that there's nothing in the world that we can't talk about." He pulled her back in his arms and licked his lips. He did not like the sound of her voice.

"I don't care, Joe," she almost whispered the words.. "I'm afraid you will not understand, will take it the wrong way, will not understand. I know I don't understand it. I don't think anyone in the whole world could understand it. I am sick with the thought that you will leave me and we will never see each other again."

"Honey," he squeezed her, "there's nothing on the face of the world that would make me never want to see you again..I love you, my darling, and nothing can drive me from you except you yourself."

"Are you sure? Absolutely sure? Positively sure?" She sat up and turned to look directly into Joe's eyes.. She took a deep breath and continued. "Joe, I've missed two of my periods. "The silence on the roof was so thick it could be cut with a knife. It was awesome. Even the sounds of the traffic far below seemed to have ceased.. Mary felt as if her heart was trying to leap out of her chest.. Joe had loosened his hold about Mary as his mind was trying to grasp the meaning of the words that Mary had just spoken.. A cold breeze enveloped them causing them to believe that old man winter was still trying to make a comeback. Darkness had wrapped its arms about the city, and in retaliation, the city had bathed itself in artificial light, the glow a deep yellow coming up to the roof.. It seemed years to Mary before Joe pushed her from him and came to a sitting position.

"Mary," his voice was low and kind of husky. "Are you trying to tell me that you are..are..pregnant?"

"I don't know Joe, I feel like I think I would feel if I were pregnant."

"B..b..but.." He tried to expel the words calmly, "You know that we have…that you and me, we never,,you know you and me never did anything." His face felt crimson.

"I know, Joe, I know. I have never let any man or boy touch me that way. I swear to you, Joe, I never have. I'm saving myself for you."

"Me. too, even though the fellows poke fun at me for it."

"I know, Joe. I know. that's why I was afraid to tell you. I was afraid you wouldn't believe me."

"Me believe that you are pregnant?"

"No,,believe that I had never been with anybody."

"I could believe you, Mary," Joe stood up and turned away from her. "I would believe you, Mary, but Mother nature simply doesn't work that way. It always takes two"

He walked over to the edge of the building and looked down. His face, bathed in the yellow light was a study in agony.. Mary sat still, not recognizing Joe's face. It had an expression she had never before seen him wear.. Joe thought rapidly. How could she have done this to me? He must have courage to handle this. He remembered having read somewhere that even angels had to have courage or else they became impotent to carry out their assigned tasks. Joe's whole world had suddenly collapsed. His every waking thought had always been for Mary.. He took a deep breath and he could hear Mary crying softly. He could not force his body to walk back to her. Instead, he quickly ran to the stairway and ran down the steps and to the next building and up the stairs to his small room. Here he spent the next hours, the very worst of his entire life, in silence and in racing thoughts that made no sense.. He made fists of his hands and in a rage beat his pillow, his handsome face was contorted and his whole body shook, and then he began breathing in short gasps as if his lungs were starving for oxygen.

"How could this have happened to me? He had been celibate all of his life and was looking forward to a happy life with Mary as his wife.. It was too much for anyone to bear.

He slept little the rest of the night. When the small window in his room became alive with light announcing a new day, he got up and dressed. As he washed his face in the small basin, he felt better.. He looked at his beaten alarm clock and saw that it was time for Mary to be leaving for school. He bounded out of his building and stood by the steps of the building, and when he saw her coming down the steps with her arms full of books his heart leaped with his love for her.. He could see the signs of her sleepless night, but she was still incredibly beautiful.

"Hi, Mary," he smiled.

"Oh, Joe, I never expected to see you again..ever. When you ran away, my worst fears were realized and I knew I had lost you."

"Darling," he took her books and began walking beside her. "I don't claim to understand, but this one thing I do know,.." They stopped for a light, and when it changed, they quickly walked across the street.

"And what might that be, this one thing you understand." She smiled.

"There's no doubt that I acted like a jackass last night. I was a perfect slob. You are walking beside New York's biggest fool., but there is no doubt, not one iota or shred of a doubt that I love you above all others in this world. Of course I do not know what happened, but," he stopped and turned her to him and looked deeply into her eyes., "It is fine with me, and my mind is made up of on one thing."

:What is that?"

Again
If Christ Came Again

"If you will have me, and I wouldn't blame you for turning me down, but come this Saturday, I'd do it today, but I have work to do, but come this Saturday, you will become my wedded wife."

"You mean it, Joe? Really?"

"Yes, I mean it, and from this moment, we will never discuss this thing again." He kissed her as people skirted around them.

++++++++++++++++++

Joe's heart pounded as he lifted Mary's legs exactly as she told him. He placed one leg on each of his shoulders. He did not miss the agony that etched her face and her lips tensed and she took her lip between her teeth to choke off the scream.. She took a deep breath and strained with all her might and her face reddened.. She got her breath at last and then the air was shattered by her piercing scream.. Her face became contorted and the agony painting her features could never be understood by anyone other than a mother who had given birth. Joe cursed the fat doctor and wished him dead in agony, and again he swore to kill him if Mary died.. He looked down between her legs and saw a definite protrusion. Oh why hadn't he paid more attention in class, especially on birthing? He, like most teenagers had been more attentive to the beginning of a baby than in its birth.. He did remember that the baby lived before birth inside its mother's body in a sac filled with water.. He remembered, too, that the sac had to break, but what then? His mind was a blank.

Mary arched her body again so severe that he almost dropped her legs, and as she screamed, he again wished the doctor would drop dead in the same agony as Mary suffered now.. "Push, my brave darling,push as hard as you can. The baby is coming." Now why, he thought, had he said that? He felt like a fool. This had to be a nightmare..it couldn't be really happening., no way.

Suddenly there was water everywhere., and Joe looked down and his heart leaped as he saw a tiny head coming into view.. He kept her legs apart with his shoulders, and then he gently reached down and with great care began to ease the head farther out.. He almost shouted as two tiny shoulders appeared and then the baby was free in his hands. He placed the baby aside and ran for the hot water and the scissors and string. Mary was seemingly unconscious He never knew how he knew exactly what to do. He took one piece of chord and tied the long umbicle cord as near the baby's body as he could. He was glad to remember his boy scout training and tied a square knot.. He took the other end of the cord and tied the umbicle cord as near as possible to Mary's body. Fearing Mary would feel the pain, he cut the umbicle cord in two places. He saw that he had a son. He washed the baby with warm water and checked to see if his mouth and nose were clear and wrapped him in a small blanket. He was thinking of movies he had seen and was about to give the baby a slap on its posterior when it gave a lusty cry.. He placed the baby on the bed and cleared the afterbirth away and washed Mary, finishing with some powder she liked.. He placed a fresh gown on her and covered her just as she awoke. He placed the baby in her arms.

"Let me introduce you to your son, my darling."

"Oh, a boy. Just what I wanted. Thank you, doctor!" she grinned.

"Just call me lucky." He bent over, took her hand and kissed her. "Do you hurt any more?"

"I'm fine, my darling Joe. Just fine." She lifted the blanket and smiled. "Look, Joe, he is just perfect."

"What did you expect with such a beautiful mother and handsome father?"

+++

The following morning, Joe was up early. He had spent most of the night checking on Mary. He got up and checked the baby. He had placed it in a dresser drawer and covered it snugly.. He put on a pot of coffee and the aroma waked Mary.. He saw her stirring and brought the hot coffee to her. She was more beautiful than he had ever seen her. What caused a new mother to taken on this aura, this god-like look after the birth of a child? It was as if God Himself had put it there as a badge of bravery for having brought a child in His image.

As Mary drank the coffee she assured him that she was fine and everything was just perfect. He went to the one closet in the room and reached on the very top shelf that he had known Mary could not reach. He took a clumsily wrapped package down. He had found the

Again
If Christ Came Again

beautiful paper in a garbage can, a discard from an early Christmas party. He had saved pennys,and dimes for three months to buy a small bottle of perfume Mary had seen in a store window and had wanted, knowing she could not have it. He took the package to the bed and exchanged it for her empty coffee cup and replaced it with the package.

"Oh, Joe, what beautiful paper. Wherever did you find it?"

"Never mind, young lady, open the package."

The light from the window, morning sun, reflected by new snow fell on the bright gold box inside the package. Mary squealed as she opened the box and saw the fancy bottle. She opened the bottle and put a daub behind each ear and on her wrists.

"Umm, smells good. Like it?"

"I love it. I only wish.."

"Wish what, sweetheart?"

"I was wishing I could have bought something for you"

"Forget it, little one. What more could a man want than to be presented with a son, a beautiful son from his beautiful wife."

"Joe, open the bottom drawer on the dresser please. He found a package wrapped in the colored comic pages from the Sunday *Daily News* and tied with Mary's hair ribbon.. He carefully untied the ribbon and his heart raced as he unwrapped a beautiful scarf of knitted wool.

"It's beautiful, Mary, so very beautiful." He wrapped it around his neck." Wherever did you get it?"

"I made it myself.' She grinned.

"But the material, the wool, that costs money. Where did you get it, and how could you have made it without my knowing about it?"

"The people down stairs gave me an old wool sweater. I unraveled the wool and rolled it into a ball. I worked on it when you were working. Once you almost caught me when you came home early, I barely hid it in time. Do you like it?"

"I love it. It's the most beautiful scarf I ever saw. I wish I had had it this morning plodding on that ice and snow," He leaned over and kissed her passionately. "This scarf, which is one of a kind, and this baby which is one of a kind, and the most wonderful wife who ever lived, what more could any man expect or deserve?" He walked over and took the baby from the drawer and placed it in Mary's arms where it quickly found her breast and began nursing noislly.

"You know that we have to record its birth at city hall. We have to name him. Any ideas?"

"Sure. I've had his name picked out for months."

"And the name?"

"Joe. Joe, Junior." She smiled. "Named after the most wonderful man on earth, my husband."

Joe blushed like a teenager. "Guess I had better start on our Christmas dinner." He had to be coached on almost every step by Mary. He managed to follow instructions, and to his great surprise, he did fine. He had found some sweet potatoes near a fruit stand, and he had bought some large white potatoes. He had spent scarce pennys on some brown sugar and a huge turkey leg. A friend in a vegetable stand had given him some spinach. He made fresh coffee and managed a sort of dressing and some gravy.. As he brought a chair near the bed and placed the meal on it and the family enjoyed this meal more than the most wealthy family in New York. Happiness ran rampant in that small room on that day.

Somehow, word spread quickly throughout the tenement. Perhaps a neighbor had heard the baby cry. Neighbors began to trickle in after their own meals were over. The building manager was the first to visit, all smiles."

"I hope you kids know that it is against the rules to have children in this building." He walked over and looked at little Joe. "But, I don't know of any rule that says you can't keep a doll.." He patted the baby's hand and smiled at his wife who was already making all kinds of mother noises.. "And for a fact, this young'en is sure a doll." He stepped back and pulled a package from his coat pocket. "Here," he handed it to Mary, "this is for the little one."

Mary opened the box, and on a square of white cotton lay a tiny gold ring. She placed it on the baby's finger, and choking back tears said, "It is so very beautiful. We thank you so very much."

"It belonged to my son who was killed in the war., in Korea. It was his baby ring.. He was saving it for his son. I think he would have wanted for you to have it." He scratched his bald head as he started

Again
If Christ Came Again

for the door, trying to hide the tears. "See that that little doll doesn't disturb anyone."

They had not been gone long when the knock came. Joe opened the door and invited the couple inside. "Hello, Mr. and Mrs King. Please come in."

"We just had to see that baby" She rushed to the bed and Mary lifted the blanket. Joe was still sleeping his meal off.

"Word is out, Joe," Mr. King grinned, "If anyone needs a doctor, especially for birthing a baby, just to call on you."

"God was with us, and we were lucky. I don't know how we managed, but there is the proof." Pride colored the young father's words.

"Oh my, my, my," cooed Mrs. King. He is so very very beautiful. Could I please hold him?" She took the baby gently and nuzzled him softly. Mary knew that Mrs. King could not have children and now she did not miss the longing etched in the older woman's face. Mrs. King reluctantly gave the baby back and nodded to her husband. who reached into his pocket and handed Joe a package. Joe handed it to Mary who opened it carefully. Her fingers trembled a bit. Inside was a small vial of perfume, and even unopened, the air in the small room was filled with a pleasant aroma.

"Oh," cried Mary, "what a wonderful aroma!. How very sweet of you."

"Think nothing of it. We won it as a door prize at the Christmas party last week.. I wanted you and the baby to have it. I never use scent, and I wish we could have given the baby more, but you know how scarce money is."

It is so very nice. Mary noticed the name printed in gold on the bottle and she smiled. *FRANKINCENSE*

Joe and Mary spent the rest of the day enjoying their good fortune. Many times that day, Joe silently prayed for forgiveness for his lapse of faith earlier in the day. However, he could not dispel the deep hate he still harbored for that fat doctor.

CHAPTER TWO

It was almost two years later and Joe had been working just enough to pay for rent and food. Little Joe was growing like a weed, and Joe and Mary were more in love than ever before. Ever present in Joe's mind was to devise a plan to get his family out of the City. Crime was even worse. It seems that during the past two years, criminals were getting bolder each day. The police were worked to a frizzle, and drug dealing was seen on almost every street corner.. Joe longed for freedom from this crime-ridden city. He often thought of it. He had been thinking that there was little freedom in this life. for the base nature of man was vileness.

Actually, he thought, coming home from work in March, freedom was an illusion, or perhaps a delusion. If one looked at it closely, man was a slave to himself to his own carnal desires., and it was the nature of a slave to recruit other slaves. In effect making the adage 'Misery loves company.' true. Why did God send his Son to come to earth when he knew what his fate would be. It was unthinkable! Perhaps God saw more in man than did Joe.

So absorbed was he in his thoughts that he crossed a street on a red light and the shrill whistle of the policeman; brought him back to reality. He waved at the cop and the cop shook his head. Winter was still in charge, but it had waned a bit the last few weeks.. The bank thermometer read 42 but in a few minutes when night fell so would the numbers. A bit of isolated rain hit him in the face and he pulled his scarf tighter and hurried home.

He was about to finish his present job tomorrow, and his last week's pay would pay another month's rent.. It was almost dark when he reached his building. The sky was clear and he looked upwards and saw the huge pearl fingernail shaped new moon riding high knowing it would be full grown in a few weeks. Now a blast of cold wind came and ran down his collar before he could stop it with his scarf. He tightened his coat and his depression was trapped inside. hugging his body as if refusing to let go.

He climbed the three flights and knocked on the door to his flat. He had forgotten his key again.

Again
If Christ Came Again

"Who's there?" He heard movement inside.

"It's me, Joe, your husband."

"What is your wife's first name.?"

"Mary."

"What present did your wife give you two years ago, for Christmas?"

"A scarf she made for me. I have it on now."

The door opened. "Oh, Joe, I am so glad you are home." She quickly closed the door and shot the bold before turning for a kiss.

"What's wrong, Mary? Why all the questions?"

"I guess you have not heard. Someone stole a small child, about little Joe's age. They took it from the tenement next door. It was only a month older than little Joe. The Police found it on the roof of a vacant building. It was lying in a pentagon, and it had been stabbed, and its little heart was gone.. They said it had been sacrificed in a Devil ritual.: She ran into his arms and cried.:"Oh, Joe, I am so afraid.They might try to take our baby. Imagine how that baby's parents feel." She placed her head on his chest and wept.

Joe felt her body against his and desire came on uninvited. He felt his wife growing more beautiful every day. Her breasts had returned to their youthful shape since little Joe had quit nursing.. He looked down at her face and saw again her incredible beauty, the sculptured loveliness of her slightly raised cheeks. He noted her gorgeous eyes, their long lashes dripping with tears. He saw again for the first time her mouth that looked like a ripe plum. He saw her even teeth, white as snow, behind her lips. He hugged her tightly, trying to ease his own panic, for this news shook him to the bottom of his feet.

"Hey there, honey, Let's not get into a panic. Those people are far gone by now. They wouldn't try the same thing twice in the same neighborhood." He gain hugged her tightly. "Um, something sure smells good, could it be waiting for a hungry man? Let's eat supper and then let's do some discussing and some planning."

Mary nodded her head and went to the stove to place the meal on the table.. Joe washed his hands and then he and Little Joe romped a bit. He saw that his son was growing fast and his vocabulary was extensive. His teeth were strong, and his skin was taking on a ruddy hue. His hair was the same shade as Mary's.

Afterwards after he helped Mary wash the dishes, they sat down and tried to analyze their situation.

"Mary," he began. He was sitting in the rocking chair he liked so much. He had removed his shoes. "I've been thinking a lot lately about trying to get us out of the city.. See what you think of this plan: If I work hard tomorrow, I should be finished with this job by noon. I will then be paid for the week, and we will have a little over $100. Why don't we sell what little furniture we have here, and when I come home, we can get on a bus and leave this place. We could leave late tomorrow. The bus station is just a few blocks away. I could tell that second-hand furniture dealer on my way to work. He can come and we will take what he offers. You can fix a sack lunch and we will be on our way. We can sleep on the bus and the further we go the warmer the weather will be."

"Where will we go?"

"As far as our money will take us. We can save back thirty dollars and we can rent a motel room and I can find a job and we will be fine."

"Oh yes, Joe, yes, yes." She came over and sat on his lap and rumpled his hair.. They were oblivious of the rising wind outside or that the sleet was trying to get inside their room. Winter was making a last stand. "I just want to get away from this horrible place."

The following morning while it was still dark, Joe carefully stepped down the icy steps to the street. He bent into the North wind. Winter laughed at those who thought that spring was here.. He glanced back at the tenement and breathed a sigh of thanks that Mary and the baby were safe.. He was elated that this would be the day when they left this place and headed for a better life down South someplace. About an inch of snow had fallen last night and the trees tried to shake loose from the white burden.

He noticed a yellow cab inching its way up the street. Joe noticed the money-hungry cabbie and the driver inside. each looking for a number likely buried in a white grave. The sun was just coming up and he saw that each roof overhang was covered with sparkling diamonds by the millions. The rays of the sun caught the snow as if to show off the incredible beauty. Blue-white smoke belched from besieged chimneys. Gusts of wind would grab the coat of an unwary pedestrian and hang on like a fighting dog.

Joe walked extra carefully this morning. He surely did not want a broken limb to spoil their departure today.. He had allowed for an hour to get to work so he would not be rushed and invite trouble. He met some touted street people astir in quest of food, their eyes showing their anxiety. hoping that they would find food quickly and then return to their lair whether it be a packing crate or a subway corner.

The city was beginning to come alive: to emerge from a frozen tomb. A mounted policeman rode along slowly, letting his horse make its own pace.. His yellow Parka reached to his stirrups. Off to the east, a deep-throated fog horn sang a duet with the shrill whistle of a tug boat. bring in its ship or going after one.

Joe moved softly, his worn coat flapping in the wind. He liked the warmth of the scarf about his neck each time the wind tried to get in. His thoughts went to the death of that innocent baby. What kind of sick mind could take an innocent child, a gift of God, and murder it so senselessly as a sacrifice to Satan? He wondered about the future of his son. Each day he saw teenagers running rampant, turning over garbage cans, breaking street lights, defying authority.. At what moment did a child leave off being an innocent and join the ranks of the wicked? Where did his innocence change into the ranks of the wicked? In behaving like a depraved animal, disregarding the rights of other people. Explain, if you please, how a child in school, say the fourth grade, even the fifth, a child who took no part in in vandalism, who was not a known thief, even to his peers, why is it that society forces such a person to become a hermit, a loner, long before reaching the teens if he did not join the unruly he would be ostrasized by his classmates. Why do people hate virtue and goodness? Explain, if you can, how a girl reaching her mid teens and was still a virgin is ridiculed by her peers, both boys and girls. Are all human species by nature evil?

These thoughts crowded the mind of Joe on that frosty morning as he edged himself to work. If I were God, he thought, I would simply eliminate those who sought to live on the blood and sweat of other people..

"Well," he thought as he had to jump as he crossed an street to excape the path of a sliding car, its white faced driver trying vainly to get control. "no fiend is going to get little Joe, for this was his family's day of liberation., the day they went south where most people expected to earn a living the hard way, by working for it.

Joe reached his place of work and by noon he had finished the last cabinet and had cleaned the entire place so that it could open for business at any time.. Within fifteen minutes he had his money and was inching himself toward the bus station. His young heart was filled with high speculations and anticipations. His boss had paid him the balance of the contract and had handed him an extra hundred dollar bill. The boss sort of blushed and said it was good to find a man who took pride in his work and was not afraid to do something extra even no pay was in store for it., and "besides," the man went on, "I wish you well and the very best of luck."

"One hundred eighty-six dollars!": Joe said the words aloud as he moved carefully along. He felt as if he were walking on air. He reached the bus station and was elated that there was no long line at the windows. He approached a window marked *Information* and asked the man how far $150 would take a man and his wife and baby. Joe's luck held, for he found that they had reduced fairs just that morning.

"Where do you want to go?"

"Any place South where's there's little or no snow.." The man consulted a book and used his calculator.

"I can get you to Bethany. That's a little over 1500 miles south. How does that sound, young man?"

"Sounds great. I like the name. It's in the Bible."

Joe walked home as fast as he could for in a little over two hours the bus was scheduled to leave. He found Mary sitting on a packing crate, and little Joe was asleep on a small quilt.. He knelt beside his wife and kissed her luscious lips and explained their good fortune.. Mary squealed in delight, She proudly told him that she had gotton $50 for the furniture. He quickly shouldered the box and told her to stay in the apartment until he got back from the bus station. to check the box for *Bethany*..

He returned and they had less than an hour to make it to the bus before it left. Mary clung to Joe's arm as he carried little Joe. She clutched the paper bag containing their lunch.

+++

Four days later the bus opened its doors with a swoosh and Joe and his family got out and after Joe was sure his box was put off, the bus drove away with a belch of diesel smoke with the characteristic smell that was part of it.. As the watched the bus drive off, Joe and Mary felt as if they had landed on another planet.. It was cold, but nothing like the cold of New York. Thankfully, there was no snow. No wintry blast tried to rip the clothes from their bodies., and best of all, no mugger gave them the eye.

He sat Mary on the box and went inside the bus station to inquire about the location of a motel. The bored girl at the counter said between smacks of bubble gum and an occasional bubble that there was a motel a few blocks away that rented rooms by the month. She eyed Joe up and down, and then when she glanced out the window and saw Mary and the baby, she lost interest.

Joe placed the box on his shoulder and with Mary and the baby clinging to his arm, they made the short journey into a new life. The journey was pleasant because he did not have to watch out for slippery ice and snow.

To one who lived in the north, the motel would have been termed 'seedy', but to Joe and Mary, with their history of living in a tenement situation, it looked great. It was very clean, and they saw that there was a tiny kitchenette with a bath all its own. The rent was fifty dollars a month (payable in advance) and the widow woman who owned the place fell in love with little Joe.

They unpacked their sparse belongings and Joe took Mary in his arms and saw that she was still lovely despite four long days and nights on the bus.. He told her once again of his love for her and the baby.

"You know, Mary, God is good to us. We have a place to stay for a month, and I will surely find a job before the month ends. We have a few dollars for food. Yes, God does exist. I have read, and I agree whole-heartily, that a person can prove the existence of God in all sorts of ways: in a dream while asleep, in his private thoughts when awake,. If one looked, he could see Him in a wild flower by the side of the road.. God's thumb print could be found in the clouds at sunset. One might tremble at the vociferous sounds of a storm, but God was there too, reminding man of His awesome power. If a man's arrogance got in the way of the worship of God, he was made fearful in the mightiness of a storm that caused even mighty mountains to tremble.. Man is afraid when he sees the ocean leave its assigned place, and then when he remembers that God is in charge, his fears go away.

He paused when he saw the love in Mary's eyes. He thought rapidly: I saw the hand of God in the deliverance of little Joe. I saw His hand in the bonus the man gave me. I see His hand in our coming here to Bethany, this roof over our heads. Here we are, with a little nest to keep us safe, the rent paid for a month, and a new life before us." He kissed his wife with all his might.

Yes, as the sign on the highway read *BETHANY, population 2504 and one* old grouch" The sign would have to have three added to those figures.

CHAPTER THREE

On a bright June day in 1962, a youth walked along the dusty street in Bethany. The lad was tall and sort of gangling. He had shot up like a stalk of corn, his mother often said, especially the last year. His step was lively, now aping the plod most kids showed, the result of a lifetime of sitting in front of a TV set. The air was warm and free from smog. The leaves on the trees along the street were thick and were giving out wonderful music from the tiny throats of the birds. Now and then a squirrel leaped from one tree to another.. The air was filled with the odor of honeysuckle vines.

The boy brushed his dark hair from his eyes, for he wore his hair longer than his mother liked, but she allowed it because he liked it and the other boys wore their hair longer than adults liked. His cheeks were the color of a ripe peach, his skin was without blemish, his red lips smiled almost constantly, showing two rows of white even teeth. His eyebrows were thin and met above his small nose. His eyes were of a bright blue.. His arms were strong and larger than an average. Biceps showed through the thin short sleeved shirt he wore. The regular clothes of the teens were Jeans, and his were hitched closely around his thin waist.. They were cut slim and it made adults wonder how kids managed to get into them.

Most of the girls in the seventh grade thought the boy handsome and dreamy as they described him. Some used the words 'the most' as they giggled when talking about him. They almost swooned when he smiled at them and the dimple in his left cheek came to life. He knew how to use that smile, especially against his mother when he wanted something. The only thing Joe did not like about his looks were his eyelashes. They were so very long. He felt it was sissy. His lips were healthy red and his young tongue was forever darting out of his mouth to keep his lips moist. He had dazzling white, even teeth. He was fast on his feet and he could out run, out box and out wrestle any kid in his class or even older.

Like other kids in Bethany, he was still enjoying the time of year when the schools were closed. He often sang with other kids:

Lee Roy Neal

**No more school
No more books
No more teachers'
dirty looks!**

He, like most other boys, had had a bout with ruebella measles, and he had been unfortunate enough for them to have hit him the first day of summer vacation.. He had been kept inside the house by his mother, and today his usually olive skin was sort of pale.. He tightened his belt holding up his jeans around his trim waist. his blue shirt was faded and had a torn pocket., Some kid had grabbed it in that touch football game this morning. He refused to wear an undershirt and this gave his mother, Mary, some misgivings. Today he wore a pair of sneakers and a pair of sox left over from gym class. His hands were regaining their brown color and they were strong.,. A couple of fingernails were broken, and some had dirt beneath them.

Joe did well in school. In fact, he actually liked school, but he was careful to keep this secret from other boys.. He hurried home after school when it was in session. He liked to help his dad in the wood shop.. He had been doing this since he was five or six.. His dad had converted the double garage on their house into a cabinet shop. They lived in a small house just east of town. His father had become well known in Bethany this past ten years. He had customers from other towns who had heard of his beautiful cabinets.

The twelve year old boy liked to work with wood. He loved the smell of the sawdust and he loved to see a sharp saw go through the smooth wood.

Joe's life would have been perfect in his sight except for the tragedy of a year ago. In front of his house, a car had ran off the road into a ditch and had rolled over on its side. His father had run out to help and in trying to pry the car up,another car had run off the road and right into the disabled car. Joe's father had been killed instantly.

The loss of a father is devastating to shy boy especially to one who had enjoyed the closeness Joe had had with his dad.. Joe had been completely thrown off his stride. Mary was, of course, almost inconsolable. Her love for Joe had remained steadfast through the years, and she, for a while, lost all interest in living., When she

Again
If Christ Came Again

thought of her four boys and one girl, she got control of herself. Fortunately, the insurance had paid her $40,000 for her husband's death. She had paid off her mortgage and was managing to live on the interest of the balance.

Joe managed to help out by taking odd jobs around town after school and on Saturdays. He loved to make money, and he was at present saving up for that red ten speed bike down at the Western Auto store., just across from the post office down town.

Today, Joe was enroute to one of his regular jobs. He felt the sun seeping through his shirt. He gulped huge breaths of fresh air. He loved to make his lips flutter as he expelled air. He was careful to do this only when alone for fear that he would be called a horse, As he moved along, he could smell the peach orchard in old man Max's land, He did not fail to see ripe peaches peeking out from deep green leaves,. A bee brushed past his head on the way to its hive. He could hear the big eighteen wheelers on the Interstate a few blocks away.

Every other week, Joe would mow the grass and clean up the rest of the yard at the house of Deacon Bandy. Mr. Bandy, like a lot of people in in the First Baptist Church, liked to have young Joe do their yard work. The boy was always happy and cheerful and he always worked to please his customers. Without being told, he always raked the lawn and put the mower back in the garage, If something was broken, the boy seemed always to be able to fix it, expecting no extra compensation. Most people remarked that they felt good just being around the lad as he worked.. Deacon Bandy was waiting for Joe when he arrived.

"Hi, Joe," the man called.:"Glad that you could come."

"Me, too, Mr. Bandy." He saw that the lawn mower was already out of the garage as if Mr. Bandy was afraid he would not show up. "I'm a little late, but not to worry, I'll be through before dark and that's a fact." He smiled a faint dimpled smile and went to work.

Mr. Bandy was not much taller than Joe. He was grossly overweight and he liked to eat and hated to exercise.. His head was large, even for his chubby body, and his brown hair was sparse. He let it grow long and combed it over the bald spots on top.. Actually, his hair was thin all over.. His chubby belly had a noticeable bulge. He was clean shaven and his hands seemed to be moving all the time..

His plump features were what most folks would term as ordinary.. It took no imagination to decide that the man's head was out of proportion with the rest of his body.. He seldom laughed and Joe had never seen him smile Actually, Joe thought he looked as if he had indigestion all the time. His nose was large enough for two faces., and his cold brown eyes looked sort of dead.. Had he been dressed in clothing from Good Will, he could have passed people on the streets passing for one of the factory workers of the town., enroute to a tract house filled with cheap *bric a brac* with a cheap rug on the floor. But, Deacon Bandy did not wear cast off clothes. He loved to wear suits that were tailor made. And the furniture in his house was anything but cheap.

When Deacon Bundy did laugh, it wasn't really a laugh. It could frighten someone who was not used to it.. His entire face seemed to take on a different, foreign expression.. The skin of his face got tight, and his eyes became sort of scary., with a sort of demonic look.. His eyes bugged and his eyebrows lifted from the ends nearest his ears. His nostrils enlarged and even his ears seemed to twit.. If one took an instant photograph of the deacon's face when he was not laughing, then took another when he was laughing, then show the two pictures to strangers and they would be unable to identify it as the same person.

Joe went to work and the grass flew as his young legs guided the mower over the lawn. The smell of the freshly cut grass was pleasant, and the catches of the phrases the boy hummed or sang was recognizable only to another teenager. He worked rapidly, and when he had finished he cleaned the mower and put it in its place in the garage.. He raked the lawn, savoring the smell of the newly mowed grass that was mingled with the fresh smell of ripening fruit from the tree by the porch., The climbing rose was also making its contribution to the country air. The limbs of a Mimosa tree were swaying in the slight breeze. Clouds were already coming to escort the sun to its resting place for the night.

Mr. Bandy came to the door just as Joe put the rake away and closed the garage door. He called Joe to come inside. On the kitchen table Joe saw the usual plate of oatmeal cookies and a glass of milk. Joe liked this part of the job best of all.. He sat down and took a

Again
If Christ Came Again

plump cookie and sank his perfect teeth onto it. Already the childhood gap between his two front teeth had closed. and his mouth looked like an advertisement in a dental magazine. He drank the milk as if he really liked it which he did; not just because it was said to be good for a growing boy.

The Bandy's were active members in the First Baptist Church of Bethany. In fact it was the largest church in the entire county. Mr. Bandy was a deacon and superintendent of the Sunday School. Mrs. Bandy taught the *Rebeccas*, a class for older women. Both man and wife would be what the people called pillars in the community.

"Joe," Mr. Bandy sat down and took a cookie, "I am proud to see you in Sunday school each week.." He tried to smile and stained teeth showed trying to look out of his mouth. The lips made a reflective effort to hide the secrecy.

"Yes-sir," Joe wiped a crumb from his lips. "I like to study the Bible. I guess I always have, ever since I learned to read. I read the Bible every day, even though I don't understand it all. I do know that I don't always agree with what some preachers say, even those on TV."

"What things do you not understand or agree with, son," Mrs. Bandy placed a fresh plate of cookies on the table and brushed a few crumbs from the cloth.. She then sat and placed her hands on the table making a childlike tent of her fingers.

"Oh, Mrs. Bandy," Joe took another bite. "I would rather not say.. I'm just a kid and am not supposed to know very much. I do read my Bible and each time I do not understand something, I ask God to help me to understand it."

"Oh come on now, son," Mr. Bandy tried in vain to become a 'a good old buddy'. You are here among friends. I like to think of us as your very best friends.. I like to consider myself a father-figure to you since you lost your own dad. Mrs. Bandy and I are teachers. We have taught Bible classes for many many years.. I guess it would be impossible for anyone to ask us a Bible question that we could not answer. The Bible is filled with many many different stories. For example, I'll bet you did not know that there's a story in the bible about a woman who killed a man by driving a tent spike through his head while he was asleep.. Do you know her name, Joe? Huh?"

Lee Roy Neal

"No, sir, I haven't read that.

"It's in there, Joe, it's in there! Her name was Jael. She killed the enemy captain of an army that was destroying her people. His name was Sissera." He looked pleased with himself.

"That's interesting, sir."

"Now then, Joe," Mr. Bandy patted Joe's arm and lowered his voice. "What particular thing is it that you don't understand or agree with. I can help you."

"I'd better not get into it, sir." Joe drank the last of the milk in his glass and took the last cookie and stood up. "Mom says I should keep my ideas to myself, especially around grown people." He threw a dimple at Mrs. Bandy.

"But son," Mrs. Bandy took her fingers apart destroying the tent, She brushed a stray hair from her face. "You are among friends. We are friends first, and adults last. It would give us great pleasure to answer any questions. Let us know. We really do want to help.. How can we help if we don't know what things you are in doubt about are?"

"Well," Joe sat down again. "I will bring up one thing, and then I have to go home. Mom will be worried about me, She worries if I am out after dark." He licked crumbs from his lips. and then caught his lower lip between his teeth for a second. "It's about the commandments. The Ten Commandments. God said that we should remember the Sabbath Day and keep it Holy The seventh day of the week is Saturday, yet we have church on Sunday, the first day. The Jews kept the seventh day religiously. Jesus kept it too,, yet today most churches meet on Sunday Most business places stay open on Saturday but close on Sundays. I just can't understand why."

"Mr. Bandy you answer the boy. I thought he had a real problem." She patted Joe's arm. You'll see son. She smiled.

"Sure, mother, he tried to smile at the boy. "When Jesus came to earth, he was crucified and rose from the grave on Sunday morning. This changed the Sabbath to a new day in honor of the day He came out of the grave.. See how simple it is. If you have any questions at any time, you just bring them to me. I'll set you on the right road."

"But what about the law, the Commandment that says 'Remember the Sabbath Day to keep..'"

"Son," Bandy quickly interrupted, 'it says, remember the Sabbath. It does not say which day of the week, it says the Sabbath day. It does not say which day of the week. For hundreds of years we have kept Sunday, the first day of the week."

"But, Mr. Bandy," Joe tried to keep his voice calm," Jesus said that he did not come to destroy the law but to fulfill it." Joe smiled, showing the dimple. "Moses told the people that he got the laws direct from God, and that God said to keep the seventh day. The original sabbath day was Saturday." He looked calmly into the deacon's eyes.

"But Joe," now the deacon's words were tinged with irritation. "I explained it to you. It was changed when Jesus rose from the dead on Sunday, the first day. This is the new Sabbath."

"And that's why it was changed, to commemorate the day Jesus rose from the death?" Joe asked.

"That's right son." Bandy's voice was cheery, "I'm glad you got it straight. Don't ever be afraid or ashamed to bring any of your questions to me, and I will set you straight. No problem." He patted Joe's arm again.

"But, Mr. Bandy," a pixie look covered Joe's face, "What if Jesus did not rise from the grave on Sunday. What then? Would we still have a first day sabbath?"

"I am afraid that you have been listening to some nut, Joe. Was it in school? I am sure you do believe in the Bible and what it says, don't you?"

"You know I do. That's ridiculous. I love the Bible, and I love to read it every day."

"Then you must know the story of Mary and Martha on their way to the tomb to anoint Jesus' body."

Sure, Mr. Bandy, sure. It's told many places in the Bible.

"Fine, now what day did they go to the selphchur to anoint the body of the crucified Jesus?" Again he tried to make a smile cover his features and failed.

"That's easy. The Bible says 'Now upon the first day of the week..''

"Stop, Joe," Bandy's had delight in his voice, "stop right there, that is enough: Triumph colored his eyes." You said it right there, the

first day of the week. Now what day is that, son?" His voice was conciliatory.

"But Mr. Bandy," Joe's seemed so naive. "When they got there, did they anoint Jesus' body?"

"No, they did not."

"Why?" Joe asked.

"Because He had risen. Our Lord had risen! Hallelujah. He had risen back to life."

"Mr. Bandy, you say his body was gone. How long before Mary and Martha got there had he risen?"

"No one knows, Joe. All we know was that the grave could not hold him. He had risen!"

"Could He have come out of the grave an hour before the women got there?"

"Well, I suppose he could have, son. Sure, he could have come out an hour before.:"

"How about three hours before?"

"That too, stretching things some. What are you getting at, Joe?"

"Mr. Bandy, please understand I am not trying to get smart, but I am really wondering, Could it have been possible for Jesus to come out of the grave…say…twelve hours before Mary and Martha got there?"

"Joe," Mr. Bandy's voice had a harsh quality now. "I know what you are getting out. You are trying to twist the scriptures to make them say what you want them to say. That is a sin, son, a grievous sin.. I am so happy you brought this to me, for I am happy to set you straight. You ran into a road block that time son."

"Please straighten me out on this, Mr. Bandy, for it really concerns me."

"Gladly, my boy. Gladly." He poured some tea and Mrs. Bandy got Joe some more milk. "You see, Mr. Bandy, the Pharisees asked Jesus for a sign to prove that He was the Son of God., the Messiah, the Christ. Jesus said he would give them just one. He stated that even as Jonah was in the belly of the whale three days and three nights, so would the Son of Man be in the heart of the earth three days and three nights."

"Yes, sir. I remember that."

Again
If Christ Came Again

"Well, if Jesus rose twelve hours before the women reached the tomb, it would be Saturday. He then would not have been in the grave three days and nights. Friday and Saturday. We need Sunday. See how simple it is?"

'Where are the three nights if Jesus died on Friday as most people believe. The Catholic Church pushes Good Friday and all that. Where are the three nights? Friday night and Saturday night."

"You are young, Joe, and don't read carefully. Jesus said 'three days and nights'" Bandy faltered, his heart racing. He felt disaster creeping into his mind.

"Beg your pardon, sir, he said three days **and** three nights."

Bandy got his Bible and flipped some pages and then closed it and put it on the table. He flung a glance at his wife and sort of hung his head. "I never thought about the three nights. All I know is that for hundreds and hundreds of years the Christian Church has known of Good Friday and the Sunday resurrection. I'm sorry, Joe. I will have to do some research before I can explain it."

"Mr. Bandy," Joe took his lower lip between his teeth and then let go and moistened his lips. "Will you please not be mad at me if I say something else?"

"Course not, Joe."

"Suppose Jesus was crucified late Wednesday, say at sunset.. Then we could count Wednesday night, Thursday night, and Friday night as the three nights, and we could count Thursday, Friday, and Saturday as the three days. Wouldn't that work fine, Mr. Bandy? Huh?"

"I'm afraid not, Joe. You need to know more Bible before you can argue Scripture. For you remember that Jewish law said that a body could not hang on a cross on the Sabbath, and as the Sabbath was drawing near, the soldiers came and broke the bones of the two thieves, but the found Jesus already dead. See, the next day was Saturday." Mr. Bandy was elated, glad to put this kid in his place."

"I can tell you this, sir, I was really up a tree on that and then one day I was reading in *John* and he said that the next day was a *high Sabbath*. I looked in the Jewish encyclopedia in the Bethany library and it said that a *high Sabbath was an annual Sabbath. It was the Feast of Unleavened bread and it happened on Thursday that year..*

Lee Roy Neal

You see," Joe smiled. *It makes everything work out. There were two Sabbaths that week, the weekly Sabbath and the annual Sabbath."*

"What about Good Friday?" Mrs. Bandies asked.

"I don't know that. The Catholic Church started that, and everyone just sort of followed what they said."

Before any more was said the door bell rang. Mrs. Bandy went to answer it and returned with Joe's mother.

"Joe!" Mary was angry. How could you stay so long and cause me to worry so. I didn't know what had happened. I imagined all sorts of things.. You could have called."

"I am so sorry, mother. I just lost track of time. Mr. and Mrs. Bandy are so interesting to talk to. I just forgot. Please forgive me."

"It's all right. I just wish you could have called." She smiled at the Bandys, "I hope he has not been a bother. or any trouble."

"No, no. He has not been any trouble at all. We are happy to have him here any time. He does such a good job on our yard."

Thank you. I have to hurry back. The other children are alone."

They left Mr. Bandy with a look of an enigma on his face.

CHAPTER FOUR

With a blood-curdleing scream that imitated almost perfectly the scream of a wounded animal, the young woman flung her emaciated body against the steel bars of the hugh gate that closed the gap in the ten foot wall surrounding the estate of the richest man in Bethany.. Her fingers turned white as she grasped the steel bars, foam coming from between her clinched teeth.. Again and again the air was covered by the pathetic wails of the helpless creature.. The cries sounded a lot like bestial cries of rage and helplessness.

Millard Hunt, M.D. who happened to be taking his daily stroll inside his estate. The stroll had a three fold purpose: to get needed exercise; to inspect his estate and to spend some time with his young daughter, Emily, who usually accompanied him on his daily rounds of inspection. He happened to be near the gate when the screaming began. He stopped and stooped slightly to get a better look at the creature hanging on to his gate.. He stepped back suddenly, for the stench from the creature was overpowering. causing him to grab for a linen handkerchief and put it over his nose. He began backing away from the unwashed creature, holding tightly to Emily's hand. His daughter snuggled very near her father, unable to take her eyes from the horrible scene before her.

"You see, Emily," the doctor hurriedly moved out of reach of the awful smell. "that creature is one of the inmates from the mental hospital at Herald. She was released by the hospital in order to prey on the innocent taxpaying people of this county. The public raised a hue and cry that these creatures be released to make room for other such creatures." He shuddered and moved up the driveway to the house. "I'll call the sheriff and get her away from my property."

Joe was at that time just leaving the estate of the good doctor.. He had completed work on a magnificent pecan bar in the doctor's new cabana which graced the southern edge of his Olympic swimming pool just completed.

"What seems to be the trouble, Dr. Hunt?:" Joe asked, shifting his tool box to another shoulder. "I could hear screaming just as I left the pool area." Already a crowd of about fifty had gathered to watch the excitement.

"Oh, it's just one of those state hospital inmates released recently. She seems to be in some sort of cataleptic trance." He held the handkerchief even closer.

"Did you try to help her, doctor. Shall I run to the house and get your medical bag?" He placed his tool box on the ground and started toward the gate.

"Why should I? She's not a patient of mine. Likely she doesn't have a cent to her name."

"But you are a doctor of medicine. You are also a deacon in our church. I hope for either of those reasons you would offer assistance."

Joe had grown taller these past fifteen years, and since graduation from high school had filled in his frame to the point where he was not lanky anymore. He approached the gate very slowly. It was at that instant that the creature gave forth another cry causing those in the crowd to fall back a little way. Joe was tall and strong and his oval shaped face had lost all the child-look he had had as a youth. He looked a little younger than his thirty years. His brow was smooth and his face had escaped the ravages of acne endured by a lot of adolescents. His cheekbones were high and bronzed by exposure to a lot of sunlight. His eyebrows were a fawn brown, and beneath them were the bluest eyes, more compelling than anybody could imagine. His dark hair was abundant and it reflected a sheen in the waning afternoon sun.

"I pay my taxes and should not have to be bothered by creatures such as this," the doctor seemed to be trying to justify his action. Anger slipped in, however, to color his words. The doctor had known Joe for years and years, and he disliked the young man's ability to make a person feel guilty over the slightest thing.. He would never have hired him to build that bar except for the fact that Joe was the finest cabinet maker in the entire state., yet the man seemed to have a knack to make a man feel guilty over the smallest thing.

Joe opened the part of the gate that the woman was not touching and came slowly to her side. The crowd could not take their eyes from the scene. Yet they drew as near as possible so as not to miss a single word or deed. They had the many rumors about Joe: how he was 'different' how he had a way of handling situations that confronted him. Some deemed him a nut, others a remarkable man.

"There, there, little lady," Joe's voice was hardly above a whisper, "I want to help you. Don't be afraid. Are you able to stand up?" The creature rolled her eyes, only the whites showing. "Take it easy. I will help you. Please don't be afraid. I wont let anyone hurt you." He put one strong arm about the filthy body and with the other hand pride her fingers from the bars. At last she stood, tottering to get her balance. She eyed the crowd and gave a screech causing the crowd to fall back, some on top of others. Joe saw that the doctor had reached his house and had entered and slammed the door. Somehow, he knew the doctor had not gone to get his medical bag.

"Stop yelling and moving around, little lady. I am going to help you." Now the woman's eyes rolled in their sockets and then upward so that only the whites showed again. He continued in his soothing voice and she seemed to calm down and relax.

At thirty, Joe was an enigma to the residents of Bethany, now a thriving metropolis of over 50,000, over double the size when his parents had first moved there. He had graduated from Bethany High School as valedictorian. The school year book had dubbed him as 'one who wants to help other people.'

His social life had been reduced to almost zero since the death of his father and it seemed that his younger siblings were always in need of something. Mary was always trying to get Joe to let up, to relax, and take life a little easier, but he found that he could not do this. He should have spent more time with his peers, but somehow he felt as if his calling was to see that his siblings wanted for no needful thing. He did have a few close friends whom he saw often since he had graduated in 1973. His friends seemed to accept him as he was despite the fact that he was branded 'different'. They did not fully understand his frantic devotion to his family. Joe would not even buy an old car for fear it would take from those he felt responsibility for..

Joe did take great pride in his skill as a carpenter and cabinet maker. He was never happier than when he ran his fingers along the edge of a piece of wood knowing that hidden inside the wood was something of beauty, just waiting to get out. Joe made a lot of his co-workers mad at his almost frantic desire to never do a shoddy job.. He insisted always that the job he was hired to do be of the very best his hands could make it.

Joe secretly thought that most of the people in Bethany were a little on the ignorant side…not book-learning' ignorant but 'common sense' ignorant.. He knew it was sinful, but he got a lot of joy (for which he prayed forgiveness) in backing Deacon Bandy into a corner on some phrase from the Bible, and then watch the man squirm to try to prove some dogma or tradition he had accepted as true all his life. Nobody could ever correctly accuse Joe of being a religious fundamentalist. He often smiled as he remember the many times that Bandy had grabbed his Bible to prove Joe wrong only to have the deacon's face redden when he found that Joe had again been right. Joe remembered one case in point when the deacon had chided Joe for working so hard.. Joe remarked that he only wanted to supply the needs of his family.

"Don't you know, Joe," the deacon tried to smile, 'that money is the root of all evil?"

"No, sir," Joe had smiled as others crowded around to see the fun, for never had the deacon proved Joe in the wrong. "I don't think that you can find that in the Bible." They were going down the church steps when people stopped to listen. They smiled as Bandy's hands trembled as he sought the passage.:"Here it is right here!" Bandy was triumphant.

"Please read it to me, sir."

"'…for the love of money is the root of all evil' see, Joe, for once I have proved you wrong."

"Mr. Bandy, it says the *love* of money is the root of all evil, not **money**." Joe smiled and continued down the steps.

"Joe," his mother whispered to him, "I wish you wouldn't bait that poor man like that".

++++++++++

Joe now held the woman gently still talking to her.. The crowd drew closer and the siren's wail from the Sheriff's car split the air. Joe acted as if he had not heard. He saw that the woman was now very calm. He placed his right hand on the woman's head. The crowd held its breath. They had heard things. Then Joe cried in a loud voice:: "Woman, in the name of God, in the blessed Name of Jesus, I command that you be healed!" He placed both hands on her head and repeated, pushing hard," Be healed!"

Most people, that night, when retelling over and over what had happened, agreed that at that instant the woman stopped trembling. She had stood up straight, the saliva stopped coming from her lips. She looked around the crowd and then she looked at Joe.

"Where am I?" She looked around. "How did I get here, at the doctor's place?"

"You were evidently trying to get him to help you. You are safe, little lady. You are safe."

The sheriff's car rolled to a stop, its siren running down to a lower and lower growl. The antenna whipped back and forth, a ripple of voices coming from the scanner inside the car.

"What's the trouble here?" the deputy got from his car, his hand cuffs and pistol balancing each other on each side of the man's waist. "Oh, hello Joe" He recognized his former class mate. "We got a call of some sort of disturbance at the doctor's gate."

"You can see that everything is fine here, Frank" Joe and the woman walked side by side toward down town Bethany."

"I feel so good," the woman said as she tried to keep pace with Joe. "I have never felt better in my whole life."

Word spread like a wild prairie fire throughout Bethany. Most of the people knew the striken woman and that she was subject to seizures. When they heard what the young carpenter had done they wondered. Deacon Bandy heard it and simply shook his head.

When Joe reached home, he told Mary what had happened. She said that he had done the right thing and that what he had done was a gift from God. She wanted to tell him of the circumstances of his birth but thought it was not yet the time. She further felt that when the right time came she would know it.. How could she ever tell her son that he had been born of a virgin and had no earthly father, a scientific impossibility.

When Joe got up the following morning, he realized that he did not have a job to do. He decided to take a long walk alone. His favorite place was about half way up the side of his 'mountain' as he liked to think of the large rise just North of Bethany very near where State 19 intersected the I-20 free way.

As he walked, he again was enthralled by the early morning art show. The burnt orange color of the horizon was breath taking as the sun chased the night away. It was as if someone had pushed a button and the music of a hundred birds filled the sweet smelling air. The soft spring wind was little more than a gentle breeze, and it was pungent with the aroma of spring blooms.. As he walked near the foot of the mountain and began his ascent, small creatures scurried before his feet. The Mountain in its green dress was the color of jasper against the now vivid blue of the morning sky. Its majesty seemed to pulsate in its serenity. The nearby trees seemed to run up the hill showing off myriad colors running from shades of green to aqua marine to emerald to olive.

Today, Joe felt as if he were standing on a precipice: the very edge of life itself. Somehow he felt that a change was near. He knew he was almost thirty and he had yet to solidify the goals of his future. He had a feeling that he knew his future, and then again doubts came and nothing was definite. Nothing that had a one two three aura about it. He knew, he felt, yet he did not know. He felt that there was something, some goal, he would do, not something he **must** do.

He climbed slowly for over an hour and was nearing the top when he found his spot. Here he often came alone just to be with himself and his thoughts. He wanted to quiet the raging thing within his being. Even as a teenager he had come to this, his 'secret' place. Here he was out of reach of those below who called him 'odd'. Why was it so vital to make folks see and understand what the Bible really said? Was it sinful to be elated each time he got the best of Deacon Bandy?

Why was he so different from other men? He remembered when he was still in high school the place down below where fellers brought their girls on Friday nights. It had been when he was about sixteen when he had taken his girl along with another couple to the trysting place. It was there he had received his first kiss. It was while sitting beneath the 'kissing rock'. He had felt a strange feeling rising within his body. It was a feeling he did not understand. He had thought it was his imagination. He had taken the girl in his arms and kissed her soundly as he was supposed to beneath the 'rock'. Fire had raced throughout his body. It must have effected the girl too, for she began unbuttoning his shirt, When she reached his belt and unbuckled it he stood up suddenly, his heart racing. When the girls said 'why not?' he could not answer her for he did not know the answer. All he felt was that it seemed wrong. He then had another name to add to all the others. He was a 'cold fish' or 'gay' or whatever.

Joe had been born in a generation that embraced all kinds of beliefs: cultish and otherwise. "If it feels good, do it" was a common theme. Many teens bragged about their atheistic beliefs. Some said "have no beliefs at all" Don't be burdened with a conscience, it holds you back from enjoying life."

Joe remembered a conversation with one of his friends who said that he was an atheist. Joe had tried to reason with him. He had said: "Only a fool would fail to believe in a Power greater than himself. The very fact that man is here on earth, a breathing, living entity was indeed as miracle. Of all the millions of spermatozoa cells present in one ejaculation, why was one specially targeted to penetrate the egg of the female and thus began a new life, a new person?"

"Go to your science books," he had continued, "you will find that nature adheres to rigid rules. The sun and the moon must keep in their orbits to the fraction of a second. Throw a rock into the air, and at some point, the rock ceases its upward flight, and for an instant is dead still. Does it stay there? Of course not. The law of gravity draws it back to the earth. Not only does it return to the earth, but it comes at a pre-ordained speed.." Joe had then looked into the eyes of his best friend, Gary, He wanted so much that his friend believe.

"Gary, compared to the stars, man is just an insignificant speck. Man did not make the laws of gravity or any other law of nature. Man is a stupid creature, taken as a whole, He really has no idea as to why he is here on earth; in fact, he doesn't give a damn." When Gary had said nothing, Joe had continued. "Man tries to change nature. He tries to defy the heat of summer and the cold of winter by hiding inside some building, and when the utility bill comes, he curses the utility company."

"Can a man make a mountain disappear?" he went on, Oh I know in the Bible Jesus said that if a man had enough faith he could make a mountain disappear, but I believe Jesus did not mean a literal

Lee Roy Neal

mountain, but he meant some problem in a man's life that seemed to have no solution. He could have even meant a real live mountain.. I haven't heard of anyone doing it. Oh sure, a man can move a mountain with a bulldozer, but I am speaking of miracles, the results of faith. Doing something with the mind a lone is called *telekinesis.*

"A person cannot say to the sea, 'hey tides,stop coming in' and they would stop. I might say that to the sea and then put my sleeping bag near the edge of the water and go to sleep, I will soon wake up with a bag of salt water to keep me company.. No judge on earth can give an order that no rain will fall that no hail will come or that a volcano will not explode. Man is powerless against the laws and forces of nature.

"Gary," Joe had continued since Gary seemed interested, "Man denies the existence of God in many different ways. Man doesn't have to just say, 'I don't believe in God' I once read where a man named Robert Ingersol, the first famous atheist, said that there was no God and there was no devil. Yet, when Ingersol died he had to be held on his bed for he screamed that the devil was there ready to take him away. That man was a famous atheist, even had an atheist church, but when he died, he died in fear. They say that the site of his church is today the site of a large Baptist Church."

Gary had then told Joe that the meanest and sorriest, the biggest crooks and liars that he knew where in church each Sunday. The boys he knew in school who had not missed going to Sunday School for ten years straight, these boys boasted of bedding a different girl each week..

"That's right, Gary," Joe had replied, "and the Devil uses that to his advantage. A person doesn't have to go to church to become a child of God. I am of the firm belief that a child of God can worship any time and in any place. I personally believe that if I attend church regularly and worship God when I go and praise his name, I have found God.

"An humble, uneducated man who delights in fishing in the moonlight or who loves to watch a beautiful sunrise or sunset in glorious technicolor, who quite possibly doesn't have his name written on a church roll; he might have never been inside a church; if

Again
If Christ Came Again

he believes in a great Creator, who puts his trust in Him, surely God is fair and imputes faith in him.

"A highly educated preacher who does not meditate daily to find God's will in his life, or he puts his faith in book knowledge, this man is less in God's sight than the uneducated, non-church going man.

"You see, Gary, it's when man realizes that the knowledge he has doesn't supply all of his needs and answers, and then he looks upwards to heaven, it is then that his real understanding begins. God can't teach a person who knows it all who has all the answers. When a person will humble himself before God it is then that he is able to be taught: to learn.. At first, the teaching is just a flicker in the night like in a well or a dark tunnel. As a person begins to be drawn to that light, to in fact make a movement toward that light, it is then that understanding begins to take root..

"Gary," Joe talked faster then, "I believe that we can find the will of God only in daily, almost constant prayer. When Jesus said 'a little child shall lead them' He knew exactly what He was saying So many preachers stumble over this simple truth. A small child is filled with belief and innocence, but then he is exposed to traditional church teachings and his belief and innocence are swept away and even unbelief takes over in its place.

"Some people believe only in their conscience. Many preachers with half the alphabet after their names stifle childhood beliefs. The American Indian, whom we treated like savages and stole their lands and their way of life, many had a quaint belief: he believed that each man had a heart shaped like a triangle with sharp corners. Each time the Indian did wrong, the heart spun around and hurt and the Indian knew he had done wrong and stopped. After many many wrongs and many many spinning, the sharp edges of the triangular heart were smoothed to where when it turned it brought no pain. He could do wrong without pain. God gives us all the inner feelings when we sin. We don't need some ranting preacher to till us or remind us of our sins. This is a private thing between a man and his God."

"But Joe," Gary had asked, his eyes showing his sincerity, "doesn't the Bible teach that because of Adam's sin in the Garden of Eden that man is tainted forever more? He is conceived in sin, born in sin and is naturally a living sin machine If I understand what you are saying, man can commune with nature and has no need of church attendance: just commune with nature..isn't that Pantheism, a worship of nature? Surely the august Joe is not panthesistic!"

"Gary," Joe had replied, "you have just given a prime example of man's efforts to place everything into little slots or cubby holes. Just because I enjoy a painting by Van Gough or some other famous artist doesn't make me oblivious to the fact that someone sometime took a piece of canvas and a paint brush and painted the work of art.

"A man who communes with Nature as did David Thoreau who wrote *Walden*, looks for God and then begins the tortuous journey toward the perfection God meant for man to reach.. Someone once said 'The mighty sun obeys God's law, and I, as a mere man, should strive to know God's law and obey the best I can.'"

+++++

As Joe sat on the rock, he smiled as he remembered this conversation with Gary. His best friend seemed to understand what Joe was saying. Gary had often attended church with Joe since then and they were still the very best of friends.

Joe idly looked across the vast expanse of greenery between him and Bethany. He saw the large trucks rushing in both directions along Interstate 20. It was like watching a silent movie, for the sounds of traffic did not reach up here. He saw a yellow butterfly kissing a bunch of wild violets. He tried too shake off the feeling of restlessness that permeated his entire being.

Suddenly, in an instant, there was a great wave of light. A radiance fell over the area where Joe sat. For a moment, Joe was blinded by the brightness of the light. He sat still, scarcely breathing, and to him he seemed to feel that he was leaving his body and slowly rising up, up, up. He was not frightened; rather he had the warmest, most peaceful feeling he had ever known. He was conscious of the great light and his feeling of peace blended together. He felt there was no limit, no boundary where he was. It was just a peaceful euphoria. He felt both peace and ecstasy. Joe knew he had not lost consciousness, for suddenly a thought took hold of his mind, filled ever fiber of his being. He could hear the Voice, actually hear it though no sound came to the mountain. No bird song, no insect sound, for some reason he felt he heard the words: *"Be Still and know that I am God."*

Joe was fully aware of what was happening. He was fully awake, it was no dream. He felt such a vastness.such glory, such an opening of his mind to understanding...of promise and a love for all mankind. He felt incredible hope and compassion. He felt as if he were looking into the heart of eternity itself., a place without walls without boundaries.

He felt like shouting. A warmth such as he had never before experienced seemed to fill his mind and his body. In fact, he felt as if he was released from his body, even from the world.. Perhaps he had died! He knew his surroundings, yet he felt no part of this earth, he was a part of some vastness beyond this life.

He felt expanded, not his body, just his mind.. The blinding glow swept him into a feeling of rapture, strength, tenderness. He felt as if his future was being installed in his mind like data on a floppy disk of a computer, never to be forgotten. Nothing needed explaining, he had no questions. Somehow he felt no fear. Before he knew it, Joe was crying. The tears that engulfed his body were not of sorrow; rather they were of extreme happiness and elation.. Suddenly, the light left him and he was on his knees by the rock on which he sat a few minutes ago. Had something really happened? Was he just coming out of a dream?

He felt elated.. He again looked down on Bethany. He could recognize the belfry of the Baptist Church and thoughts of the self-righteous Deacon Bandy entered his mind. He suddenly breathed a prayer for forgiveness of the things he had done to to rile the old man. A light breeze fanned his forehead and he lifted his thick hair to let some cool air reach his scalp.

Joe knew suddenly that he could not join the commercial part of the world. He knew his mind was agile enough that he could make a good living in the secular world. He had already met and made some tough decisions since graduating from high school. The several scholarships offered were indeed tempting He felt that the devil's offer of a life of riches and pleasure were indeed tempting. He breathed deeply and sat back thinking of Stella, his first girl who had given him his first kiss. It would be pleasant married to Stella with his own little house and his own job and his own settling down to a life very much like those of his peers.

Joe sat there for a while. He couldn't shake off that light of just moments ago. He could not fool himself. He knew exactly what it meant. He did not feel ready for it to take over his life. He stood and walked around for a while. He climbed a little higher up the mountain, almost to the summit. He noticed a gnarled Oak tree that really should not have been where it was growing. It had survived the onslaughts of nature for over 100 years, yet it still lifted its weathered head. A red bird sat proudly on the highest branch and sang loudly and even sweet and nastologicly. He watched the bird with fascination seeing the tan throat move up and down and quiver, keeping time to the music.

He returned to where he had sat a few moments ago and took his place there once again. He leaned against the rock and suddenly he was praying. He was praying aloud yet he could not understand the words. He was almost frightened as his lips uttered the strange, though pleasant words. He talked on and on, each word clipped from his lips in a slow rhythm. Then all was quiet, and Joe closed his eyes in prayer. Suddenly, he came to with a start. The time had become lost, and already the sun was looking for its bed in the western sky. Had he slept all that time? What was happening to him? Now the sun was settling behind the Bethany water tower. He must get home or his mother would worry.

He was so engrossed in the setting sun so lavish with its scarlet and shades of green and white on a canvas of blue, he almost tripped over a rock in the path. Once he saw that the stone was large and he had to hop and skip in order to regain his balance. He laughed loudly. He was happy. He felt as if all the cares he had ever experienced had been swept from his mind and body.. He actually whistled as he hurried down the mountain side.

The moon hanging loose in the sky looked look a skull he had examined once in science lab. It hung high over the Bethany courthouse bathing the tower in an eerie blue. As he neared home, he kicked some dust into the air and it looked like cobwebs in the dim light. All around him were sounds of the coming night.. Animals.

insects. birds, even man began robotic actions in preparation for the coming time of rest. He heard the shrill voice of some woman commanding her children to come into the house at once. From one house as he walked along, shrill laughter came from the living room. The boob tube was in full swing. In another house, he could see another family gathered around the TV, trays of food on their laps, the one-eyed monster holding their attention. Joe often said that television was the scourge of the the twentieth century.

Joe was outspoken on the uncontrolled use of TV. The average American family no longer was able to hold an intelligent conversation among its members.. This art had been sacrificed on the altar of television. In fact, Joe often mentioned an article in a recent magazine that was appearantly well-researched.. The article stated that the average youngster reaching eighteen, had spent more hours in front of a TV than he had spent in a class room.. He shuddered as he thought of fertile, young and untrained minds exposed to all the violence and sex that was served up daily on TV.. Kids viewed the killing of a fellow human being as just an every day occurrence. He abhorred the acts of men and women in bed as horrible fare for tender minds.

"God have mercy," he whispered. He sighed and breathed deeply as he passed a lilac bush and the heavenly scent filled his nostrils. He stopped for an instant and took several more breaths, thanking God for this gift.

As Joe neared home, he wondered how Mary would take his new status in life. Oh, his life was forever changed, and he knew he was powerless. He was compelled to do this thing. He felt that he had no choice, and if he had, he would choose the path anyway. How would his friends react? He had always tried to be tolerant of other people's beliefs and actions. should he expect the same tolerance from others? He tried to treat other people's beliefs with dignity, yet he felt that he would be granted the same consideration. He was used to being the butt of some of his peers jokes. Why did most people hate virtue? Or goodness in any form whatever? Was it because man's nature was basically evil? Why was it that people tried to destroy a person if he tried to live a decent life, one pleasing to God? Why was it that those who flaunted the laws of God were most times the most popular?

A good example was that star athlete who got on TV and bragged that he had bedded over 1000 women before he caught the Aids virus. This man was tauted as a hero, He was even invited to the White House. He was on many talk shows. He supposed that most people considered virtue a weakness. Perhaps it was just a ploy to hide their own depravity. This sophomoric attitude must be permanently affixed to the human brain at birth. Joe realized that he had been called odd for years, both by his peers and adults as well. He realized that when words of this new turn in his life was known about Bethany, his detractors would have a field day, knee deep in gossip.. He knew that this was one of the prices he was bound to pay for doing what he knew to be the will of God. He knew his future plans, and like King Solomon he had prayed to God for wisdom above material wealth. Not worldly wisdom, but wisdom not found in books: wisdom to be in God's divine will.. He was well aware of the fact that the average man had more interest in the area between a woman's thighs than he was in knowing God's will for his life.: wisdom for living a successful and happy life.

Joe knew that a lot of people did not like him. He felt that a lot of them had already allowed the circumstances of life geld them and hold them prisoner to public opinions. He felt a warm feeling knowing that most of the people who disliked him were in fact not like him., they were not what he was for which he was thankful.. He tried to remember his history classes, had he ever read of a man whom everybody liked ever amounting to anything? Even as a lad he had felt that if the world approved of something it was almost certain that God did not approve of it.. Jesus Himself had stated (as told in John's gospel) that anyone who loved the world hated God. He felt that meant that a man who loved the ways of the worldly people hated God's precepts.. Someone said, he remembered, "The mighty sun obeys God's laws, and I as a mere man, should strive to find God's will and do the best I can!'"

Joe had little use for those would use the Bible to enhance their own wealth or views. If more people spent less time trying to invent excuses for their actions and more time seeking God's will in their lives, they would indeed find the elusive happiness man so futilly seeks. Just last week, Joe was really suprized that someone actually put their thoughts into words. The man had stated that he had grave doubts that the Bible was in fact the Word of God.. Someone added that since the writing of the Bible things had changed and that the strict moral codes of the old times were not valid today.. This guy went on to say that Jesus approved of prostitution. He cited as proof the instance when some people brought to Jesus a woman caught in the very act of adultery. They stated that according to the Law Moses had gotten directly from God that the woman should be stoned. They asked Jesus' opinion.. Jesus knew it was just another of the traps set for him by the Pharisee party. He said, "Let the one among you that has no sin cast the first stone." He then stooped and wrote in the dirt at his feet.. One by one the members of the mob looked over His shoulder and read and then dropped the stone he held and silently went away. Jesus asked the woman where were those who would condemn her, and she shall 'none'. He then said "Neither do I condemn thee" The man had said that because of this, Jesus was in favor of prostitution. And because of this, Jesus does not condemn sex outside marriage. Joe was asked to respond to this and he had stated that to indulge in sex on any occasion other than the marriage bed, was defeating the greatest joy and gift that God had given to man. The fact of reserving sex for the one you loved enough to marry. Many did not like Joe's answer, but none challenged it at that time.

Joe always was plain in what he believed regarding sin. He often said that Christ said many times that all sin would be forgiven man except one: the sin against the Holy Spirit, Christ was talking of everyday sins. Joe said further that anyone who sinned and contritely went to the Father and asked forgiveness, God would forgive him. "I honestly believe," Joe had once said in that Bible class for young adults "that God will forgive a man of his sins, but I also believe that before a man can ask God to forgive him of his sins, that person must first forgive himself. I do not believe that contriteness can come before a man has settled this with his own soul. Only then will full forgiveness come."

It was just such statements as these that people felt too deep for their personal understanding. Many stated that they had never understood Joe and would probably never understand him. Deacon

Lee Roy Neal

Bandy had once said to his wife that he thought Joe was demented and would end up in the State Hospital for the insane.

At last, Joe reached his home and turned up the walk to this front door. He found Mary putting the final touches on the evening meal. He kissed her cheek and helped carry the bowls of steaming food to the table. As the family gathered, they held hands around the table, and Joe again thanked God for his wonderful family and the food. He also resolved not to reveal his experience on the mountain that day.

++

The following morning, Joe came from the shop into the house. It was about mid-morning.. He could see the flowers on each side of the walk way between the shop and the house. On the lawn toward the street, he could see the grasshoppers playing on the tall daisy stems, leaping on a stem and then riding it back and forth until it stopped. The sun reflected from their shiny bodies. He saw some birds lustily singing in the tree near the driveway. He saw the singing stop as a bird dived down to get a worm that had come up to see the sun. He saw the small rabbit that the kids had tamed drinking from its water pail, its cotton tail moving in time with its swallows. He entered the house and found his mother in the kitchen ironing clothes.

"Mom," he smiled, "can we take a break and talk for a while?" She put the iron in its bracket and turned the power switch off.. "I don't feel like working in the shop today. I just want to talk to someone, and you are the one."

"Sure, son, sure." She opened the refrigerator door and took a pitcher from it. "I just made a fresh batch of tea. Want some, or some lemonade?"

"Tea will be fine,, Mom" He went to the living room and sat in his favorite chair. Mary placed the glass on a napkin on a small table near him. The kids had all gone down town and they would likely not be disturbed for a while. Mary felt down deep in her mind that her life was about to change: that Joe was going to reveal some news.

"Mom," Joe took a healthy drink of the amber liquid, wiping his lips with the side of his finger. "As you know, I went up the mountain yesterday."

"And I am glad, son. You need to relax more." She looked carefully into the eyes of her first born son., Her heart was racing, for she could remember Joe in so serious a mood as he was then.

"Mom," he set the glass down again, his heart raced, "yesterday something happened on the mountain. I can't explain it, for I don't really know myself. I don't know if I fell asleep or what. I do know that hours passed that I could not then and cannot now account for." His eyes glowed and he had that warm feeling as he remembered the experience. "Suddenly I was aware of the brightest light, brighter than any I had ever seen, brighter than the sun at noon,. This light seemed to cover only the area where I was. Mom, I felt that I was in the very presence of God Himself." He licked his lips and smiled as the dimple showed and he took his lower lip between his teeth. "If Deacon Bandy ever heard me talking like this, he would have the district judge fill out commitment papers for me. Soon the men in the white suits would come for me."

He got up from his chair and went over to his mother seated on the couch. He knelt before her, taking her hands in his. "Mom, please try to understand. I feel in telling it to you will help me get it more solidly in my own mind. To hear it spoken out loud will make it more real. I hope you won't think me crazy. I am utterly sincere".

"I could never think that of you, my son." She swallowed and remained silent, feeling his tension through their hands. Outside, through the open window, a bird began to sing, and far off a dog barked.

"Mom, I want to give the rest of my life to a very special work. I feel compelled to do all in my power to make people understand exactly what the Bible says. I have to try, somehow, to make people follow the laws God meant for them to follow."

"But, Joe, that's why we have churches. To teach the people."

"The churches today are most of them perverted by tradition and other things just as ungodly."

"Joe," Mary spoke quickly, "If all the churches are doing this, and I can't say I believe that they are, how does this have anything to do with you?"

"I plan to organize a group of men and somehow, either from town to town, or organize another church, just something. I am sure

God will reveal what to do. I aim to preach and tell people exactly what the Bible teaches: the very things meant from the beginning."

"You mean, son, that you are going full time at this, that you might start a new kind of church?"

"Perhaps, Mom. I don't know at this point. I want to find a few good men who believe as I do and will do as directed by God Himself. If it means organizing a church, fine. If it means going from town to town like the old time medicine show did, then that will be it. I know only that I must do something concrete.

"You see, Mom, I feel that most people who go down the church aisle and make a profession of faith have absolutely no knowledge of what they are doing. Sort of like when a couple get married. They say the words 'till death us do part' and then get divorced a year or so later. Perhaps that's why one in two marriages fall apart. If they truly understood what 'cleaving only to him (her)' meant there would be less fooling around jumping from bed to bed.

"When a person, young or old, goes through the motions of 'accepting Christ as his Savior' he must truly realize that Christ did die for *him: that he really gave His life for him*, he must be willing in return to give or dedicate his life for and to Christ.. He must be willing to put all his likes and desires, his plans, everything after Christ. The surrender must be absolute. From then on it must not be me and mine, but yours.. Christ must be the center of his mind, his thoughts and his life from that moment on..

"Mom," Joe returned to his seat and took another drink of tea, "If people really took that view seriously, they would be more apt to follow the leadings of God in their lives. Christ must be the King of their lives. Understand?"

"Son," Mary stood and walked over to Joe, placing her hands on his head. "I want you to realize that whatever you decide, whatever you do, you have my full approval and support."

":Thanks, Mom, thank you very much." Mary poured some more tea in his glass. "But you surely know how a lot of people in this town already feel about me. I can take it, but what about you and the kids? They will surely be affected.. I just feel that I will be hated by more and more people as time goes by. More people will ridicule me for the step I am taking."

"Joe," Mary took a small ottoman nearby and sat on it looking into her son's eyes. "My prayer for you is that you will be happy regardless of the feelings of the world.. You must reconcile your self to living while you can not looking back and try not to let small people hurt you. Be grateful for each day, Joe. Try not to remember that hamburger you had at McDonalds last week or what meal you will have next Tuesday."

"Sure, Mom, Jesus said much the same thing, but He also taught planning. Remember about the man who started building a house and did not plan the cost? One just can't let things happen. You must plan for it too."

"Joe, I have no quarrel about planning for tomorrow. But such plans must not be set in concrete. Make sort of 'write in' plans, tentative plans for a while. Many people give up their whole lives because their plans are all for tomorrow. Such people deny themselves the pleasures of today because they are planning of pleasures for tomorrow. Don't fall into that trap, my son. One day the man who lives only for tomorrow wakes up and find they have lost their entire lives." I am for planning, Joe, but not to the exclusion of today.

"Go for it Joe, do what you feel you must do. I realize that if you stray very far from the traditional paths of church dogma, the world will act up. People will not like being told and shown and taught that all that glitters is not gold., so to speak.

"Remember this, my son, with all your heart and all your mind and all your soul.. Do what you feel God wants you to do.. Do not submit to the world. People will forgive a person almost anything but submission: submission inflaming into a worn rut or the path of least resistance. This is weakness, son. This is another 'no-no' of the world. The world is ever eager and ready to forgive the robber, the rapist, the embezzler. Forgive everything they do but never forgive the victim for being there to tempt the evil doer. Even though the world perhaps does not realize why they are unwilling to forgive the victim is because the victim had been weak.. I am sure that you know that death is the inevitable fate of all living creatures, especially man. How a man dies is most of the time his choice. He meets death fighting like a tiger, or he simply lies down and submits." She walked back over to the couch.

"Joe, I have something I have wanted to tell you for many many years. I just have never felt the right time until now.. Now, I feel like I know why I have waited all this time…

"I never did understand it when it happened nor did your father. In fact, to be perfectly candid, I still don't understand it." She drew in a full chest of air and was silent for a moment. Joe waited silently. The dog began barking again, and they could hear a car or two passing on the street.

"I loved your father so very very much, I still do. When I was thirteen, we became engaged. I was so happy, and so was my Joe." She got a far away look in her eyes as she remembered. In a moment she breathed deeply again and continued. "Then one day, a year later," she paused, reluctant to relive those moments of long ago, "I found out that I was pregnant." She could not help seeing Joe's head lift suddenly and his eyes come alive. "Now hear me out, son. I knew that this was impossible. You see, Joe, never had I been in bed or anywhere with any man or boy, not even your father.

"When I told your father he became angry. He did not believe I was a virgin, he left me, but not before accusing me of being a whore. I'll tell you, son, that night was the most miserable of my life. After he had said 'It takes two' and slammed the door and left, I spent the most miserable night of my life."

"Wow, Mom, I can understand why Dad was bowled over. My what a predicament to be in. Dad must have come around since you were married after all."

"Yes, he did, bless his heart, The very next morning. I came down the steps of my building on the way to school and there he was waiting for me, that sort of crooked grin on his face. Oh, Joe, he was such a wonderful man. He took my books as I walked to school. He asked forgiveness, and said that the believed me and that he did not understand anything except that he loved me and he said we would be married the very next week. We were so very proud when you came and we never mentioned it to each other or anyone again. I know Joe, I am perhaps being presumptuous, even vain, but I keep comparing my situation with another Mary long ago.,"

Again
If Christ Came Again

"I immediately thought of that Mom, Jesus and his mother Mary. People did not believe Mary's story either. Many called her a fallen woman. Many goons today even name a Roman soldier as the father of Jesus A noted minister in the largest Baptist Church in New York, Dr. Fosdick, I think his name was, he advocated such a tale and even named the soldier.

Many call Christians stupid for believing in the Virgin birth, but that is the corner stone on which all our creed are based.. Did you know that there is written records of at least one girl who became pregnant while still a virgin. It happened in Chicago in a tenement where several families used the same bathroom. Well, a young man relieved himself sexually while taking a bath and drained the water and this young lady took a bath and became pregnant with his sperm."

"But such a thing did not apply to me, Joe. I lived with my aunt and we had our own bath."

"Mom," Joe smiled. This might seem silly, but do you suppose that I might not really have an *earthly* father"

"I don't know, son, I don't know. I do know that God who made me for some reason, could have made my body function as it did with no help from mortal man. All these years I have accepted it solely on faith. Joe, you and I are the only people on earth who know this. I hate to think what people would do with this knowledge if they ever discovered it."

"No one will ever know, Mom. I know I could never have loved Dad more than I did and do, even if he had been my biological father. And, Mom, let's agree here today never to mention this again. Okay?" He stood up and took his lip between his lips and paced the room. Mary sat quietly. "Mom, do you suppose. Do you think that.. Could it be that that is why I am so against the traditional church? I know that Jesus often said that man makes null and void the Word of God by their traditions." Joe paused and looked out the window. Then Mary saw that his eyes got a sort of distant look in them. He shook his head. "You know,Mom, I don't find it hard to believe that I have no earthly father. It's as if…no, it couldn't be. I am not worthy..yet why am I so adamant in my calling?" He went to the couch where Mary had re seated herself. He knelt and again took her hands in his. He kissed them softly. "Why am I so possessed? What can I, a poor man do to make a noticeable change? Why must I be compelled to devote the rest of my life to the Heavenly Father? Could that have been God on the mountain yesterday? Am I, a simple poor man to be like John the Baptist, simply a 'Voice crying in the wilderness'? He stood and paced again, the tea forgotten the sounds from without the house unheard. He hit his hand with the fist of the other. Outside the sounds of the children began as they were coming home.

"Joe," Mary stood and put both hands on his shoulders and looking quietly into his eyes, "I simply want you to know and never forget that I believe in you, and though I understand very little, I believe in you and will stand by you no matter where your feet lead you. I love you, my son, I love you."

"Thanks, Mom, thanks a million You know, I love you more now than ever before." He gave her a boyish hug. "You have any cookies? I have to get James who I hear coming in. We have to deliver that Elkin order this week. It is the last one I will do."

"Then, you intend starting your crusade at once?"

"Sure thing, Mom. Sure thing."

++++++++++

The next day, Joe went over to his best friend's house. It was after work hours and Joe found Gary in his back yard spading a garden plot.

"I know, Joe, I should have dug this earlier, but Mom wont give me any peace until I get her garden ready to plant. I tried to explain to her that it was too late for a spring garden, so this can be a summer-fall garden.." He laid the spade down and shook hands with Joe.

"How have you been doing, old buddy? Haven't seen you for some time now. Made a million yet?" He smiled and dusted dirt from his knees.

"Things are super, Gary. At least, I think they are. I just felt that I wanted to talk. Want me to help finish this digging?" Joe picked up the spade.

"No, Joe, there's enough garden space to feed a dozen people, and there's only mom and myself."

A gust of wind blew dust in their eyes causing each man to close his eyes against more dust. The grass on the lawn was getting over the early spring spurt of growth and was settling down to early summer fare. The fruit of nearby trees was almost ready for harvest, and the flowers that Gary's mother had planted were in full bloom. Joe noticed his favorite, Shasta daisies. He had given Gary the start of these plants. A blast of wind scooted a few leaves left over from winter, moving them along Gary's driveway very like the wind moving a small sailboat on a calm body of water. The traffic on the freeway made a subliminal roar.

"How about a cup of coffee, Joe?" Gary cleaned his shoes carefully before entering the house. Joe followed suit. "I think Mom just made a fresh pot. She told me some time ago before she left the house for that meeting at the church. Looks like she left it plugged in." He reached for two cups from the sink.

"That will be fine, Gary. But I came over mostly for some chit chat."

Gary put the cups on a small tray and they soon found themselves in the living room, coffee in hand.

Gary," Joe set the cup on the coffee table. "Do you still hate your job the same as you always say?"

"You had better believe it, Joe. It seems I am really stuck in a rut there. You know what a rut is, I'm sure: it's a grave with the ends knocked out. Here I am thirty years old, and people say I am too old to train for a new job, especially a technical one. I sometimes wish, Joe, that I had gone to college. It might have led to a job I like better than the job I have." He took a sip of coffee and Joe heard the audible sigh escape his lips.

"Gary," Joe's voice was serious. I really came over to throw a few thoughts at you. Things you will very likely think are 'off the wall'. I guess I want to use you for a sounding board.. You and I have been best friends since sixth grade. We have always thought nearly alike."

"Sure, Joe." He put his cup on the table and leaned back. "Lay it on me, old friend." Gary had not failed to notice the strange look in his friend's eyes. It was a sort of deepness that he had not seen there before.

"Well, Gary," Joe licked his lips, a habit he had had all his life when he became tense or thoughtful. Joe was trying to find the right words, to find the best place to begin. He took a deep breath. "You are not the only person in this room that has been dissatisfied with his job, his lot in life. Of late, and I've told no one until now, I have lost the joy I used to have in carpentry work. The satisfaction seemed to have gone away someplace. The work has suddenly become a chore instead of a pleasure of just a few months ago.

"Yesterday, Gary, I did not feel like working at all. The kids were off to Vacation Bible School at the church. I played hooky from work."

"Trying to be a school boy again, eh?"

"I have had my share of playing hooky as well you know since we usually did it together. I wonder how many fish we have caught over the years while playing hooky from school. Any way," Joe sat back and still searched for the right words., "I felt that I had to get away from Mom, the kids, the shop, away from the world I guess. I climbed old Smoky and went up past the kissing rock and sat in a place I often go just to think." He decided to plunge into the whole thing. "I was just thinking and thinking, and suddenly." He stopped as he saw Gary sit up straight. He was silent for a while.

"Go on, Joe, go on. What else?"

"Suddenly a bright light covered the space where I sat. Somehow I was not scared. I don't know how long the light was there.. I could have fallen asleep, for time passed that I was not aware of.. It was if I had left my body and gone on a trip…that I had returned, and a different person was inside my skin. It was as if..as if..I had been reborn with a different brain. I had a warm, glorious feeling. I felt a surge of knowledge within my mind leaving not one *iota of doubt about what I wanted..no that's not the word, about what I had to do.*

"Gary, it was not only what I **had** to do, it was what I **wanted** to do and had wanted, unconsciously, to do all of my life.

"You know, Gary, of my many 'run ins' with Deacon Bandy, and how I have always maintained that a lot of things the traditional church does and teaches are not done according to the Bible."

"I know, Joe." Gary smiled, "how well I know. You have no idea how often you have made my day when you made Bandy look like the egotistical ignoramus that he really is." He smiled and took a sip of coffee. "So, you had some sort of 'experience' on the mountain yesterday. What comes now?"

"Gary, you must hear me out before calling for the men with the white coats and the large nets" He picked his cup and drained it, licked his lips and leaned back in the chair. A look of expectancy covered his handsome face. "Gary, this will really take a lot of understanding." He managed a smile.

Joe, you insult me. You know I'll understand."

"I fervently hope so. Oh I truly hope so, Gary." He paused for an instant. "Gary, I want to organize a group of men, no particular number, who think about like I think. I will want them to be in a position to give up their jobs, give up their way of life and throw in their lots with me. I haven't worked out the details yet, but we could go from town to town, or we could settle in one place, but the purpose of the organization would be to spread the true Gospel of Jesus, to tell the people the true things that God meant all along for His people to know and to follow. Now, Gary, don't take this wrong, but I plan to follow the steps of Jesus, even though I am unworthy to kiss the bottom of one of His feet. In spite of the organized church, the **traditional** church. I want to start a real, honest to goodness church adhering to the true principles for which Christ died."

"But, Joe, surely you know that you will have a powerful built-in enemy, an enemy full grown and ruthless and jealous of any hint of anyone trying to usurp its hold on people.. If you reveal to a group of people that perhaps they have been wrong about something, they will stop at nothing to mash you like a bug. They will go all out to eliminate you, and I am ashamed to say that they will not care how they accomplish it. Do you know, I think you would be safer sticking your head in a den of rattlesnakes."

"Sure, Gary, you know that I have thought of that, but I still think that God wants me to do this, but I also feel that God will guide me in finding a way to do it, and I also feel that He will protect me from serious harm.

"Look at what happened to Jesus, the very Son of God. He was framed and executed by the high and mighty church officials of His day just because their power base was threatened.. You see, Gary, you can fool around with a man's wife and he is likely to forgive you, but if you start fooling with his wallet, he will never forgive you for that. Jesus was cutting off the money supply.. That's why it will be difficult to assemble a staff of men, perhaps 10 or even less. I hardly know where to begin."

"You have one already Joe"

"You mean, Gary, that..just like that?" He smiled broadly.

"Yes, Joe, just like that." Gary's eyes shown. "I want to be your first recruit.!"

"But what about your job, your mother?"

"To the dickens with the job, and Mom doesn't need my income. She has social security, and the house was paid for before Dad died. She will be fine, Joe, just fine.

"Diffugere nives,redeunt iam gramina campis/ Arboribusque comae!" one smiled as he remembered the Latin class when he had to memorize it.

"There you go, Joe, with that Latin stuff. I can't see how you remember that from over ten years ago. What does it mean?"

"I would not remember it if Mrs. Lipes hadn't made us memorize it. As well as I remember it means: The snows have scattered and fled, and already the grass comes again in the fields and on the trees.\ Gary, as long as man lives and as long as man has a worthy goal, winter will come and the grass will too each year. I don't mind telling you that I secretly hoped you would be my first recruit. You have come a long way since you gave up atheism. But God has provided me with you and already I feel that the load is only half as heavy since you are holding up one end..

"Jesus sent out his disciples and they began with nothing, only the clothing on their backs. God provided for them."

Joe, we will not be flat broke. I have a little money in the bank and my old car, that's a start. Your comments please." Gary was like a small boy.

"I have a few dollars in the bank, but I feel I must leave that for Mom. She has Dad's social security for her and each of the kids, so she will be okay. I think we could trade your car for a truck, say a one ton one. We could rent a tent and get some chairs and hold church in the tent, and at night we could sleep in the tent."

Again
If Christ Came Again

"You mean that we would have to live on what we took in in offerings?"

"Sure!"

"We would receive no salary, no stipends?"

"None, unless you could get Bandy to donate some money each month" Joe laughed as did Gary. "That's why the men we choose will have to be a very special breed. Dedicated men. Not lovers of filthy lucre as Paul put it.."

"Well, Joe," Gary stood up and put a hand on Joe's shoulder. "I know of two candidates for the loony farm and both of them live in Bethany.. Wow! I This is really something. I'll likely be stabbed by Bandy personally, but count me in, Joe, count me in."

++++++++

A week later, the word of Joe's latest caper was widespread over Bethany. Many was sure of it at last. Joe had quietly slipped over the edge of sanity. Not only had he fallen over, but he had taken that fine young Gary with him. Bandy laughed as best he could and glee colored his words as he spoke to his wife. "Didn't I tell you? I told you long ago that Joe was a nut. Imagine, a man who did cabinet work so good he had a waiting list. He could name his own price. Wonder how long before he is standing in line for food stamps?"

If Joe and Gary heard the gossip, they seemed unaware of it. They had managed a nice trade for a three-quarter ton Chevrolet truck. So far, their funds did not provide for a tent. They decided to apply to the County Commissioners for a permit to use the county fair grounds for a temporary meeting place. They had decided on meeting each Saturday. Joe had discussed this in detail with Gary.

"I want us to hold services on Saturdays. I firmly believe that this is the real Sabbath, the seventh day God meant for us to observe. By doing this we will take one club from the enemy's hand: taking people from their churches to attend this one."

"Good thinking, Joe, that's smart." Gary. You convinced me of that long ago. Let's go to the County Judge right now, and let's go from there."

"I went yesterday and he said we could meet here for twenty-five dollars each week. There are restrooms near by and the weather will hold for weeks now."

"You are wasting no time, Joe."

"I think we are many many years behind schedule."

Joe went to a spot where he felt the platform should be. It was on higher ground, and a beautiful oak tree would spread its branches in a beautiful way. Gary had gone to see about getting seating. He closed his eyes and talked to the Father giving thanks for progress thus far. He did not see the young man approaching him until he was only a few paces away. He opened his eyes and the man was suddenly kneeling before Joe.

"Master," the man said softly, "bless me and let me become one of your helpers."

"Don't call me Master, sir." Joe was embarrassed, "And don't kneel to me, please. I am nothing. I deserve no honor. I can't bless you or anyone else. All I can do is to ask the Father to bless you."

"Please, oh please, sir," the young man stood up. "Please ask God to bless me."

"Father," Joe placed one hand on the man's head and took the right hand of the man in his other hand, "Father, Almighty God, I ask that you look into the mind and heart of this young man, and in the blessed name of Jesus, I ask that you give a special blessing to him. Help him to understand what following You will cost him in time and effort and reputation. Help him to love you enough to place You and Your cause above all else in his life." Joe then loosed the man's hand and raising his hand high to heaven almost shouted, "In the Name of Jesus. In the Name of Jesus, have your way in this young life." He pressed his hand firmly on the man's head and was silent for a few seconds.

"Thank you, sir, Oh thank you." Joe saw tears in the man's eyes.: He noticed that the man was tall and thin, his skin pale as if he had spent many days out of the sun's rays. He had a smooth, healthy skin despite the paleness. His eyes sparkled and were larger than average. They were a sharp blue and spoke when he spoke. Some might call his features effeminate, but Joe thought of the term regal. The wrinkles around his mouth gave evidence of much laughter and of a happy person.. He was smiling now, and as Joe removed his hand from the man's head, he noticed white even teeth showing no smoking stains.. His curly blonde, almost copper colored, hair was cut longer than Joe wore his, but he knew the present generation liked long hair. Everything about the man showed breeding and culture. He was a stranger to Joe. He judged the man's age around twenty. For some reason Joe sensed a stability and seriousness about the man who stood before him.

"What is your name? Do you live in Bethany?"

"My name is Mark, and I live here in Bethany. I just moved down here from Chicago. I have been here about four months. Do you remember that poor woman hanging on the doctor's gate a few weeks ago?"

"Yes, Mark, I do remember it well."

"That's the first time I ever saw you. I could never get it out of my mind."

"What do you mean, Mark?"

"What you did for that poor woman. You actually healed her!"

"Only God can heal, Mark."

"All right, you asked God and He healed her. I have wanted to come talk with you, but never had the nerve. I work at the mobile home factory North of town." He smiled and Joe relaxed. "I wanted to know more about you, and now I want to be one of your active followers."

"What makes you think you want to do that?"

"Oh, sir, it is all over town, what you and Gary are going to do. A lot of people at the factory say you are nuts, but not me. You really healed that woman."

"You are wrong, Mark, God does the healing. I was just the conduit."

"All right, but I still want to follow you. My life since high school has been a drag. I want to be out there, where the action is."

"Mark," Joe looked into Mark's eyes closely, his heart pounding. Could this indeed be another Gary? "The Bible said that a follower of Christ must deny himself. Do you know what I am planning to do?"

"I think so. I know that you are different. I know you don't believe in the church as it is today. I have been attending the First

Baptist Church though I have never joined. I saw one Sunday when you made a monkey out of Bandy.. I am convinced that whatever your beliefs, they must be different from people like Bandy. I am willing to learn."

"Mark," Joe's voice was stern and business like. "Are you willing to give 24 hours a day to the work? Are you willing to be numbered with a minority cause? Are you willing to be painted with the same brush I am and will be painted with?"

"I truly believe that I am."

"Then meet me here at this time tomorrow>"

Mark left, his loose jeans flopping about his legs. He was almost running and leaping, joy showing in ever step he took. Joe had not said no. He had a chance!"

The following day was Thursday, and Joe and Gary were discussing the coming premier service. They had used some of their dwindling funds to buy lumber and the two men had fashioned some crude benches for the audience which might or might not attend the service.. Joe told Gary about Mark and was pleased to know that Gary already knew him. It was at this moment that Mark arrived, slightly out of breath for he had jogged from town.

"Mark," Joe said after greetings were exchanged. "I see you know Gary, and after praying about this I am very pleased to tell you that you are now a member of our little group" He took Mark's hand and so did Gary and the three had a brief prayer for thanksgiving and guidance.

"Mark, you will have to grow a thick hide rather quickly, for the darts and arrows will soon be flying about all our heads."

"I am used to it, Joe," Mark said. "In school, I was what you would call a loner. The other kids did not like me, and at times it hurt and was a problem."

"That's fine, Mark," Joe smiled at the man. "When people don't like you that's pretty good proof that you are not like them, that you are not what they are. You should be elated, boy. I never heard of anyone that everybody like who was ever anyone important. I think that if the world approves of you you are where the Devil wants you. Remember what John's Gospel says, 'He that loves not this world is

Again
If Christ Came Again

no enemy of God' Be glad when men 'dump' on you, Mark, you must be doing something right."

"Mark, you never asked for any details, so perhaps you and me and Gary should sit for a spell in these nice church pews" They sat down, and the bright summer sun warmed their heads and shoulders. A squirrel was playing tag with another squirrel, and some blue jays were having a heated argument about something. The slight ammonia odor from a nearby horse barn tainted the air just a bit, and then suddenly a slight change in wind direction brought the wonderful summer odor of wild flowers in the pasture near by.. Gary had managed to get an old fashioned coffee pot and had made a camp fire and had come up with a fresh pot of coffee. Each man poured a cup of the steaming brew and Mark spoke first.

"It's all from Odd-ball city, Joe," Mark began, taking a healthy gulp of coffee. "When I woke up yesterday morning, I had the strongest feeling that I did not want to go to work that day. I felt, for some strange reason, that I should try to find you. I had gone to bed the night before and was thinking of all the talk and how stupid you were and Gary no better. I felt that I did not want you to be alone, facing the mob. I knew then that I wanted to join forces with you. I guess I should have my head examined, for I have enough sense to know that you will be a sitting duck, a target for anyone wishing to make brownie points with the mob. Strange, that did not bother me a bit. I knew I had to find you and join your crusade if you would have me."

"Mark, I had no problem when I prayed last night. I knew before I opened my mouth that you were to be one of us. I actually knew it yesterday, but I wanted to be sure. When I told Gary this morning he told me that he knew you and felt you would fit right in.

"I told Gary about it, but I will repeat it briefly. Not long ago I went up on the mountain to relax, and I had some kind of an experience. It was if God Himself came down and made His will known to me. I knew from the time I started off the mountain that I was committed for the rest of my life. Your being led here is just another sign." Joe stood up. He walked over to the crude podium and then turned and looked at his 'flock'.

"You have or we have a built in, ready-made enemy: the leaders of the traditional church. For years and years people have left their brains at home or outside the church and have gone to church and have accepted every word some preacher has uttered with no thought as to its validity. People simply did things without knowing why.

"About ten years ago, I took a bunch of boy scouts on a vacation to a National Forest. There were many flocks of sheep grazing with their shepherds. One shepherd moved his flock from one pasture or area to another. The sheep passed very near where I was standing. They passed through a narrow gorge between two rocks. As they were passing, I placed a stick across the path and the next sheep jumped right over it: no problem. Then after about twenty sheep passed, I removed the stick and a unusual thing happened. The sheep still jumped over the stick that was no longer there. They jumped because the sheep in front jumped. Then needed no reason, they did no thinking, they asked no questions. They jumped because the one in front jumped. I thought, how like those sheep is the average church member today. they do things exactly as they have been done for hundreds of years.

"I read in the papers about a young high-school girl who had won first prize in a cooking contest. The prize was for $25,000 and her recipe was baked ham. The local paper sent its food editor to get the recipe for its readers. When the editor met the young girl and congratulated her she asked for the recipe The girl began by saying that she took the ham from the wrapper, washed it and cut about four inches off the end of the ham and went on by giving usual things to do to bake a ham.

"When she finished the editor questioned the reason for cutting four inches from the ham. The young girl said she did not know, but her mother taught her and that's why she did it. The editor went to the mother and after congratulating her on her daughter's win asked her her recipe It was the same as the daughter's and when the editor question the four inch cut, the mother remarked that she did not know why, that her mother taught her to bake a ham that way.

"The editor found the grandmother and the same thing happened. She told the editor that she felt like an idiot, but that was the way her mother taught her. The editor found that the great grandmother was in a nursing home in California, and she got permission from her boss and soon found the little old lady rocking contentedly in a rocker. The editor soon had the little old lady talking. She remarked that she went to the smokehouse and chose a good ham and washed it and cut about four inches off the end. It was then that the excited food editor stopped and asked her why she cut the end off the ham. The little old lady smiled and said that it was because her pan was too small to hold the ham so she cut the end off of it.

"You see, Mark," Joe sat down again, "I find that to be a perfect example of people in the traditional church today. They simply do not question, they do not think, and if some preacher says so, that is the truth with no questions.

"I hope I have made myself clear. I want to organize a church where the people will not leave their brains at the front door. I want people to question and search the Bible and if ever I am in error, I will ask forgiveness and mend my ways."

"A church," Mark cried. "You called it a church!"

"So I did. I hadn't really thoughts of it before. Of course it will be a church. I want to find some more men who will, together with you and Gary, be a board of directors. Someone who will put their talents to work and together we will seek God's will in all that we do. In that way, how can we fail?"

"Gary, how about you and Mark and myself walk down town and see what is going on. I feel that it is important. You have a pretty good start so far, don't you?"

"Sure, Joe. Things will be all right here. Let's go in the truck." They climbed into the truck after Gary had made sure the campfire was out and that there was no danger to any of their things. They soon drove the truck was to downtown Bethany and they stopped near the park..

They got out and entered the beautiful park and the warm weather had brought many people out to enjoy the fresh air. They came near a group of about fifteen people and Joe was surprised to hear his name mentioned by a man he knew from the church.

"Hi, Joe," the startled man was not expecting to see Joe in a park. He was always working. "We were just talking about you. I was telling the folks how you healed that poor woman at the doctor's gate a few weeks ago."

"I didn't heal her! please," he took in all the people in a brief glance.." give the credit to the One who really healed her, our God in Heaven. God healed the woman, not me. I was only the instrument He used."

"Can you really heal people?" A man about thirty asked, seemingly not understanding what Joe had said. The man was young, yet he seemed tired. He wore blue overalls and had a red bandanna tied loosely around his neck.

"Sir," Joe tried to make each word crisp and plain, "I can not heal anyone. God does tell us in His word that if we ask anything in His Son's name, believing, He will grant it."

"Please, Sir, listen to me. My brother is sitting on that bench over there," the man pointed a thin finger to a bench near by, "He was born blind and," the man faltered, trying to choose the right words, "please, sir, give him his sight!"

Joe's heart raced for an instant. He did not know why they stopped the truck at the park. He did not know even why they got out and entered the park. He began to believe that the very God had led him here. Something was about to happen. The hairs on the nape of his neck stood up. He felt that a test was about to fall on his shoulders.

"Bring your brother here, sir." As the man left, Joe saw that the crowd had grown to about fifty people, all staring, some mouths agape. The trees were dressed in their mature green, and in one tree a redheaded wood pecker was playing a tat-a tat melody on the bark of a tree in search of a worm or bug. A large fountain about twenty feet in diameter was gurgling pleasantly, throwing water high in the air where each drop magically turned into a newly faceted diamond. The flowers, the grass, the bushes, all looked brand new even though fall was knocking at the door. Joe could hear the traffic on State 64 that ran through Bethany. It was filled with cars of people going home from work to nearby towns and farms., In a sort of subliminal haze, the huge trucks on Interstate 20 could be heard. Joe saw the man bring another to the center of the circle. He was about mid thirties, and he was dressed as was his brother. The overalls were clinched tightly around his narrow waist. His chestnut brown hair was thick and cut short, and already streaks of gray were evident. His temple hair was almost white. His facial features were remarkedly like those of his brother. He was taller than Joe, and he looked massive. He had the appearance of one who did hard exercise every day. His eyes were a dark brown, but the had that unmistaken look all blind people seem to have, giving his face a sort of moronic look. Soon he stood straight and tall before Joe. The only sound was of the water falling back into the fountain.

"Sir, this my brother and he has never been able to see." The brother's face was filled with hope and expectancy. Joe could feel the faith in the brother's voice. Joe's felt a tenseness and he placed a hand on the blind man's shoulder.. As Joe spoke, the vacant eyes looked toward the sound of Joe's voice.

"Sir," Joe's words were low and kind, and yet it seemed that all the people could hear. They held a collective hope that perhaps they were going to witness a..a..something. Just something was about to happen. "do you believe that God can heal you?"

"I do believe, sir,as much as my faltering human faith can believe." The voice had a slight tremor.

Joe took a handkerchief from his pocket and dipped it in the nearby fountain which was less than an arm's length away. He squeezed it dry and then folded it neatly into a rectangle shape. He placed it over the man's eyes, and told him to hold it there with both hands. He then placed his left hand on the blind man's head and lifted his right hand high in the air. Joe felt Gary and Mark lift both their hands high in the air also.

"In the Blessed Name of Jesus Christ, I command that your eyes receive their sight. In the name of Jesus! In the Name of Jesus!" He paused, keeping his hands still.. He closed his eyes and the crowd saw Joe's lips moving and those very near heard strange words coming softly from Joe's lips. Now Joe placed both hands on the man's head and shouted: In the Name of Jesus!" Back at the edge of the crowd that had grown to about sixty people, someone whispered, "This is a lot of hooey. He wont make it, but it's a good show. Better than those TV re-runs"

"Shut up, you idiot. What you need is to get Joe to pray for a brain for you." A woman was barely able to keep her voice down. Joe stood still and tall, not moving, then the people saw his expression change.. His face almost glowed. It held such an assurance such a confidence, that no one doubted. "Thank you, Jesus, thank You Father, he whispered. He carefully removed the cloth from the man's face.

"Open your eyes, my brother," Joe said.

The man slowly tentatively opened his eyes, and every eye in the park was glued on the man's face.. Slowly, the vacant look was gone, and the expression racing over the man's face told them all that they had witnessed a miracle.

"I can see!" the man screamed. "I can see! I see the trees, I see the sky, I see the people, and he grabbed his brother who was weeping large tears. He then turned to Joe and taking Joe's hands kissed them and then looked deeply into Joe's eyes. "I want to pay you, sir, I want to pay you."

"I want no pay, sir." An inspiration came to Joe. "If you like, come out to the fair grounds this Saturday at ten in the morning.' He raised his voice to take in all the people. "All of you are invited to the very first meeting of a brand new church called **Our Fathers House**. You are all most welcome."

The crowd dispersed quickly, each person wanting to be the first to tell of the Miracle that happened in the Bethany Park. Later, that night, Joe's name was uttered in almost every house in town. Many knew of Joe and the names he was called. They knew of his disputes with the religious leaders in town. Was a new day dawning in Bethany?

CHAPTER FIVE

SATURDAY dawned bright and clear. The eastern sky was burning crimson, painting everything and the belfry of the court house looked as if it had been dipped in red paint. Even for a late summer day, the birds in the trees near the fair grounds were furnishing the music of springtime. The only man-made sounds came from the great trucks on the distant freeway as they fled toward many different destinations.

The first thing Joe did on arrival at the church site was to compliment Gary and Mark for the preparations they had made. They had managed for a mower and had mowed the grass, and the ten benches were steady, and at the front, they had managed a podium and three chairs behind it.. They had taken four picnic tables and had fastened them together to form a dais on which the podium and chairs were placed. Joe meant to ask but forgot where the two men had managed for some artificial grass on top of the tables. It was like that used at grave sites to cover the mound of dirt to hide it from the eyes of the family.. Why did people refuse to face reality? All knew that the cold earth was piled in on each casket, so why try to hide it?

Joe was a little surprised to find people had already started to gather an hour before the scheduled hour to begin.. Most people in Bethany knew of the site, for it was here that the annual appearance of the traveling circus pitched its tents.. Perhaps the people were here to see a different kind of circus. He pushed the thought as unworthy from his mind. Joe had sat himself in the cab of the truck parked a short distance from the gathering.. He was there, but apart. He had noticed several drinking fountains scattered around, and there were two rest rooms conveniently near. He saw an old school mate, Johnny Harris parked in his squad car near the entrance to the place. He wondered if the Sheriff's department expected trouble, or was it curiosity?

By ten o'clock, the benches were filled, and many sat in cars parked near the deputy's car.. Some people had brought blankets and were sitting on the ground. The people were silent, a few small children acted up but were quickly silenced by their parents. A slight breeze wafted over the heads of the audience, and the smell of the flowers from the near pasture were pleasant. Even the bees, flying over head were non-threatening as they went from flower to flower to hives. The breeze got lower and the people could see back of the dais the wild flowers were waving at the audience. The Indian Paint brushes, the sun flowers, the wild daisies and wild clover were moving in unison.

The seats were filled, and most of the place around the benches was occupied. About ten cars held people. Gary estimated that a little over a hundred people were present.

Promptly at ten, Joe came to the platform together with Gary and Mark. Joe sat for a minute with his head bowed in a silent prayer. He held his Bible firmly in his brown hands.. At exactly ten, he stood behind the podium. He gazed over the people, and for an instant was seized with stage fright. Joe was flabergasted to see several members of the Baptist church including of all people Deacon Bandy and his wife. He had no time to wonder why they were here. Deacon Bandy was very imposing, sitting on a bench at the back. He had an unfriendly expression on his face. He was dressed in his everyday clothes, not his Sunday Best he always wore on church days.

Joe imagined that Bandy was here with others who hoped to see Joe fall flat on his face. Other people had come to see the successful launching of a new Christian movement, others were ambivalent as to what they expected. They wanted to be present if anything did happen. Those who had been fortunate enough to be in the park when the man received his sight were sort of heroes to the rest of the town. Some expected nothing, for after all wasn't this a local man? Wasn't this that carpenter and cabinet maker who lived just past the grammar school? He was practically born here. He attended Bethany schools. He was just one of the locals.

Others considered Joe with awe. The man who had received his sight just a day or so ago was there and so were many of his friends. Of all the people in front of him, Joe felt that here was one who was really on his side. It made him feel less alone. Joe stood silently, and his piercing blue eyes searched every face. When he looked at Bandy, the man dropped his head.. Over to Joe's right were several people in wheel chairs. Two women were on crutches, sitting in folding camp chairs.

There was a sort of sternness on Joe's face, yet there was something else there that made every mother want to fold her arms around him and keep him from all harm. Joe stood a moment longer, confidence flowing through his body with the speed of light. A small baby began whimpering, but a bottle thrust in its mouth stopped that. Joe took a deep breath and began in a loud clear voice.

"Friends, we are so happy that so many of you have come out for this initial meeting of **Our Father's House**. We have chosen this name in order that any member, present and future would not be prone to forget whose house this really is. Here, as long as I have anything to say about it, God's will and His way will be held high for all to see. The will and the Words of God will be clearly expounded as well as this feeble man is able to decern and expound them. My one aim is to preach and to teach the perfect will of God. This church is affiliated with no denomination and is beholden to no man or group of men. We are accountable only to God and Him alone. My aim and my prayer is to lead the people of this body to know and to follow the perfect will of the Father.. It is hoped that whoever stands here to lead this church will follow the will of the Holy Spirit until the end of time.

"It is impossible for me to embrace all of the things in my mind and on my heart at this initial meeting.. Each week we will explore different facets of the Christian beliefs and Christian living. I will say or do nothing unless it is perfectly clear that it is of God.. I want to make myself perfectly clear up front that I have no animosity toward any church, any man or group of people. None. I begin this work with the greatest humility I can summon. Please forgive this egotistical remark, but it explains clearly my aim: I plan to be, like John the Baptist, a Voice crying in the wilderness.

"The Bible plainly states that by tradition, the church has made null and void the word of God., so the main thrust of this ministry is to make known what the law and the will of God really is.". Joe held the Bible high. "We will not search any place at all except between the covers of this Book. This is our guide, and the tenet of this church is to seek and follow it." Joe paused for he saw that Deacon Bandy had risen. Joe nodded for him to speak.

"It seems to me Joe, from what you have just said, that you are setting yourself up as a pastor. Please tell the people here where and when you were ordained to the ministry." He began with a sort of squeaky voice, but soon it became firm as he finished. Joe took a breath and Gary was ready to go wipe the sardonic expression off the deacon's face.

"I was chosen and ordained in the same manner and by the same Person who chose and ordained Jesus."

Many in the crowd clapped and cheered. Bandy's face became brick red. He wondered how Joe seemed ever ready with an apt answer. He stood up once again.

"And please tell these good people here the college or seminary where you graduated that qualifies you to be a minister of the Gospel." He trembled a little as he waited.

"Mr. Bandy, may I answer your question by asking you one? What college or university did Jesus attend?"

The crowd breathed a collective sigh of relief as Bandy took his seat and Joe noted that he turned to the man next to him an whispered in his ear. The other man smiled.. Joe continued.

"**Our Fathers House** has two members beside myself. Gary, please stand, and Mark, will you stand.. This is sufficient, for three is a magic number. It was the number of days that Jonah spent in the fish's belly. It was enough days to straighten out his thinking. Jesus was in the heart of the earth three days and it was sufficient for Jesus to Save the world from sin. From we three, we hope to build a power house for the enlightenment of what God's word really says. We will grow, for God will add to our three here today. You just can't come up here and say I want to join **Our Fathers House**. You can't just join, you have to dedicate yourself, your will and your resources to the cause of Christ and the Father. The members here must be dedicated to promulgating the truth of the Gospel as Christ taught it. Upon joining this church, the member must be burning with a desire to further the truth as revealed to us by God Himself.

"I could not care less as to what clothing you wear here, or to the color of the skin you live in, or to your money or lack of money.. God has plainly said that he looks not on the outside of a person but on the heart. In no way will I fall into the trap of saying whether or not a woman may wear jewelry or make up or whether the jewelry touches her skin. You will never find me pouncing on some little thing in order to make you feel guilty. I will, instead, concentrate on those things that make you feel good. I will spend my time in helping each of you get your minds and your spirits in tune with God.

"People attending this church will never be concerned with whether or not you brought an offering. Personally, I care not if you bring an offering or if you don't bring an offering., now or ever. I care more that you bring a contrite will and an eager heart to follow the will of the Holy Spirit. If you are compelled to bring an offering, Gary has a receptical you may use as you leave.

"We are meeting on the seventh day of the week which I truly believe to be God's Sabbath, the day God gave to Moses, the only day God created that he gave a name to. I believe that the Bible plainly teaches that God sanctified the sabbath day and made it Holy, and I believe He expects to continue in that same way.. The traditional church has ignored this Just because the commercial world is geared to a Sunday sabbath doesn't make it right.

"I know that many people in Bethany call me a kook, and I must hasten to warn you that any who join this body will be painted with the same brush." Joe paused and wiped moisture from his face, and saw that Mark or Gary had placed a small cup of water on the podium. He took a sip and ran his tongue over his lips. "I personally like meeting on Saturdays, because we will not be competing with churches meeting on Sundays. I also believe it is the day God commanded us to meet."

"Joe", a man stood and spoke as he rose to his feet, "I want to confess that I came here as a supporter.' He bent his legs slightly to get the circulation going. He was well dressed and spoke in an authoritative voice. "I came to support you, but I must confess I had heard you healed a blind man this week, right here in Bethany."

"It's true", another man stood., Joe saw that he looked ten years younger. His eyes were clear and seemed to sparkle. "I am that man." Joe wet his lips and waited for the clamor to die down.

"You are both wrong. Sir, I did not heal your blindness. My Heavenly Father through the name of Jesus healed you. I am nothing. I was just like a copper wire that carries the power to make a lamp burn. I am a pipe or a wire through whom God flowed his Grace to you. It was, my friend, God's power that healed you. Please, please," Joe walked around the podium, his voice raised. "Please never never give me credit for healing you. I can't heal anyone. That domain belongs exclusively to God."

"Sir," a woman stood. She was near the wheel chair of a little girl about ten years old. "Healing that blind man was not the first time you were involved with a healing. That poor crazy woman at that doctor's gate a few months ago. That woman happened to be my sister, and she was out of her mind. Say what you will, but you were responsible for my sister getting her senses back and is now back with her husband in another city.

"I will confess that I came to this meeting today with my little crippled daughter. She has Spinal Befitidata I brought her here to day to be healed. Will you please let me bring her to you I truly believe she will be healed if you just touch her."

The two men had reseated themselves, and the silence that came over the crowd was so heavy it could be felt giving pressure on the people. Deacon Bandy smiled and whispered in the ear of the man by his side.

"This is great. When that upstart falls on his face, it will be curtains for this church. I couldn't have planned it better."

Joe stood absolutely silent for a moment and said nothing but he bowed his head, his dark hair falling over his face. The silence was complete. Even the creatures in the wild had, for an instant, ceased movement or voice. At last he lifted his head and brushed his hair aside. He gripped the edges of the podium, He looked to the side where Gary and Mark sat. He breathed deeply, and with an almost inaudible sigh nodded to the two young men..

In a moment, the two strong men had lifted the chair and the little girl up on the dais. Joe walked over to the chair and knelt where his face was even with that of the child.. Joe knew her, for her family attended First Baptist.. The child lifted a lovely face and looked quietly into the face of Joe. He noticed her dimpled cheek and bright blue eyes with long lashes. Her skin was like a ripe peach. There was not a single blemish. Her lips were as red as a strawberry, and her blonde hair reached almost to the arms of the chair.. It was tied with a pale yellow ribbon. She wore a white knit dress tied at her waist with a matching yellow sash. He saw her twisted limbs from her waist down and her little legs hung useless toward the bottom of the chair..

The sun had disappeared a few minutes, but suddenly the cloud moved on just enough for a shaft of bright light to illuminate the scene before the people. Every eye was on the wheel chair, and people had gotten out of the cars and were moving as closely as they could. People on the blankets were now standing. Oddly enough, a faint odor from a nearby exhibit barn drifted over the crowd. Later Joe said he likened it to those present who were unbelieving. Somewhere up high a squirrel gave a chatter to its mate, and somewhere a baby began to whimper.

Joe knelt by the chair a little closer "Minnie," he spoke loud enough that Johnny Harris could hear where he sat on his squad car fender. "Do you know who I am?"

"Sure, Joe, I have seen you lots of times."

"Minnie," Joe repeated her name, "how old are you?"

"I am nine and a half. I'll be ten in January.' She smiled and the dimple showed clearly.

"My young friend. Do you know who Jesus is?"

"Sure. Jesus died for my sins and is in Heaven with God."

"Minnie, do you believe that God can heal you, can make your legs as good as new?"

"I know that I want to walk like other girls I try with all my might to believe I can be healed. Jesus did it lots of times." She paused and then when Joe said nothing, she looked him in the face and said "I know that God can heal me."

"Amen and amen." Joe placed one brown hand on Minnie's head and lifted his right toward the sky Gary and Mark fell on their knees and lifted both hands toward heaven.

"Father," Joe began "I ask that you look down on this beautiful child. And I ask that you accept this child-like faith in your Power." Joe raised his voice. "Father, in the blessed name of Jesus, in the name of Jesus, I ask that you heal this child who trusts in you."

Silence covered the scene. Bandy sniggered and punched his companion with his elbow.. Joe now stood and placed both hands on Minnies head and yelled "Be healed! Minnie, in the name of Jesus, stand up and walk over here to me."

It seemed that not one pair of lungs took in a breath for the next few seconds. For an instant, almost everyone really expected a miracle. Bandy punched his companion often enough that the man shoved Bandy's elbow away. But then rationality took over the minds of the people telling each one how ridiculous this was. That little girl really had no legs. Doubt replaced faith in the minds of many present, a favorite ploy of the Devil Lucifer.. The birds and squirrels seemed to have stopped talking and were intent on what was happening below. Miraculously the sounds of traffic was still. All time seemed frozen in space. Every eye was on that wheel chair. The rays of light were still strong. The girl's mother had come to stand by Joe. They saw Minnie look at her mother, tears oozing between the lids of her eyes. She focused on Joe who held his hands toward her, nodding his head and smiling. Time literally stood frozen in time and space.

Minnie suddenly gripped the arms of the chair that had been her prison all of her life, and slowly pushed her body upwards. As she rose, her legs seemed to inflate like a rubber raft. She tentatively placed her weight on one leg which she had moved to the floor. Then very carefully she placed the other foot to the floor and with a final push stood on her feet. Her face held a puzzled look, for this was the first time she had ever had feelings in her legs. She carefully made a small step, throwing out her hands to keep her balance. Joe backed up a few paces as did Minnie's mother. Minnie took a step or two in much the same manner a baby does in taking its first steps. Her spine was straight, and she had no trouble keeping erect.. Then as she came nearer, Joe backed across the dais and Millie quickened her steps and at last ran into Joe's arms.

Minnie's mother screamed and this set off the demonstration of the people present. Bandy stopped punching his neighbor, Johnny Harris stepped a few paces toward the dais, Joe placed Minnie in her mother's arm and bedlam busted loose in the fair grounds at that instant. People began shouting and some idiot stepped on Bandy's new shoes. The deacon just sat there with an incredulous look on his face. He shouted to his companion, "It's a fake, if it did happen, he did it with the power of the devil. Many people were shouting, "Jesus! Jesus! Jesus!" Others were weeping, others were kneeling. Some started for Joe, but Mark and Gary stood in front to keep them away, fearing the make-shift dais would collapse.

It was some time before order was restored, and Officer Harris breathed a sigh of relief as he sat back in his squad car. It was a little while before the crowd was reseated. Even longer until Joe could be heard.

"Friends," Joe smiled. How Bandy hated that man as he sat and glared, thinking of his scarred shoes. "Let each of us always remember and never forget that our Heavenly Father is always great and is always good. I had prepared a sermon for you, but nothing could illustrate more the power of God that what you have just seen. We will have church here next Sabbath day at ten in the morning. I do hope you all will come." He turned and walked off the stage and on behind the stock barn. Mark and Gary followed quietly.

+++++++

Thus began the ministerial career of Joe of Bethany on the 8th day of September 1987.

CHAPTER SIX

Alfonso W. Pritchett, Pastor of First Baptist Church, Bethany, did not have the appearance of a minister. If a stranger met him and tried to guess his occupation, he would fail. No one would 'tag' him as a minister of the church. Yet, Pritchett always introduced himself as a 'minister of the Gospel'.

He was tall and made a very impressive figure in the pulpit. When he had been elected to pastor the Bethany church, he asked that the pulpit be replaced. The old podium had been there since the church was built. Pritchett gave as a reason that it needed updating. He also specified that the new pulpit be six inches lower than the old one.. He dictated that it be made of heavy Oak timber.. He did not tell them that such a pulpit made him appear more imposing and in command.

His facial features were blunt, and his nose a trifle hooked.. His sandy hair was worn longer than the deacons preferred, and a year ago he actually began growing a beard. He was striving to let it grow real long for he fancied it made him look like Moses or Abraham, the father of the Jewish people.

When he stood behind the pulpit, his eyes darkened and sometimes had the trace of wildness.. He frightened the young who usually occupied the front pews.

Each time he rose to preach, he carefully adjusted his lapel microphone, and took a sip of water from the crystal glass always at hand.. He would moisten his lips before reading the first words from the Bible. When he got 'warmed up' he would pace the length of the dais and sometimes pound the lectern He had read that this were the antics of the famed Billy Sunday, the famous baseball-converted evangelist of long ago. Once he got so wrought up that he, like Sunday, picked up a folding chair he had conveniently placed nearby and slammed it to the floor where it shattered.. He loved it when things happened like that, and on that day, he had 'scared' four people into the Kingdom. Yes, he thought, Billy Sunday knew his stuff.

However, Pritchett had, on advice of his deacon board, 'toned down' a lot of his antics. The board had explained that such actions were not in keeping with the dignity expected of the pastor of the First

Church. In fact, the board had suggested buying some fancy pulpit robe or gown to use in the morning worship service at least. He agreed, and picked out a fancy purple robe complete with 'degree stripes on the arms, and a heavy gold chain complete with medal, around his neck.

Pritchett's face was well lined although he had not yet reached fifty years of age. His frame, in the past year had begun to fill out in the waist due to his craving for rich foods, a condition that did not escape the notice of the board. When he did walk the streets of Bethany, he always held his head low as if trying to pass unnoticed or if he was looking for any lost coin along the way. He rarely spoke to anyone he met unless a member of his flock called his name. His wide mouth, which the beard failed to hide completely, always appeared cruel, and few smiles had been born there.. His entire demeanor never would have invited small talk..

Today, the chairman of the deacons had called a special meeting of the board.. After the short walk from the manse, Pritchett entered the board room and saw that all members were in their places. Bandy was the first to notice that the pastor's face looked as if sleep had eluded him most of the night. But, Bandy thought, didn't he always look like that? Pritchett took his place at the head of the large polished conference table. When the minister spoke, it sounded as if someone had tossed a pail of rocks into the room. Certainly the voice was louder than was needed for the place. His irrationallity was plain at this special called meeting by the board. Pritchett's walk of the two blocks to the church accounted for his obvious impatience. The hot, muggy heat had taken its toll. He had noticed the trees swaying in the rising wind, and clouds had begun to frame the belfry of the court house. Small bushes had begun swaying and they looked as if they were trying to hide from the coming storm. A bolt of lightning had split the heavens and Pritchett had hurried to the church. When thunder made the ground shake, he almost ran the few remaining yards to the doorway, his childhood fear of storms causing him to be afraid.

He shifted in his chair after his first remarks, and he was anxious to get to the business at hand.. He nodded to Bandy who was

Chairman of the Deacons and Bandy rose. He took a deep breath and began.

"Brother preacher and fellow deacons," he brushed his hand across his thick lips, and he scanned the faces of those around the table making sure of their attention. Some knew of what Bandy had in mind, but he had to get it formally on the table.

"I have called this meeting to have a formal discussion of that upstart so called preacher who meets weekly at the fair grounds. I had hoped that someone else would broach the subject, for my animosity toward Joe is no secret.. Some would call me prejudiced and try to say it is all personal on my part. Since no one has done this, I felt that I had to lead the way.

"Joe is a dangerous man. A very dangerous man. He is a danger to the peaceful existence not only of our church, but to all other churches that have been in existence for hundreds of years. Churches in this city and in this county and in this state, and even in all the world." Bandy paused for an instant.

"What is Joe doing, Brother Bandy," one deacon asked. He knew what Bandy was getting at. He wanted it out in the open., to put it in words.

"The man is gaining a serious following.. A lot of simple people are swallowing the hog wash he is spouting. He peddles heresy, and even though I have no facts to support it, he is making inroads into our very membership, into our own congregation. He is preaching beliefs that serve only to confuse the simple people of our city., beliefs that endanger the very salvation of the people." Bandy paused to wipe his forehead with a linen handkerchief.

"I don't know about the man endangering anyone's soul," said Fred Burns, owner of the local Western Auto Store, "I'll admit that I attended one of his meetings, and I could not see any harm in him."

"Neither can anyone see any harm in a newly born tiger, but only a fool would fail to realize the potential.. I feel danger in every fiber of my body." Bandy's face was red from his rising blood pressure.

"How many of you men have attended at least one of Joe's meetings?" Bandy began counting as hands raised.. He saw that all hands were raised. "See," he chortled, "he has each of you on the way of being hooked on his garbage."

"Well,", the District Clerk of the county said, "I go because he really seems to be gathering a following. I attended his first meeting last September, and he had about one hundred people there. I attended last week and there were over three hundred people there." The man looked at his pastor, "in fact, there were more people at Joe's services last Saturday than were at our service yesterday. He has to have a public address system so everyone can hear."

"I'll say one thing," the owner of the City Cafe spoke quietly, "He heals someone at every meeting, sometimes more. That alone will make the people come." He turned to his pastor, "Brother preacher, I think we have nothing to fear. The people just go to see the show. It is surely a passing thing. The new will wear off and the people will stop coming. The newness will fade away and so will Joe."

"Well and good," Bandy cried, "well and good, but the man is a menace. Many of his regular people are from our flock."

"Yet," the District Clerk said, "he does not meet on Sundays. If the people were not at his services, they would be fishing or shopping or something. How can he be a threat. I feel that what people do on Saturdays is their own business."

Bandy interrupted with a shout: "Is it any concern of ours when our own people attend his services on Saturday and then the next day feel as if they don't need to attend church on Sunday making it two days of church in a row. A case in point: When have any of you see the Wilson family in one of our services? They used to be here each time the doors opened. I see them every Saturday at the fair grounds. Need I say more?" Bandy tried to smile.

"But the Wilsons have every reason to be one of Joe's followers. Their daughter Minnie was healed by Joe and now she runs and plays like the other children.

"If a tiny crack shows up in the dam out at the city lake, what will happen if it is ignored?" Bandy had their attention now," Besides, I believe that Minnie would have walked any way, doctors are doing wonders now a days." He changed the tone of his voice, "I think that this group of men, this governing body of our church, should do something to rid us of this cancer that is eating away at our very life. This rebel has to be gotten rid of.." Bandy's face was red again as he sat down.

"Brother Bandy," the pastor's voice was calm and conciliatory, "am I right in assuming that you have some kind of plan." He spoke as if he were the Great White Father speaking to an Indian savage.

"Yes, pastor, as a matter of fact, I do have a plan.. It is simple. We have to put a stop to Joe's weekly meetings."

"He has just as much right to meet as any other church. The Constitution of the United States gives him that right." His voice was louder than necessary.

"First," Bandy rose again, "we must stop him from using the fair grounds as a meeting place. It is public property, and we can legally do that.."

"Since I am Road Commissioner," a deacon offered, I can do that. The county judge will go along with me.. He can get the court to pass an ordinance forbidding the using of the fair grounds for religious purposes.. Right now, Joe pays $100 each week for the use of the grounds and for electricity and water. It actually is a profit to the County, but he'll have to go along."

"Well, Bandy," he stood up. "That's a start anyway. We can also make sure he is not allowed to use a school or the football field.."

"Fine, fine.," the pastor gulped. "You men can do that. Let's get down to other matters the board needs to consider."

++++++++

An unexpected shower early Saturday morning that July day freshned the air just seeming to bless and freshen the area. The sun dried the moisture leaving the air almost septic and ready for the service.. When Joe walked into the arena a few minutes to ten, he saw that all the benches were filled and also about a hundred donated folding chairs were filled. Many people sat in cars, and many had spread blankets all around the chairs and benches. It was actually pleasant in the area now.

Gary and Mark had placed the people carefully leaving a space near the front for the crippled in wheel chairs.. Birds were chattering their love songs, and the wind again waifed wild flower smells over the audience. People had gathered faster now that ten o'clock was nigh, and Deacon Bandy was grumbling because he had to park a few

Again
If Christ Came Again

blocks away. He carried a folding chair for he knew all the seats would be gone. One Saturday he had to stand all during the service. He was dressed unobtrusively today in hopes of not being recognized so readily, His big fat face with the pig eyes and ears relished the fact in a few minutes, the young upstart would be informed that he could no longer meet here. He felt that the church would fold immediately.

Bandy's hatred for Joe bordered on the manical. He realized that he hated this man with a venom that his wife told him was unhealthy. He hated Joe with all the power of Satan himself. He missed seeing the field of yellow flowers just over the fence. He missed hearing the birds and the squirrels. He missed seeing God's paintings in the sky. He was missing out on God's gifts through nature because his whole being was saturated in hate.

By the time Joe stood behind the crude lecturn, every available space was taken. He could see many in cars, many with their own folding chairs. The sun was getting warmer, and clouds began to form, but old timers looking above knew that the clouds were for decoration purposes only. No rain on this parade was eminent.

Joe, as usual, stood quietly for a moment until he had full silence. He wore a blue suit, obviously new, a gift from the man who had been blind. He could hardly believe that nine months had passed since that day in the park. Joe's hair still had trouble staying in place. His head turned to the wheel chairs. His blue eyes dripped with compassion for each one. He stood loosely, leaning on the pulpit, and many a young girl's heart began to beat rapidly. he smiled at those in the handicapped section, and all at once they relaxed, happy that they had been noticed.

"My friends," He began with a smile, his mouth a few inches from the mike. "I am so happy that you could be with us here today." He spoke softly into the mike for Gary had said not to shout or his words were not clear if shouted words went through the microphone. Joe noticed that the Sheriff himself had come today instead of a deputy. He was sitting on the hood of his patrol car. "I am so glad that all of you decided to find your way here today. I do hope that you are here for the single purpose of worshipping God. God is indeed kind and merciful. He is a generous God. He is One who will supply your every need.. Today, I wish to read a few verses from the book of Hagaii..

"If you will bear with me, I would like to set the stage for the verses I am about to read. It is indeed an interesting story. Hagaii was one of the minor prophets, one of the obscure men hardly remembered to day. The book of Hagaii is one of the shortest in the bible, having only two chapters.

"Hagaii is mentioned in only two other places in the Bible outside his book he wrote. and that is in Ezra 5:1 and in Ezra 6:14. God has obscured this prophet and has left us only his prophesies.

"You will remember that Solomon built a magnificent Temple in Jerusalem. It was the earthly dwelling place of God Himself. Jesus Himself worshipped in a later Temple on that site. Remember when He drove the crooks from the courtyard? In 586 B.C. Nebuchadnezzar completely destroyed the temple that David's son, Solomon, had built, destroyed it even down to the bare rock. He then took the Children of Israel into captivity."

Hagaii began his ministry in 520 B.C. after some of the Israelites had been permitted to return to Jerusalem. This remnant of a once mighty nation had returned with high hopes. They reinstated the annual feast days and began rebuilding the Temple. They worked for a year or two and then seemingly lost interest.. For ten long years, the work lay dormant. Not even one wall was in place. Hagaii saw this deplorable condition and we read his words about it today. I am using the paraphrased Bible." He saw many Bibles opening all over the crowd. He waited a moment and then began reading:

"Chapter 1, verse 1: 'When in late August on the second year of the reign of King Darius I, Why is everyone saying that it is not the right time for rebuilding my Temple? asked the Lord'

"His reply to them is: is it the right time for you to live in luxurious houses while the Temple lies in ruins? Look at the results: You plant much but harvest little, you have scarcely enough to eat or drink, yet not enough clothes to keep you warm. Your income disappears as if you were putting your money in pockets with holes in them.'"

"God's people have always been good at starting things and then stopping after a short time..after the new wears off. I can't say they back-slide or they just stop. It might be something worse than back sliding.

"Many people come to the church and become avid in their new found interest., then suddenly they stop and all that they do is fill space in the church on Sabbath mornings. I think this is worse than being a back-slider. At least a back-slider is moving, he is going some place.

"These people of Hagaii's time were typical of a lot of church members today. These Jews had been held captive for seventy years. They had been taken to Persia, present day Iran. The time of their release had been foretold almost to the day, and when the time was up, when their days of slavery had ended, Cyrus, in the first year of his reign, right on God's time, issued an edict that allowed the Jews to return to Jerusalem. Their enthusiasm was red-hot. The long journey home through present day Iraq, did not seem long and hot. They were going home. they had a purpose in life. Home lay at the end of the trip They were going to rebuild God's house, the Temple. They made the long trek which took four months with little or no complaining.

"They were not dismayed when they saw the pile of rubble, grass growing up through the rocks, wild animals hiding in small crevices. Weeds were everywhere, snakes slithered before them. That was okay. They were home! They could hardly wait to get started. They had a reason to live.

"They quickly cleaned up the rubble and hauled off the trash. They did not go to a Rent-all place for machinery, they did it with their bare hands They quickly laid the foundation and was ready to start up on the walls. Then what happened?

"They decided to throw a big party. After all, they had been working hard, hadn't they? They threw the party and let their guard down and then the enemy came, It always happens. Once your guard is down the enemy always comes." Joe gazed over every corner of the audience Bandy and Pritchett who had joined him looked sheepish, The preacher was thinking of some way to use this story in one of his sermons. Joe was continuing, emphasizing each word carefully.

"I don't care what you try to do, it must be some unwritten law or something. God lets you have a victory or a partial victory as in this case. He lets partial success come and then enter the Devil. Don't be misled, the Devil is everywhere. He is ever ready to whisper 'sweet nothings' in your ears, convincing you that you deserve to let up, to rest.. After all, he says, you have done something. Suddenly you find yourself compromising a little here and a little there and before you realize it you will come to a fork in the road where a clear-cut decision will have to be made..

"Let me digress just a moment. Any individual, any ministry that has only an upward spiral with no valleys, no set-backs, is not a life nor a ministry for God. I will repeat this and read my lips: Any individual life or ministry that has no defeats or set-backs and moves only upwards is not God's ministry, it is not God's life.." Joe moved to the side of the podium.

"My friends, I am certain that you are not going to like what I am about to say, but you must realize that there is a war out there. You are the infantry soldiers., the foot soldiers, the soldiers who are first in battle. I know that Jesus said *'I will build my church and the gates of hell shalt not prevail against it.'* Believe me, dear people, there will be set-backs.

"The Prince of the Power is no mean adversary. Look at the wickedness in high places. All kinds of evil is there just waiting to happen.. Even some of God's so called anointed, such as Jim Bakker and Jimmy Swaggart that at one time drew people to God must now take the blame for many defecting Christians.

"What did Jesus promised his followers? A frugal, fragile life with many people hating them without just cause.. I want all of you who have made a commitment to God's service. You will have many miserable hours in your life doing the will of God. I refer you to the prime example: Jesus Christ Himself.

"God sent His Son, His only beloved Son to take on a life in the human flesh and dwell among sinful men. No matter where He went, no matter how much good He did, no matter how many he healed, he always managed to engender hatred each step he took.

"Each of you have heard of the trials that have come the way of a true follower of Christ.. One clear cut clarion assurance you can have that you are indeed a true Christian is when adversity comes and jumps on you with both feet.. I cannot understand it but Satan somehow is there always and makes a true follower of Christ an alien among his peers.

"You can expect opposition as did the people in Hagaii's day." Joe slapped the podium with each word: "everytime you start to do something for God, the Devil comes right in and starts to beat up on you." He paused and took a drink of water. "Jesus said it best when He said: *'If you are of this world, the world will love you, but if you are not of this world, the world will hate you.' You must realize that if you are truly of the army of God you are marching to a different drum beat.*

"The Jews did not return to rebuild the Temple as an investment. They did not make a market survey; they did not use a projection of the rental income or lease income. They came" again Joe slapped the pulpit: they came to rebuild the Temple because God wanted it rebuilt.. I always get a kick out of it when someone says 'What part about no did you not understand?' The task of Hagaii's people was so simple that it was impossible for anyone not to understand it.

"At the risk of being redundant, I repeat: Any effort for the cause of Christ will have its ups and downs., and Satan will fight you tooth and toenail each and every step that you take.. Please do not misunderstand me, my friends. I am not saying that failure in your life is a sign that you are in God's will, but any ministry needs to have its mountains and its valleys. You remember that Christ fed 5000 people at one time, and when adversity befell Christ, how many of them were at His side? The fair weather converts had fled to such an extent that only his eleven disciples were left. Jesus was so broken hearted that he told them: 'Will ye also go away?' What I am trying to say and very poorly, I'm afraid: After failure, its just a hard thing to draw a crowd. Everyone likes to be joined to a winner.

"When Jesus came back to life after the Crucifixion, he told his followers to go to Jerusalem and to wait and after a time they would receive great power. A whole horde went, but after a few days some went back home, a little later others left, and after seven weeks, when the Power finally fell. Only 120 people were left to receive it.. But get this: The Power was so potent that 1000 people were converted that very day.

"Remember this: The church was so persecuted that it had to go into hiding, meeting in secret, and even in the catacombs, the sewers of the city. Those discovered worshipping the risen Christ were killed in some cruel manner.

"Now Hagaii's Jews were gung ho. They were going to build. They began, and then a set-back came and they marched off the job. Ten years passed and when the old Hagaii entered the picture, he was flabbergasted.

"He told the people, in effect, that if they thought Satan was a punisher, wait until God showed them His brand of punishment. Wait until God showed what He could do. He pointed out to the people that although they planted their seeds, little or no harvest resulted. They didn't have enough food to live on. They made clothes that did not keep out the cold. They were drinking but their thirst was never slaked.. They were working at jobs full time, and putting their money in pockets that had holes in them.

'Cheer up!" Joe yelled "Fellow Christians, it's gonna get worse!" He drilled his eyes into the crowd, and as they paused on Bandy, the deacon felt a cold chill run up his spine.

"These Jews had the horrible feeling of having God pulling up and Satan pulling down, so they did what came naturally: they quit. They quit for ten long years.

"I would like to give an example of just what I am trying to say.: Here's a person who had come to the front in some church service. He has professed Christ and has truly repented and has truly become a Christian. He is baptized and becomes a member of some church. He is faithful in tithing and in attendance. Then enter Satan. The devil daily whispers in his ears, and soon the convert begins missing a few church service, he does not tithe regularly. Soon he stopped getting the answers to life's problems from the Bible and instead started trying to find the answers in the six o'clock news.

"The traditional churches teaches that all you have to do is walk an aisle and accept Christ and from then, an easy life, a bed of ease and you are assured a happy and successful life. **Phooey!** Everything is not rosy and peaceful and successful, my friends, that is not the way it is at all. You walk that aisle and you have just volunteered as a foot soldier in God's army. You are in a war!" Joe stopped for a moment

Again
If Christ Came Again

and then lowered his voice for effect. "Listen, my dear friends. If you get nothing else from what I am saying today, hear this and hear it well. Get it straight, for undoubtedly it will be quoted all over Bethany this week.. Perhaps you will be shocked at this next statement, but hear me out. **Coming down the aisle to accept Christ is probably the worst thing that could happen to you!** I will repeat it: Coming down the aisle to accept Christ is probably the worst thing that could happen to you..at **first**. By making a public profession will automatically put you on Satan's hit list. You are enlisting in a battle to the death, but keep this other thing in the front part of your mind: He paused, moistened his lips, lowered his voice a little more "One thing God is unable to do: He cannot lie, and He has promised to be with you to the very final play of the game.. He has given an iron clad guarantee of glorious victory to each one of His warriors.

"So you started out, you walked the aisle you were breezing along and you stubbed your toe. Someone in the church told a lie on you. You never got that much deserved promotion. Your best girl said no to your proposal of marriage. You stopped. Just like Hagaii's Jews stopped. You stopped going to church, you stopped paying your tithes. Now, how goes it with you today, my friends. Is your bank account healthy? Should be, ten per cent more money. Everything fine at work? At home? 'Well,' you say, 'if that battery in the car hadn't blown up, if that lottery ticket had won, if that stock had gone up like it should, if if if'

"Consider your ways!" Joe now shouted, and Bandy almost fell off his chair for he had been almost asleep. "Does anybody feel as if there were holes in his pockets? I will be the first to admit that it is bad for the Devil and his Imps to get on your case, but, my friends, I can tell you something worse than that, much worse.: Wait until God turns His wrath on you.

"I hate to tell you this, but there such a thing as turning God into your perennial enemy. Please listen, my friends, don't let your thoughts leave me now." Joe walked around to the edge of the pulpit.

"If God is God at all, get this:If God is God at all, He does not exist because of His love; it is not God's love that makes Him God. Know what it is? **It is His power! If God doesn't have more power than the Devil, who do you think would be in charge?** If and when

God turns His wrath on you to bring you back in to line, the antics of the devil and his angels will seem petty and tame to you. Some people have not realized that as long as God is boss, He will do exactly as He want to do. God is exactly what He is because that is exactly what He wants to be. Never forget that it is not dependent on us for Him to be God. God is today sitting on His throne, and our getting to be there with Him someday has to have His approval.

"What Hagaii is saying here to each of us today 'You are putting your money in bags with holes in them, compliments of Satan. Remember what Job said: *'Though He slay me, yet will I trust him!'*?

"Ask your self this question" Joe stepped back behind the pulpit and looked at his notes. "How are you doing since you stopped paying your tithes? How goes it since you stopped getting up early on the Sabbath, getting the kids ready and bucking traffic in order to go to Church on the Sabbath? How goes it since you started attending Church in front of the TV screen? How goes it since you stopped doing volunteer work at the church? How goes it since you stopped helping a neighbor or someone in need? I don't mean to get personal, but how are you doing?

"I wish I could tell you how much I hate to preach a sermon like this. The devil will whisper 'don't go to hear that nut. All he wants is money' **WRONG!** Do you think that God, who owns all the wealth in the world needs your tithe? God could speak the word, and a thousand pounds of pure gold could fall in the back of that old pickup truck out there by the barn. Did you know that he could suddenly make it rain 100 dollar bills all over the place here? God does not need your money, actually His money. You need to give it to Him if for no other reason other than you love Him, or to show Him you do not put money before God.

"Serve God and the only enemy you will have is the devil. I hate to belabor this point." He paused and once again walked to the left side of the podium. "I must be sure you understand. I love you people. Many have put your trust in what we are trying to do. God bless you. Before you heard God's call, you had few or no enemies, but once He called and you responded, you automatically became a buck private in God's army. I hate to tell you this, but you became open game for

Satan and all his Imps" Joe paused and returned to his place behind the pulpit.

"You say, 'but I liked it better the other way, I liked the blissful life I had before Christ.' Remember old Jeremiah: God said to him: 'While you were yet in the womb I called you!' You know that that old prophet did not have an easy life.

"As I have said, once God calls you and you accept the call, you have a slew of built-in enemies. You try it for a time, and you say 'I want out' and if you follow that lead and slide back, believe me, the Devil will then let you alone. That's fine, but then God enters the picture. You can not leave you promise. You are in the army, and just as a soldier becomes AWOL, you are AWOL in God's army. He comes for you.. If you train a horse to be a race horse, he will never be happy just as a pasture horse. He will be a race horse until he dies. Once you say 'yes' to God and then succumb to the pressures of the Devil which are bound to come, the Devil will let you alone but God wont.. You might stand up out there and say 'Brother Joe, the devil never gives me any trouble.' Then I hate to tell you this, the devil has you exactly where he wants you. He would be a fool to waste any energy on you. He spends all of his time on those who are still faithing.

"Do you want to get God off your case? It's simple. Put God first in your life.. Hang in there and fight the good fight. Remember, *God said that my grace is sufficient for thee!*' Believe it, my friends, believe it." Joe was getting tired. He took another drink of water.

"What is this message all about? Stop blaming the devil for what God is doing to you. I am almost finished. Please bear with me just a while longer. Look at verse 12: *'then Zerubbabel, the governor of Judah, and Joshua, the High Priest, and the few remaining people in the land, obeyed Hagaii's message from the Lord their God. They began to worship Him in earnest. Then the Lord told them (again sending the message through Hagaii, his messenger):'I am with you and I will bless you, 'and the Lord gave them the desire to build the Temple, so they all gathered in early September in the second year of the reign of King Darius, and volunteered their help, and Jehovah kept His promise and blessed the people'*

"See how simple it is? I repeat once more: you are blessed of God if God called you and you accepted. You are a member of God's family, and He will bless you and keep you, but if you ever even think of turning back, watch out!

"Any millionaires out there who became rich after you stopped tithing?" Joe smiled and a small titter went up from the audience. Then he continued in a loud voice:

"Please, listen to me. Consider your ways. Do it God's way. It will likely be the toughest time of your life, and it might go on for years, but my oh my, friends, once the battle is over and has been won, you will be glad that you hung in there. Actually, what I have tried to make clear to you, you have no choice but to hang in there and fight Satan with everything you have. Wait a second, that is not exactly right, you have two choices: continue the battle against the Devil, or quit and let an expert take over on you.

"I can hear you say, 'I don't like this at all' I ask you once more, how are you doing? Any holes in your pockets?

"In conclusion, I will try to sum it all up. The call of God is an honor and it is not recallable. Remember the words in Hebrews? *'His house we are if we continue steadfast!'* As your pastor, I will never ask you to do anything unless God has already asked you to do it. Remember what Hagaii said: *(I am with you!)* When you learn to put God first, everything you do will be blessed by God. If you ever get to the point where serving God becomes a chore and decide to go back to the old way, watch out. It is better for the Devil to be against you than God. You plus God is always a winning combination."

Joe closed his Bible and then stepped down to the area where the wheel chairs were. One by one he spoke softly to them and placed his hands on them and one by the people walked. Some of them pushed their empty wheel chairs before them, smiles etching their faces. Joe returned to the pulpit and when the crowd quieted he began.

"I have kept this news from you to the last. I have been informed that just before this service began that we can no longer use the fair grounds as a meeting place." A groan covered the audience in one breath. "Actually, I am not surprised, for it was to be expected. Now, we are forced to find a place of our own. I believe it is God's way of forcing our hand, to try our faith."

Again
If Christ Came Again

"Brother Joe," a well dressed man stood up. "I can't understand what harm you are doing. You seem to be law abiding, I have a suggestion if I may be so bold."

"Go ahead, my friend, suggest away."

"I own 100 acres over at the intersection of I-20 and State 19."

"I know the spot."

"Brother Joe," the man paused, and Bandy sat up straight, he did not like this, "I want to give that 100 acres to Our Fathers House." A cheer cut the man off. He finally could say no more so he sat down.

"My brother," Joe said after the tumult died down. "God bless you. Praise Jesus. We will meet there next Sabbath. We will need volunteers to help move all our things. Any who want to help, meet here tomorrow at nine o'clock."

Several came up after the closing prayer, and the saddest man in all Bethany that day was Deacon Bandy, for he knew he had lost the first round.

CHAPTER SEVEN

Dennis Shepherd had reluctantly celebrated his 46th birthday anniversary just a week ago. The nearer he got to 50, the more he hated it. He was tall, about six feet two inches and looked like a Dallas Cowboy tight end. His light brown hair had a reddish tinge as if nature couldn't make up her mind what color his hair was to be.. He had a perfectly round head, and a long line of eyebrow above his almost black eyes. People often told him that a person whose eye brows met was in for good fortune all his life. The eyes had a spark that seemed to come from somewhere deep within his body. His hands had thick fingers and on the ring finger of his left hand he still wore his high school ring. He was very impressive in demeanor, every cell of his body seemed to yell that here was class; here was no ordinary man.. Somehow anyone who dealt with Dennis Shepherd felt that they could trust him, even if he was a lawyer. This was his biggest asset when he stood before a jury in an effort to persuade them of the innocence of his client. Dennis enjoyed a lucrative law practice in Bethany, and even in the county and that section of the state, for he seldom lost a case.

Joe was ushered into Dennis' spacious and impressive offices in the professional building in the new mall just south of town. His offices were next door to Wal-Mart.. Sunshine played leap frog on the rows of leather bound books back of the massive desk. Joe noticed the rays of sun on the thick earth toned carpet. As Joe entered the private office, Dennis came around from behind his desk and extended a welcome hand. Joe took the hand and noticed the chubby fingers and the well trimmed healthy pink nails. Dennis pulled up a chair for Joe and then returned to his seat. For an instant, the two men studied each other, each waiting for the other to speak first.

"Brother Joe," Dennis broke the silence, his voice booming, He was leaning back in his high backed chair and playing with an ivory handled letter opener, "I want to thank you for that splendid sermon last Sabbath. It was unusual, and it certainly hit me smack in the face. I found out last week about Bandy's plans for getting you evicted from the fair grounds. If someone had told me when I left home for your meeting that I would give 100 acres of land away, I would had the judge make out commitment papers for him. I have been stealing God's money for years, and somehow, I was on my feet giving the land to Our Fathers House. I have never been moved like I was with that sermon.

"The land is a high visibility location, and you should do very well there. I wish that that message could be heard by more people, even the whole world. In fact," Dennis came around to Joe's side of the desk and leaned against the desk. "Joe, if you will have me, I want to join your staff. You have two fine men in Gary and Mark, and I could do all the legal work and contracts of the church."

"Mr. Shepherd," Joe began.

"Please, Joe, call me Dennis." He smiled.

"Sure, Dennis. We will be honored to have you. The rate we are growing, and now that we own property, we will need a lawyer..

"With you, we have three, and I still need some more as God gives them to us, just as He put it on your heart to join us."

"It would be a miracle, Joe, if you did not have a dream. Want to tell me about it?"

"You are pretty astute, Dennis. Sure, I have a dream." Joe's eyes got a far-away look. I see a large church building, something like a Crystal Building with a spire reaching upwards toward God Himself. I see a fully graded school, a food ministry, and a sort of retirement village for our senior citizens. where they can live in safety and security."

"No one can truthfully accuse you of dreaming small, Joe." He walked back to his chair.

"I serve a big God who can do big things."

"Joe, I asked you to drop in and sign these papers for the land. The County Clerk will mail you the deed after it is recorded, or if you prefer, I will make a file for the church and keep it here in the office.

"That will be great, Dennis. And God bless you for the land, and more than that, God bless you for joining Our Fathers House.."

When Joe came out of the office, Gary was waiting there in the truck.

"Hi, Gary," He climbed in beside his friend. "Sorry I was so long, but now the land is ours and we also have another helper. Dennis has joined the group."

"Super, Joe, super." He slipped into gear and they headed across town.

"Gary, do you imagine what that land is worth?"

"A bundle, for sure."

"I should not have been so surprised when Bandy came out openly in opposition to our work.. It seemed that his opposition in getting us evicted was just like pouring gasoline on a camp fire.. You know, Gary, we now number four officials of Our Fathers House. We should sort of give each man a title and some table of organization as to duties."

"How about calling us ministers of whatever, naming our field of work.

"Great idea, Gary. I want you to be my assistant pastor, and if the time comes when I cannot function, you will be all ready to step in and fill the gap. Your duties would be varied, and you could sort of coordinate the efforts of the others.

"Great! Mark can be Minister of services having to do with everything pertaining to the physical plant of Our Fathers House. Dennis could be Minister of Finances. We will need a Minister of education, a Minister of Social Services and so on. How is the moving job going?"

"We have one more load as soon as we get there we will set things in order. Saturday is speeding toward us at a fantastic rate.." They turned into the site, and Mark ran to the truck like a young child. "Ready, Gary, we got that one more load." He turned to Joe, "I hope you approve of the site that I picked out to put the meeting place. It is sort of an open air theater."

Joe got out of the trucks and was elated. It was indeed a sort of amphitheater.. The ground sloped down gradually to a flat place where already some men were building a large dais.

"You know, Mark, it's great. Do you suppose we could rent a large tent just in case we run into bad weather. They might give us a 'rate' say if we rented it for a year."

"Great, I'll get on it right away. And how about a nice sign, saying **Future Site of Our Fathers House?**"

"You guys don't need me. You are doing great. I would suggest that when we get enough money, we could manage for a sort of temporary office with a phone where we will be available to people all the time. People who, perhaps, are home bound for one reason or another.."

"Fine, I'll see to it. You know, Joe, Bandy ain't going to like this."

"Yes," Joe smiled. "I don't think he will."

"I'll cry over his mood tonight before I go to sleep." Mark smiled.

Saturday dawned a bright, brilliant day. It had rained some on Friday night, and a fresh smell permeated the entire area. Great piles of white clouds hung in the sky hardly moving. The morning sun reflected off the windows of nearby buildings of stores along State 19. The copper dome of the county court house rose majestically above all other buildings. as if to signify that justice prevailed in all the land. Already the heat of the day could be felt in the air. Joe walked over the area speaking now and then to someone he knew.. He saw that Mark had arranged for over 200 chairs. Gary is an optimist to the core, ran through Joe's mind. Joe surveyed the platform which was almost double the size of the one at the fair grounds. From somewhere, the men had arranged for a small organ, and as the time for the service at the new location drew near, a young lady was softly playing hymns. The more Joe looked around, the more he admired his helpers. He saw two Port 'O Pots placed strategically, and on either side of the rows of chairs was a barrel with a chrome spigot and a stack of paper drinking cones. The only doubt in Joe's mind was that a sudden rain, but one glance at the bright blue of the sky gave him confidence. In a huge Oak tree just back of the platform, many birds joined in the organ music and the effect was a blessing to all who heard. Even the traffic on the nearby freeway seemed sparse, and those trucks that sped by seemed to be devoid of sound.

Promptly at ten O'Clock, Gary mounted the dais and led the people in a verse of *Old Rugged Cross* and when he got over his nervousness he announced that since we had no song books we would

Lee Roy Neal

do it from memory, and then he chose *Amazing Grace* which surely fit the occasion perfectly.

Joe took his seat near the center of the platform behind the temporary podium and resolved that by next meeting he would have built a pulpit worthy of the new church He was elated that all 200 chairs were filled, and seated right on the back row was Bandy and his pastor, Alphonso Pritchett. He could not help but wonder what these two were up to now. Actually he was surprised too see them here at all. He fell that it took a lot of gall on his part to attend.

. He saw Dennis sitting near the front and he smiled at him and Dennis nodded and smiled.

Today, Joe wore his 'other' suit, a simple blue which reflected the blue of his eyes. It was a casual suit, but looked well on his trim body. His hair was brushed severly and it reflected the rays of the sun now almost directly overhead. A few people had brought fans and were using them now and then.

Joe stepped to the pulpit and Gary quickly penned a lapel mike on Joe's coat.. "I guess I will have to get used to this," he smiled. I never know what Gary or Mark will be up to next. I do want to thank each of you for coming out in the heat of the day. I am so grateful for all of those who have worked to make possible this meeting today, For Dennis Shepherd for this magnificent portion of God's good earth, for Mark and Gary and all the volunteers who worked to make things ready. With the blessing of the Heavenly Father and the generous hearts and hands of others who believe in this ministry, I offer my humble gratitude."

He took his Bible and he noticed that many other Bibles came into view waiting for him to announce a scripture.

"The Spirit of Christ is with us today You gather this same Spirit of Christ when you become a Christian.. Jesus once said, 'Ye are the Light of the world', and we who are gathered here today are responsible to God to keep that Light burning.. I have called the sermon today '**What the Church Means to Me**'. I see that many of you have your Bibles, so let's all turn to the book of Hebrews, Chapter 10 and beginning at verse 2.

"Let us hold fast the public declaration of our hopes without wavering, for He is faithful that promised. And let us consider one another to incite to love and good works, not forsaking the gathering of ourselves together as some have the custom, but encouraging one another, and all the more so as you behold the day drawing near.' Let us pray:

"Father, we humbly submit your word to You today…we submit it for the consideration of the people here today.; we submit it that it might have an eternal effect on our lives here and now. We know that if we will truly submit our lives to you, our lives will be changed. We know that each one here can come to a brand new start in life, the same as this church has come to a brand new phase of its ministry.

"Our hearts are overflowing with gratitude, blessed Father, for the blessings already falling upon Our Fathers House..This wonderful plot of your good earth, of the dedicated, unselfish help, to the trusting people here today. We ask only that Your Will be done here today and that you keep your guiding hand on our shoulders at all times."

Joe raised his eyes, and smiled at Mary and his siblings seated on his right.

"The Scriptures state in II Corinthians 5:17 *'If any man is in union with Christ, he is a new creation, old things have passed away, and new things have come into existence.'* What does the church mean to you? Let us explore some of the answers that I might get if I asked for you to respond out loud today. Some, if not all, of you would say that the Church is a place to find Salvation. How very true, but, my friends, the church is really more than that.. I submit to you that the church is a place to begin all over again. It is very important that a person not be afraid to sort of discard the old and just start over. To begin again as it were.

"You know," Joe paused and smiled at the audience. He saw that he had the attention of most of the people, except Bandy who was leaning over and whispering to Pritchett. "Some people make a lot of resolutions on the New Year which is not far away. Some people say 'I'm gonna start all over January 1.' That's not the kind of starting over I am talking about today. That's not redemption, it is merely a change of mind. In reality, it is merely stating a hope that things will be better in your life.

Lee Roy Neal

"You see, the church represents something entirely different. It's not pulling yourself up by your shoelaces. Neither is it just stating that you are going to do better, to turn over a new leaf." Joe paused, walked to the side of the podium and in a softer voice continued. "It's not waking up some morning with a hangover and promising yourself that never again will you do that. I can feel your questions, then, Brother Joe, what is it?

"The church is a place where you can trade in the old ways and pick up the new ways in your life.. In that sense, the Church is indeed a place where you can start all over.. We still know that the Church is also a place of salvation, a place of re-dedication. It is indeed a place where you can literally leave the old life and take up a new one." Again Joe paused and stepped back behind the podium. He was thankful that a soft pleasant breeze flowed over the audience. 'God's air conditioning' he thought. Somewhere a baby fretted and then before it could cry, the young mother stood and moved to the edge of the crowd.

"I tell you, beloved, I am excited about this. The church is a place for families to gather. I am so glad to see young mothers bringing their babies to church. I hope that you realize that if you are in some kind of need, and you turn to your family and the family turns you down, you can always turn to your church family. Isn't it nice to know that when you enter the door, oops! We don't have any doors, but we will." He was interrupted by loud cheers and clapping. "It's nice to know that when you walk in here, you have a new family, a big family to help you, a family of brothers and sisters, grandmothers and grandfathers, uncles and aunts, nieces and nephews who will accept you and love you and help you. That's what it is all about.

"You see, once you come to the Church, it's no longer just you and God, it's Us and God.. You need other people. We all need a sense of family, of belonging. It's part of our whole being. The Church supplies all of that. You see, that's we call each other brothers and sisters. It's not just empty words. It runs thicker than that, much thicker than human kin.

"There is some kind of commadiere, an association. There's family, there is a sort of communion owing to the fact that you have been born again, that God has put His spirit in your heart, and it is the same spirit in other hearts. It is displayed in the family feeling we all have toward each other, it is indeed a new life rooted in Christ, the moment that God touches your life, at the very instant that you truly and honestly took Jesus as your Savior. You acknowledge God as your Father, then you are a member of God's family. The conception has taken place and the birth accomplished and from then on you begin growing into a relationship that all true church members enjoy. That's what makes us brothers and sisters. That's exactly what makes us one body.

"When a person comes to the Lord and he does not feel this family relationship, this sense of belonging, he might become frustrated.. The nearest thing I can compare it with is it's like trying to drive a car with a flat tire. At first, he feels that something is missing, or is wrong. He needs something else. At this point the person must realize that what is missing is the Holy Spirit. You need the Word of God, you need prayer, and you need people you can respect and look up to, people **you can draw strength from** In essence, you need people who in turn need you. That's why the Church is a place of family.

"Secondly, the church is a place of training. Unfortunately there are some people who take their church membership the way they take their marriage. They want to be alone. 'Go away, we don't need you, we can manage all right by ourselves.' Is it any wonder that half the marriages today end in a divorce?

"I hope I can get my thoughts over to you in a way that it will be easily understand. Please bear with me. I believe that there is a practical Church action and beliefs, and also there is a theoretical action. We need some private tutoring in practicality. You see we need some good theory or we might get into trouble.

"Let's look for a while at a theoretical Christian. Already I feel some of you being turned off saying that you want no part of theory. You say you want the practical kind, but my friends, if you don't know about both kinds, how can you make an intelligent choice between the two? I'll try to give an illustration.

"In Matthew 5:48 we find Jesus saying:'Be ye *therefore perfect even as your Heavenly Father is perfect.'* Now if you don't know the difference between theory and practical, you will have trouble trying to understand this verse. Is there any one here who is perfect? If so, I want to shake your hand. You see, this verse is good theory, but try to make it practical and you are in big trouble. If you try to be perfect you will fail and you are liable to become frustrated.. You quit trying, and finally you fail in the trying and might even leave the church because you have not differentiated between practical and theory.

"You have to have a theory or you will never learn how the machine works. You see, life is filled with many things that are only theory.. You say, you mean things are not real? No, the things are absolutely real. Go back to that verse. God wants His children to be perfect, but get practical. We are not yet ready for God to makes us perfect., see? If we try to make everything real and not theoretical, we are likely to run amok.

"Let's give you an example that everyone will understand: Let's say you are planning a trip in a car. Your destination is 250 miles away. You say, 'well, I'll just set the cruise control on 50 miles and hour and I'll be there in five hours.' Nice theory, but not at all practical.. Other things have to be considered, other cars, town speed limits, weather, and many other things. You have to plan ahead. Some Christians start out and strive for perfection. The devil likes those, for he pounces and frustration takes over. The problem? You equated theory with practical.

"Thank God for what He does in our hearts. We are not perfect yet; we are not complete yet. By coming to God's Church and associating with your brothers and sisters, you will find it easier to strive toward the perfection that God wants to have. Remember, that God will do everything for us that He has promised. In the meantime, don't make the mistake of getting caught between theory and practicality.. Between theory and fact. You see, the Church is a place of training and a place to help you live a Christ-like life.

"Never forget that you must experience training in the Church. We need this place to uphold God's standards.. You must know that there is a right life and a wrong life. If you are in the wrong, expect trouble to come. It's the same thing as when a parent corrects a child. Do wrong and expect the chastening hand of God in your life. It is one sure way to know that you are a Child of God: When God chastens you. He would not bother if you were not His. In this church

Again
If Christ Came Again

I will strive with every ounce of my body and with every atom of my mind to teach and to preach the pure truth of God's Word.. When you come to church here, don't park your mind at the door. Challenge all I say. Find it in the Bible or reject it. Don't expect to come here and hear a little sermonette and go forth unchanged. And just because something has been practiced for hundreds of years doesn't make it true and correct.

"I promise you before God, I will never never compromise the truth. I am willing to fight for it and," Joe paused and again drew all eyes toward him, "I am willing to die for it. God knows my mind and my heart, and He knows that I am willing to give my life for His Truth.

"It is inevitable that many fall short of God's Glory. I fall short. I have no trouble admitting that. My dear friends, expect to fall short on the practical side of your Christian living. When some people fall short, they want to change the standards so they can reach them easier. Let's change the standards to what we want them to be and forget what they are supposed to be.

"I can't fault you for thinking like that. We are bombarded on all sides by the media and industry for each of us 'to do our own thing' or 'if it feels good do it' I tell you that if we fall for that trap of satan we might as well close shop and forget building a great Church. I believe that that is the trouble with the traditional church today. They have lowered their goals and their standards. I read recently of one church that has Bekini-clad girls who passed the offering plates. I read of another that gave green stamps for church attendance Other churches who thought that God's word was not enough to draw the people used popular rock stars and whatever to draw the people to the church.

"We must hold on to our senses. Especially relating to the church. A lot of people live in a dream world. They look forward to the hour of the day when another session of some soap opera comes on. They think of the characters in the stories as real; people. One dear lady asked her pastor to have a special prayer for Sue Ellen who was an alcoholic. For you who do not watch these thing, Sue Ellen was a character on Dallas, a TV show.

"This church is a real place. Someday you will see a building here. But it will be more than a building. It will be a place where we can meet God. I will never let this body deteriorate into a lodge hall or a night club." Joe pounded the pulpit so hard that a lot of people jumped, including Deacon Bandy who was dozing. "Someone has to say 'this is right and this is wrong'. You may rebel, set your own standards and ignore theory or go and sin, and I am here to tell you that God will forgive you. But doing what you did is wrong. I could even say it is hypocrisy. Actually, it is the difference between theory and practicality. If you discard theory, you have little or no idea where you are going. You see, you are having trouble seeing how the machine works.. You say, I don't have to come to church an listen to stuff like this. Fine. But Jesus said *'Neglect not the assembling of yourselves together.'* You say, but I can attend church on TV. I say that it's like saying you can take a bath without getting into the tub or under a shower.

"I would be the last person to tell you that this thing of practicality is easy. It most assuredly is not. Frustrations come If it doesn't come on its own, Satan will give it a good nudge. Perhaps another example in this theory-practical thing will help. The scriptures say that wives are to be subject to their husbands, and that the husband is the head of the house.. That, dear friends is theory. It does not always work that way. If all of us were in God's will 100%, then it would work. A man might say that his wife doesn't do what he tells her to do, like taking out the trash and keeping the grass mowed, shall I divorce her?" The audience laughed. Joe had them still. I would answer, no, you should not divorce her for that, it's not practical.

"Please hear this," Joe continued. "The reason we hold marriage so dear and are hesitant to break it up." Joe slapped the desk, "The reason we hold marriage so dear and are hesitant to break it up is that it is a reflection on the church. Marriage is much more important than the relationship of a man and a woman. Marriage is a reflection of God's love for His people. God is not fickle. He doesn't change his mind. In no way will He give up on Mankind and go to something different. I am going to shock some now, but it must be said. I am, not against divorce in some cases, especially where the marriage was not God-ordained. I am not here to unload criticism on divorced people, far from it. I am practical when I realize that people make mistakes and have every right to get on with their lives.

"But that's not the issue here. I am talking about theory. There's that word again. Why do we hold such high regards for the institution of marriage, and why does the church insist that their leaders lead an exemplary life. If the church does not hold high standards of marriage, who knows what the present 50% divorce rate would do. The human race would become so confused that it is likely to cave in on itself. People must realize that divorce doesn't hurt only the man and woman involved, it hurts all of society.

"Practically, we have to accept the fact that men and women make mistakes. They get married too young or they get married for the wrong reasons or they might get married to the wrong person.

"Christ has selected His Bride: The Church, and this is not a marriage 'til death us do part' but it is through all eternity.. He will never change his mind He will never go back on His vows. He has made a commitment forever.

"I have stated to day that the church is a place of theory, yet I hope that I have shown you that it is a practical place. If the church was all theory and no practicality, what a rough place that would be. I wont be much longer, but let's look at the church as a place for practicality. Turn to James 2:13-17 *'For the one who does not practice mercy, will have judgment without mercy. But if you have been merciful, then God's mercy towards you will win out over His judgment against you.'*

"I pose a simple question, friends: what use is it if you say that you have faith and are a Christian and yet never lift a hand to help a fellow being? Is that a saving faith? What James is saying here: If you see a brother or a sister in a naked state, lacking food, even for a day, and you say 'go in peace and keep warm and enjoy your meal' yet you do nothing to feed them or keep them warm, what good are you doing?

"What does it mean to say 'I love you'? It does not mean a thing unless we demonstrate that love in a practical manner. To make theory and practicality work in a Christian sense, they must work simultaneously. By theory, we are washed in the Blood of Christ, by theory, we each have a mansion in the heavens, by theory we will walk the golden streets, by theory, God has forgiven us all our sins if we have accepted His terms, yet on the practical side, we have bills to pay, we've got kids to raise, we've got that cantankerous neighbor next door to contend with, we live with all these problems and have to face them each day and face them in a real practical way. When you say to a person, 'God loves you and so do I' you must really and truly mean it., that it is not just words. We must show that we have a practical Christianity.

"In the short life of this ministry, people have come to me for help, stating that their own church failed to reach out a helping hand. That father could not have cared less about **theory**, His kids were hungry. He had a practical mind and rightly so. What did that dad want when he came to me? I could have told him to feed on the Bible the Bread of life, it's in there. No, that man wanted to see some sacks of groceries.

"Yes, the Church is a place of practicality. It's a place where what we say with our mouths and what we do with our hands come together. I would be the first to state that the Church as seen on this earth is not perfect., but I say with all my beaing that it should have some semblance of perfection. You pastor, obviously, can't always be there when you stumble, he can't spoon feed you like a baby, but praise God, when I see you in a ditch, I can try to help you get out and try to set you on your feet so you can get going again.

"I firmly believe that if you walk the aisle and rally and truly mean it, your neighbors can tell the difference. The question is not 'did you walk the aisle?' Did you give some preacher your hand?' You ask, but isn't that important? Didn't Jesus say 'Confess your sins before men'? Sure it is, its very very important. The question I want to ask" Joe paused, "**Did it change your life?**

"Please understand, your pastor is not here to condemn you, nor am I here to judge you, even, but I do mean to be candid with you and ask again, **Where you really changed?** Are you different, or did you just go through the motions?

"I must close this message. I am so sorry for being so long. Just take this with you: The church is a place of theory and a place of practicality, but I can't leave this without telling you that the Church is also a place for Committment. Right here, under the sun is a place where you can say 'I believe it. I take it. and I'm going to commit my self to it.'

"I had to smile the other day when I read of a woman who wrote to Dear Abby. and explained that she had been going with a man for ten years and he had never mentioned marriage. She asked if she were kidding herself. Abby advised her to move on that the man was no more than words.

"You tell me,'O I believe all you say so much. I feel committed when I go to church!' That's not the issue, my friend, Have you really committed yourself to the teachings of the church? Are you going to attend all the services, all of them, not just on Saturday morning. Are you willing to pull your own weight. If everyone gave as you do would the utility bills get paid? You must be willing to pay God's tithes. You must be willing to teach a class. You must be willing to mow that grass and pull those weeds. The nursery rhyme of 'sticks and stones may break my bones, but words will never hurt me' is true.

"My dear people, like it or not, the choice is here today and it will come again, but one day it will have a terrible finality. You are either going to commit yourself or you are not.. You guys going with that pretty girl and say you do not want to discuss marriage that you just want to sit in the moonlight and hold hands and look at the stars. I'm afraid that it wont last.

"I'm glad that the church is a place of commitment. It's real and God's people must get behind it and support it in a practical way. Remember the Lord's words in Luke 6:46? 'Why call me Lord Lord and do not the things I say?'

"The church can also be a vehicle to say the things you cannot say alone, to do the things you cannot do alone. The place where we can send others to foreign lands, a place where the hungry can be fed, a place to respond to emergencies. I dream, and Dennis can testify to this. I dream of a church upon this land I see a Christian school, I see a haven for old people, I see a massive food bank where hungry people can get food, and who in turn may seek food for their souls. I want our people to see and show that every man is a brother and a sister. I want each one to make every stranger feel welcome..

"Have you ever gone to a church where you did not feel right, did not feel welcome, did not feel you were dressed right?" Joe leaned over the pulpit now and spoke slowly. "We can have a church that makes strangers feel that way before we are a month older. Our Fathers House is not exempt. You can't help by brushing by the stranger to get to your seat., Why not pause and shake their hand? Their heart might be breaking at that instant. Why not do the unthinkable and give them a hug and tell them that they are welcome?

"Want to build an unfriendly church? Good, then come and don't shake hands with anyone. Speak only to the pastor and then only gripe about something. That's not Christ's way. Welcome the stranger. Invite him home for dinner.

"I see a church here that is filled with people who express their love. Do you realize that in this church people get more outpouring of love than all the rest of the week combined.? Who is to do it? Why you are! Reach out, show your love, and then God will bless.

"The church is a place of giving. Recently the media told of one TV preacher who took God's money and built an air-conditioned dog house, had gold faucets in his bath room and other glitter. I say, don't send your money where anything like that can happen to it. If you give it here, our books are always open to you. We will be accountable.

"The last thing I will mention and I will be through. The Church is a place of mercy and forgiveness. Look at Matthew 6: 14 and 15 *'Your Heavenly Father will forgive you if you forgive those who sin against you; but if you refuse to forgive them, He will not forgive you'* Just remember. learn to forgive and then try to forget Just remember, you have been forgiven, then forgive with open arms those who have strayed. Some churches have rigid rules for membership some have to apply and then be passed on by a membership committee. The story is told pf a man who tried to become a member of a large church... Each time he was turned down for some reaosn or another. Once he left the church building in dispair and he met Jesus. The Lord asked him why the gloom, and the man explained that he had been trying to get into that church for months and had not made it. The Lord said 'So have I" You say: 'But Brother Joe, you don't know who I am or the things I have done." I say, that you don't know of all the things I have done. I say to you 'Welcome'

"The Church says, I love you, I'm going to take you just as you are., but remember, the church is not a place of stupidity. We will accept you, just as you are, but we expect you to straighten up and clean up your act., we will help you in the sometimes long process of cleaning up your life with God's help. We will help you change your tune, we will help you change your language, we will help you to change your entire outlook on life. we will say to you, 'Brother, that's wrong, we can't have that here, what you are doing.'

"'Hey,' you say, 'I thought the Church was a place where people loved you in spite of what you do.' No, my friend, you got it wrong. You come to the church and you are welcomed as you enter. You are welcome to God's forgiveness, you are welcome to the church's outstretched hand, welcome to our love, are wecomed to all the church has to offer., but you are also welcome to try to clean up your life.. welcome to change your act, welcome to treat other people with respect, welcome to forgive others, welcome to treat other people as you want to be treated., welcome to show others the love of God.

"Look at Peter 4:17 *'For the time has come for judgment, and it must begin first among God's own children And even we who are Christians must be judged, what terrible fate awaits those who have never believed on the Lord.'*

"The church is indeed a place of judgment You are welcome, my friend, but you must change your ways. We are here to help you do that.. You will find all levels of conduct.

"You say, 'hey, wait a minute.I like all that love. I like all that talk of streets of gold,all of that fellowship, and now you say I have to change. You mean, I can't throw a bag of trash out the car window?' You are right. You can't, for everything you do reflects on God's church. What you do reflects on the very Son of God.

"Listen, God called you out to be a Child of the King! If you are going to be royalty, then you have to act like royalty. The church is a place to be saved, and there you, like Jonah, can hear the voice of God telling you what He wants you to do. You then have a choice. You can say no. Jonah did, and looked where he ended up, in the belly of a big fish on the bottom of the sea.. If God tells you to go to China, friend, you had better start packing your bag. God knows what he is doing.

"It boils down to this: There are people who want all of God's blessings but none of the obligations. They want all of the forgiveness but do not want to forgive.

"Believe it or not, I am closing with these few words: In spite of all that I have said here this morning, the church is also a place of imperfection. You are welcome here, but when you come, don't set your sights on the pastor or some member and follow and do as he does He could be worse than you and trying to come out of the hole. Set your sights, instead on God and then you will be led to holiness and perfection as much as is humanly possible.

"You come as an imperfect person, but God's spirit will change you from day to day. Don't put your eyes on me and follow, I am a million miles from perfection. Remember, you come to God because your sins are catching up with you. You come, God accepts you, now let Him work to change your life for the better. That dear friends, is the name of the game. Let us pray.

"Father," Joe bowed his head and the organ began playing softly. "Lord you ordained this church, and it grows each day as people come to it, willng to change their lives. I hope this church will grow stronger and larger each day than ever before. I know that it has a lot of imperfect people in it, but Lord, we are trying to change and we ask you for strength. Lord, my prayer today is that you change each of us from the inside out, not the outside in. Change our negative attitudes, helps us to love one another until we at last come into Thy Glory. Amen."

Joe stepped down from the dais to the section where the wheel chairs and people on crutches were. He placed his hands on the afflicted and one by one they rose and cried. The blind shouted as they saw for the first time. People stood and cheered, and no one except Bandy and Pritchett wanted to leave.

Enroute home, the two men were silent for a time, their thoughts not making pleasant company. Finally Pritchett spoke.

"That man," the preacher muttered, "is a menace. He must go."

PART TWO

Lee Roy Neal

CHAPTER EIGHT

Joe shook the drops of moisture from his rain coat and hung it carefully on the clothes tree in his office. He walked over to his modest desk and sat. He tore the sheet from the desk calendar and it showed April 12, 1985.

The hour was early, Joe's favorite time. He loved to witness the birth of a new day taking place just outside the large window. He gazed fixedly at the bleeding foothills just over the Interstate. They shimmered in the early light looking like some giant prehistoric animal of ages past., an animal just waking up to a new day.. He could now see the tip of the sun just becoming visible over the distant horizon., Everything seemed to have a color belonging only to it. Many hews were out there. He made out lots of red, some velvet, a sort of green and purple with a brilliant orange background. He saw yellows and blues and another shade of purple. The sky was so blue that Joe raised his hands and whispered "Thank you Jesus" It looked as if God has swept all smog from His sky. It seemed as if that sky was screaming at the clouds that brought the rain the night before were no longer welcome.. The vibrant luster of the morning lifted Joe's spirits to some sort of new high.

Joe leaned back in his chair and closed his eyes. He found it hard to believe that so much had happened to Our Fathers House the past two years.. He gazed through the window at the fountain just outside. It was flinging its own brand of diamonds into the slanting sun light. The water fell into the large basin like rain in the forest. He compared that falling water with the blessings of the last 24 months..

When Dennis Shepherd had donated the 100 acres of prime land, it indeed seemed God-ordained. It seemed the donation had caused all else to fall on Our Fathers House. The membership roll of the church expanded, and the people responded to Joe's sermons that taught that God's tithe was the only way to carry on God's work. Many people who had experienced healing, those that were wealthy contributed to the building fund. One family, whose son was paralyzed began a building fund with $500,000. This caused such an avalanche that soon over $1,000,000 was in the building fund.

Phillip Sands, an architect, had joined Joe's inner circle, and he and Joe, and Joe's staff had spent weeks planning what the permanent home of Our Fathers House would look like.. Joe was adamant that the building gave a sense of reaching upwards toward God's throne.. Gary had said he would like to see lots and lots of glass.. Phillip made dozens of sketches until suddenly, all agreed that they had what God wanted.. The building fund was soaring over a million dollars, and Phillip brought in an estimated figure of ten million dollars. Dennis had arranged financing. Joe presented the plan to the people on one Saturday morning. "I am convinced that Our Fathers House should be better, larger, more magnificent than any other building anywhere around." he had said, and the people agreed. Construction was started almost immediately, and 18 months later, not only was the building complete, but donations and gifts had made it possible to dedicate the building debt clear.

And today, Joe still found it hard to believe. He was not surprised, for he knew the power of God to move His people. The building was mostly of glass and crystal. The geodesic dome in the main sanctuary rose over 200 feet over the pews.. The walls of the building were small triangles of glass, began in a brown and toward the top where the dome ceiling was the hues were bright blue. Phillip had ingeniously designed lights that at night made the breath taking colors glow. He especially loved the prayer tower just outside the main building. It rose thirty stories into the sky and on three sides the words **O U R F A T H E R S H O U S E** could be seen in changing colors. It had become a landmark on the Interstate and could be seen from miles away.

Five thousand people could be seated comfortably, and beneath the main auditorium was a basement area seating an additional 4000.. The services could be viewed on a 9x12 foot screen. One section of the auditorium was devoid of pews and there those who were handicapped came. Each pews was equipped with ear phones, where people other than English speaking could hear the sermon in their own language. They simply pushed a button marked Spanish,French, or German.

There were several auxiliary buildings. One building was devoted entirely to the food bank, James was another member of the inner circle and he was in charge of this.. He had ten people working full time to keep records and to eleminate fraud. Joe already was dreaming of a twelve grade school to be tucked just east of the main building.. Next to the school was a 15 acre plot where a future Senior Citizen complex was to be built. This would be small, one bed room cottages where Seniors could have privacy, and yet were near the health office where a doctor would be on duty each day.

Deacon Bandy was still Joe's arch enemy. He and pastor Alphonso Pritchett were spending more time fighting Joe than they did operating the First Baptist Church.. Mr. Bandy had aged perceptively the past two years. He was now a perfect example of an egotist He seemed to draw his surroundings into himself. and absorbed them so that he felt he was both human and a computer who made no errors. He now walked with a slight stoop, his hair totally white, his eyes cold and cruel.

Lately he had begun having flashes of doubts.. His common sense often fluttered with the thought that just perhaps he was wrong about Joe. It was an uneasy fear that woke him in the dead of night. He knew he had not been happy in years, for everyone who hates, Joe had often preached, courts unhappiness. Why was it, Bandy thought late one night, that I remember things Joe says that really make sense? I remember once he said "If a man hates with all of his might chances are, he will never know happiness ever again. This is true, even if the original, fervent hate is forgive to the hater. It is there, like a deep undetected cancer silently gnawing away at the soul of the one who harbors the hate." Joe had continued, "Hate manages to get into the bloodstream like tetanus or the germs of a rabid animal where it becomes a disease of both the blood and mind and always make sure there is a fertile field ready to welcome the seeds of new frustrations, new envies, and new hates." Bandy remembered clearly and it made him sweat, "Sometimes," Joe had said, "the one who is hated suffers such as gossip, but it was almost a certainty that the hater would suffer some sort of disaster and usually lives out his days in despair and foulness and grief."

At times when Joe noticed Bandy's efforts to hurt him and the ministry, he was almost amused to open laughter. The deacon was so overt and many people remarked about it to Joe. Bandy had somehow persuaded the ministers of surrounding churches and these traditional churches had ostrasized Joe because he flaunted most of their sacred cows.. Rather than pray and search the scriptures and ask the guidance of the Heavenly God whom they allegedly served, for guidance, they had foolishly hung on to their practices for dear life. This was so similar to the Pharisees and the Saduces of Jesus' earthly sojourn.

Our Fathers House had shaken Bandy to his toes when it refused to celebrate Easter and Christmas, saying that they were Pagan holidays dating back to tree worship by the Druids and Sun worship in Egypt. Joe maintained and preached that Jesus did not rise from the dead on a Sunday and that he had not been born within months of December 25.

Bandy had been sure that Joe had stumbled when one requirement of membership in Our Fathers House had been that new members must make a genuine and concerted effort to tithe. Of course Joe had been careful to state that Our Fathers House did not need the tithes,. but that the people needed to tithe as an expression of their true love for the Master., an expression of their trust in God.. Joe had encouraged the people to begin with paying one per cent and gradually work up to ten per cent and even higher as God blessed. Most families were giving the tithe, and some more. One family had actually progressed to seventy per cent! They often testified that God managed to make the 30% go farther than the 100% had gone.

Joe's teachings were considered radical and down right crazy by a lot of traditional preachers. Joe, sitting in his office that morning, remembered the sermon he had preached in the new building. Since cassette audio tapes were available from Our Fathers House, this particular tape was played many many times in Church Board meetings. Joe had maintained that that one real proof of the existence of God in a man's life was that *he never got everything that he prayed for, things that he had worked for, had strived for and prayed for many times.* "You see," he had said, "this denial by God is part of our earthly punishment. God in His infinite wisdom knows what is best for us. He knows that if you got everything you asked for it would be disastrous for you. Why some of the things we ask for could destroy our physical life.

"When human desires permeate our every day life, we are likely to forget virtue and considerations for our fellow man. We are apt to become selfish and forget to be humble which is a Christian virtue. These traits are like God. Our hearts are ever susceptible to a tug by selfishness and arrogance. God has no intention of cramming virtue down the throats of any of His children. At times, when a man is so consumed by covetousness for some particular thing, he gets angry, and then to his horror finds that he has been the instrument of his own destruction.

"May I give an illustration," he had said., liking his lips as they still got dry when he concentrated deeply, "The story is told of a man and woman who wanted to build on to their house, but could never seem to get the money to do it. The contractor had wanted $25,000 to do the job and the couple knew that it was impossible.
"One day an old friend of the couple came for a visit. He had just returned from a trip to India. He got to talking and told them of a man he had met who was a guru and he had a talisman that would give whoever held it three wishes. The couple said they would like to see such a thing, and the visitor said he still had it. The man showed it to them and it was a gnarled and wizened and petrified Monkey's paw. The man said that anyone who had used it regretted the experience. He said he knew he had. In fact, the man said it was dangerous and threw into the blazing fireplace. The woman got a poker and yanked it out still smoking but intact. She said they would like to try it.. The visitor left after again warning the couple that danger lurked where anyone had all that they wished for.
"After the visitor had left, the man and woman sat on the couch and with both holding the monkey's paw wished for $25,000 to build on to their house. The talisman jumped in their hands as if it had suddenly come to life. They dropped it and both man and wife felt odd.
"A week later, a stranger came to their door and and informed them that their only son had been killed by a train, and that he had a check for the son's insurance for them. He handed the grieving parents the check and they were aghast that the amount was for $25,000.

"The couple was horrified, yet their wish had come true. After a week of deep mourning and after they had buried their son whose body had been so mangled that the casket was not opened, they returned to the house and their grief. Late that night, the wind and rain beat upon their house and they woke up and the man remarked at the amount of rain, and his wife said their son was out in the rain, and then a thought came to her. The monkey's paw! It had two more wishes on it. She quickly ran to the living to get the talisman and before her husband could stop her she rubbed the thing and wished her son alive again.

"Almost immediately someone or something started pounding on the door and the woman ran up stairs to get the key. The man began frantically looking for the monkey's paw and just as his wife reached the door and turned the key he made the final wish. She opened the door to the wind and rain and nothing more.

"This is a crude example of what I am trying to say," Joe had said just as Bandy had remembered it. "We pray to God for something, and God knows that the price you have to pay to get it is beyond your capacity." Bandy did not like the thoughts he was having, yet no power on earth would make him change the course he had set for himself.

Joe was becoming well known for his sermons and for the response to them. One day, Alphonso Pritchett had remarked that Joe's healing services were the drawing card of Our Fathers House. He often remarked that they were fake, and that they could easily be duplicated.

It was Sunday morning about the time that Joe had dedicated Our Fathers House building that Pritchett remarked that anyone with enough faith could heal another person. He stood beside the custom made pulpit and shouted: "Is there anyone here who is handicapped and wants to be healed?" A man bout forty came forward, hobbling on one crutch. He was helped to the dais and Pritchett looked at the creature, his hair matted and the lined face showing either pain or dissipation.

"My brother," Pritchett had shouted, the audience edging to the front of their seats.," Do you believe that I can heal you of your affliction?"

"So help me G..God I do."

Pritchett put his hands on the matted hair and shouted, "Then let it be to you as you have believed. "Be healed!:" The creature wobbled a little and then a smile came over his face and he threw the crutch down and shouted. I'm healed, O I'm healed!"

Bedlam raced over the audience. Many shouted and others wept. Bandy had a knowing look on his face.

"Go and sin no more, My brother," Pritchett had shouted. The man left the dais and he had gone half way up the aisle when suddenly he shouted. "No, No, No!" He turned and retraced his steps. He reached the dais again and the audience was stunned to a silence. The man reached into his dirty clothing and his hand held a roll of bills.

"Here," he shouted. "Here's your money back. This is wrong and I want no part of it. I was never crippled, and I'm afraid God might make me a real cripple if I go through with this farce." He left the auditorium among stunned silence. Bandy quickly went up his aisle to meet the creature outside.

"This is a perfect example of the evil in our world, my friends. You are dismissed."

Joe had given a sermon on being satisfied with one's circumstances, and try always to be in the Father's will and trust God to know what is best for you.

"I remember the story of the poor dirt farmer in Texas who barely kept his family in food and clothing. One day, Oil was discovered on his land and he was an overnight millionaire. He moved from the crude farm life and the family had a big house in the city with swimming pool; and all the rest. He gave his kids everything they wanted, and despite this fact, troubles came, he and his wife were divorced and the children went to and fro.

"One day he was sitting in his office and looked out the window on to the street. He saw a farmer in an ancient truck with several children seated in the back. The father went into a store and came back with a sack of apples which he distributed to the kids. amid shuts of delight.. The man's partner saw the vacant look on the man's face and asked him what he was thinking. The man said 'I was wishing that I had never struck it rich and was able to make my kids happy with a sack of apples."

"Do you get the point?" Joe had asked. "What you want and pray for may not be what what you can handle and is best for you. I ask that you leave it to God and when He says no, try to trust him and remember that it is for your own good."

Over the past two years, Bandy's actions, for the most part, had not escaped Joe's notice. He had seen his arch enemy build a fortress against, not only the ministry headed by Joe, but against Joe himself. Joe knew that it was impossible for a man to live a single day without erecting some sort of wall There are as many different walls as there are people. A wall built of malice: revenge or hatred or just plain meanness was a wall,indeed, but it served to be a wall about the builder. and he instead of his enemy was the prisoner.

Joe really felt a Christian pity for the man mainly because Bandy had reached a peripheral goal: Bandy had persuaded the district ministerial alliance to issue an official censure against Joe and Our Fathers House. Bandy had also succeeded in getting the IRS to investigate not only Joe's finances, but also that of Our Fathers House. In spite of or perhaps because of Bandy's tirade against Our Fathers House, the beautiful Church on the Interstate was now one of the largest churches in the entire state.

These things raced through Joe's mind that morning as he leaned back in his chair after his morning prayers. Joe learned just last week that other district ministerial associations were joining in on the effort to stifle Our Fathers House. He realized that such widespread opposition could slow down the growth of this 'different' church.. He hated being the object of anyone's hatred. He often remarked that something was amiss with mankind. Liars, thieves, rapists, killers, seemed to be the favorites of modern man. The victims of the deeds of these people were termed the 'bad guys'. Even the laws of the land were written and enacted to favor the felon. What a world to live in.. Do a favor for someone and presto you have made an enemy who tries to find a way to do you harm. They consider you their enemy.. Joe heard someone say that the reason a dog always bites the hand that feeds him is that the feeding hand is the only hand close enough to bite.

Again
If Christ Came Again

Consider a person who is gentle, kind, paid his debts to both man and to God, the very epitome of virtue. This person is the object of hate, not the murderer or other malefactor.

Joe had foregone marriage and a home of his own. He felt as the Apostle Paul had said: Some people were not meant to be married. Bandy, noting Joe's unmarried estate, had tried to pin a badge of homosexuality on Joe, but he soon learned to drop that hot potato in a hurry.

Joe felt sorry for the old man who had befriended him as a youth.. Joe often said that a man who laid down to sleep with hatred and malice was himself a leper., and when he arose, his companions for the day were foulness and decay and corruption and a broken heart. Not only had this cancer of hate consumed the deacon, but it had written its message across Bandy' face.

For some reason, Bandy began to reason that he was the victim, not Joe. In spite of this realization, Bandy refused to give it up. It was like a substance addiction.. His white hair was now thin and for sure was vanishing completely. His steps were ponderous, even his efforts to smile were no more. He was somehow aware of the fact that the more he fought Joe, the more Joe prospered. He remembered when he had connived to get Joe thrown out of the county fair grounds spot and Joe had come into the 100 acres of land where that big church stood.. In contrast, Bandy's own business had failed, and for that alone, Joe must pay.. Bandy swore one morning with his hand raised up towards heaven that as long as he lived, Joe would be the object of Bandy's ire. Bandy did not realize that he had fallen into one of Satan's most cleaver traps: If a man did not harbor hatred in his life, Satan was powerless in that life.

On that April morning, Joe again thanked God for all His blessings on Our Fathers House. Even without asking, people came forward and donated money and labor to such an extent that this magnificent plant had been dedicated free and clear of debt. It stood as a physical presence of the Glory of God. The Spirit of God dwelt here. The doors of the church were open to all no matter the need.. Joe always preached tithing, always emphasizing that God was not a beggar. He still preached that paying of the tithe and then giving beyond that was one sure way to end all of one's financial problems.

Lee Roy Neal

As Joe mused that quiet morning, he remembered one sermon he had preached about a month before the erection of the present building had begin. It was a sermon he hated to preach. In fact, he remembered, he had put it off again and again until he knew that it was from God.

He went to a filing cabinet where all copies of his sermons were kept. He found the one he wanted and returned to his desk and read it once again. It was as if he was seeing it for the first time.

"My text this morning," he had begun, "is found in Acts the fifth chapter. *'There was a man named Ananias (with his wife Sapphira) who sold some property, and brought only part of the money claiming that it was the full price. (His wife had agreed to this deception) But Peter said: "Ananias, Satan has filed your heart. When you claimed that this was the full price. You were lying to the Holy Spirit. The property was yours to sell or not as you wished. Even after selling it it was your choice as to how much to give. But how could you do such a thing. You were not lying to us but to God." As soon as Ananias heard these words he fell to the floor dead! Everyone was terrified, and the young men came with a sheet and took him out and buried him.*

"About three hours later his wife came and not knowing what had happened, Peter asked her, Did you sell the land for such and such a price? Yes, she replied, we did. And Peter said 'How could you and your husband even think of doing a thing like this—conspiring together to test the Spirit of God's ability to know what was going on? Just outside the door are the young men who have buried your husband and they will carry you out too.' Instantly she fell to the floor dead. Terror gripped the entire church.

"Friends, this man and his wife didn't have to sell their land nor even when they sold it they did not have to give anything to the church. Where they sinned was in lying. They said they were giving it all and in fact they lied.

"I tried not to preach this sermon, but I am compelled by God to do His will.. There are two main subjects that it is hard for a preacher to preach on. The Resurrection and Giving. If a preacher preaches on giving, people think it is personal, that he wants the money. Satan will attack anywhere he feels there is a threat to his work. He realizes that if people become dedicated to paying the tithe and even making gifts beyond that his work will be threatened.

"If someone is faithful and pays the tithe and even goes beyond that, Satan enters and tries his best to convince the giver that God is a liar. 'Where is the return, he often asks, even before the sun sets on the day of the gift. You must have faith, real full faith. Don't expect to pay your tithe and then watch out for manna to fall from heaven. What is faith, anyway? Well, let me try to get it where we can all understand it. Faith, as seen through eyes that has not seen, call it a fact, but call it hope. Faith is an action based upon belief sustained by the fact that God said that His word was forever settled in Heaven. When we remember that God's Word is forever settled in Heaven, we are saying that this is the hope we cling to: that what is sealed in Heaven will become a true fact on earth. I hope that doesn't confuse you as much as it did me at first.

"When faith labors to enter into the rest promised by God, we have hope of a Sabbath rest which comes in Heaven, and an earthly rest is based on the promise of God for the rest in Heaven.

"As long as faith is hope and not yet fact, it becomes a magnet to intensify the hanging on of action based on belief of God's promise to you. The hardest thing to get over to a new Christian particularly is to have patience. God said he would reward you. Wait on Him. Here is the scenario: You tithe and even give more, you wait and nothing comes. You still have trouble getting the house payment each month, the car still breaks down, and then enters Satan. He calls you a fool and you back off. Listen to Satan and you will lose all or part of your faith. It's like cutting a cord that binds you to Heaven and then you become a living dead person.

"Faith, not only in money matters but others also, has a primary purpose: to keep you looking heaven ward. You see., God has enough grace for the whole world and a million more like it for all who act in faith. Hang in there.

"Remember Abraham. God promised that he would become the father of a great nation. He believed and waited and then as the years passed, he and his wife decided to give God a hand. He took Hagaar's to his bed and produced a son. You know what happened then, Hagaar and her son were banished from Abraham's house. Then, miracles of miracles, in God's time, Sarah, past ninety and Abraham, over 100, became parents of Isaac. How happy they were until one day God told Abraham to take his teenaged son upon the mountain and offer him as a sacrifice to Jehovah.

"Did Abraham balk? Indeed not, he took the boy on a donkey with a servant and started out. Isaac asked where they were going, his dad said upon the mountain to make a sacrifice. When the lad asked the whereabouts of the sacrifice, Abraham told his son that God would provide one. Now note this, it's plainly written in your Bibles in Genesis chapter 22. When Abraham and Isaac took the wood and the flint for starting the fire and started up Mount Moriah, he told the servant in effect: 'Wait here **WE** shall return. We? Abraham had faith, and he firmly believed that if he killed his son and offered him as a sacrifice, God would raise him from the dead. See? Sow seeds of faith and suddenly God's promises change hope to fact.

"I hope that I am making this clear to you. I would like to go again to the Bible in Luke 18.: 18 *'Once a Jewish religious leader came to Jesus and asked this question: 'Good sir, what must I do to get to Heaven?' Jesus told him not to call him good and then answered the question. 'You know what the ten commandments say, don't commit adultery, don't murder, don't steal and so on.' The man replied 'I have obeyed everyone of these laws since I was a small child.' Jesus then said: 'There is yet one thing you lack, sell everything you have and give the money to the poor. —it will become treasure in Heaven. —and then come and follow me.' But when the man heard this he went away for he was very rich.*

"You see, Christ knew what the young man's true God was: Money. When the Disciples heard this story they asked then who can enter Heaven, can no rich man? Jesus said that it was easier for a camel to go through the eye of a needle than for a rich man to enter Heaven. In Jesus' time, a coarse thread was made from camel hair and was almost impossible for it to be threaded into a needle. Hard but not impossible. It could have meant that he referred to the small door in the large gate guarding the city and it was called the eye of the needle. Sometimes a thirsty and hungry camel stuck his head in that door when the main gate was closed and tried to get in. Actually what

Christ meant that what was hopeless and impossible with man was possible with God.

"When Jesus said a man should give his all, Peter reminded Jesus that they (the apostles_ had forsaken all. Jesus said that no man who has forsaken mother, father, brothers and wealth and so on would be without a reward.. He went on to say that he would get an earthly reward here, on earth, while he was alive.. I believe this is a promise of temporal blessings, actual things one can use here. A lot of poor Christians seem to miss out on the promises of these Words of Jesus.

"A lot of traditional preachers today do not preach on nor do they believe in Divine healing because they have never seen one. I personally find it a lot easier to believe that deformed bodies can become healed and perfect bodies by God's power than some Christians who fail to act on God's promises.

"I've seen many poor Christians in the past two years because they fail to take on God at His promises. Some preachers, because they themselves do not believe, avoid preaching like this.. Jest never forget what Jesus said in Matthew 19:29 *'And anyone who gives up his home, brothers sisters father, mother, wife, and children to follow me shall receive a hundred times as much in return and shall have eternal life.'*

"Was Jesus fooling? Did he really mean that? You see, he did not mean you would have 100 wives given back. He spoke of things like homes and wealth, things we can use.

"What I am trying to get across to you is that if you trust God with really what is His already, you can simply go to God's storehouse and pick what you want from His shelves. This promise is repeated in Mark 10:28.

"You must get this straight: **You give because of who God is and you give because the holy spirit leads you.. Give with eternity in view**. You see, God's promise of the hundred fold blessing presupposes the **motive** in giving If you give to the right place and for the right reason and for the right cause, when that happens, God enters the picture and keeps His promise.

"You know, it's a shame, but lots of poor Christians just can't get hold of this. Don't feel too bad, even the apostles did not get the message and it came from the very mouth of the Son of God. Each was never known to have any of the material wealth of this world.

"Ever see a wealthy man who says 'I owe my wealth to Mark 10'? How man Christians here today are living beneath their privilege? The world loves to point to the Disciples who died in poverty and say God does not keep His promises. You had better believe that this is still God's world and His word is forever settled in Heaven, and it's easy to let the weight of tradition beat you down and keep you from claiming your reward as a believer.

"Some of you have given, not in order to get, but on the value of God's word Some of you just don't expect God to keep his word. He can lay a reward right beside you and you will walk right by it."

Joe remembered that day, and the response was unbelievable. That was the day that someone pledged $100,000 to the building fund and a week later the funds were in the bank.. Joe had begin, about six months ago, to having personal counseling upon requests. Much of his time of late was taken up in these sessions people whose lives had become so muddled had at last turned to God and religion in an effort to straighten things out. The catch slogan often heard that day was 'all men are brothers'. That's all it was, Joe had remarked. The only time that the average man became a brother to someone it was when pain and despair linked them together. Oh they would go through the motions. They would come to church, they would even kneel at the altar, but unless such actions were done in sincerity, it did no good. There was no freedom from the problems that plagued ordinary mankind.

So, Joe met with these people, many just flotsam of forgotten ones. His heart went out to these unhappy people. The more counseling he did, the more he became convinced that none was free and that each one was a slave to someone or something. He did not like the picture forming daily as he met with these creatures. Man was his worst enemy and freedom was an illusion, an imaginary thing. There was no freedom as such. Man was his own slave. Joe sometimes wondered why Christ had died for all man knowing of man's frailty. He had no answer for that.

Over half of Joe's private conferences were with parents concerned with errant children. This was most difficult since Joe had no children and some parents ignored his advice justifying the advice as theoretical and that if it were his child he would have different advice. Modern education has little or no room for discipline, and even parents of this education were reluctant to invoke any type of control.

Joe's standard advice, after hearing the problem, was always prefaced by saying that having children was not always a blessing to parents. At first they seem so, but kids are influenced by peer pressure and get off track and might even become a curse to their parents, and in some cases, might actually physically destroy them. It is cheap sentiment not to see the potentially danger of a child to a parent. Even the Bible states that the heart of a child is deceitful; that man is wicked and evil from the day of his birth and has the Adamic sin in his genes.. A child is not born pure, perfect, and wonderful. Man is born a human being with all the human faults built in and must be taught. That's why God's word plainly states: 'Train up a Child in the way he should grow, and when he is old, he will not depart from, it.'

"Let a child enter a school," Joe had continued, "and the child is 'different', see how quickly the horde gathers around to pester and to hurt. A child that is always prepared for class, and who seldom runs afoul of school rules is soon ostrisized and becomes an outcast." Joe had then cited cases in his observation where some child would deliberately make poor grades in order to be accepted by his peers.

Joe felt that these people whom he tried to help needed some degree of sympathy. Many of these people never attended any church including Our Fathers House. Joe tried to show these people that this might be the root of their present troubles. He advised attending some church as a family if for no other reason than to set an example to the children. "You see," he often said, we everyone share the same fate., "we all have the ability and inclination to commit sin. We must realize that sin is not strength, it is weakness, failure: a breaking of the laws of God Almighty. Recognize the mistakes of the past and try with all your might to rectify them.. The main thing is to keep the main thing the main thing in your dealing with your kids.

CHAPTER NINE

Joe had come early on that morning, because of an early appointment with a man and his wife who were having serious marital problems. Joe reflected that he had had a lot of these of late. He always felt a bit odd about counseling married people since he had never been married, but as always, God seemed to put the right words in his mouth.

The couple were members of Our Fathers House, Jerry and Laura Spencer. He was twenty years older than she was, and it was the second marriage for both of them. She had brought two children into the marriage, and Jerry and Laura had produced two children between them. Joe remembered that he seldom saw Laura in Church, but Jerry was there with all four children almost every Lord's day. The two oldest boys were 13 and 14 year old, and the two youngsters, the boy ten and the girl eight years old.

Joe saw the couple drive up and waited expectantly for them to knock on his door. He got up and let them in. Jerry introduced Laura to Joe and the couple took two chairs in front of Joe's desk. Laura was a small woman with dark hair cut close to her small well shaped head. Her teeth showed the result of much smoking. Joe saw that she was thin almost to the point of emaciation. She must have weighed less than 100 pounds. Her face was set in a permanent frown and Joe immediately felt sorry for her for her face reflected the inner trouble from within. She wore a pouting, combative look and her gray eyes darted everywhere as if someone or something was about to pounce on her. Her nose was small, but she had flared nostrils She wore little make-up and her dress was a one-piece wool thing fitting snugly. It was a bottle green which did not go with her skin. She had an air of belligerence and she looked as if she had never smiled. Crow feet were etched about her eyes and mouth and she looked older than her husband though Jerry had said he was twenty years older than she was.

Jerry was about average sized, but a bit on the heavy side. Joe estimated that he carried from ten to twenty pounds of excess weight. His hair was light brown and streaked with gray especially the temples. He must have been a very handsome young man. Today, Joe saw the troubled look painting his face. Joe took his seat behind his desk and almost before he settled back Laura began.

"I want you to understand, preacher," she tried a smile and it never materialized, "It wasn't my idea to come here. Jerry insisted, and in an effort to have some semblance of peace, I agreed to come or I would never have heard the end of it. I doubt very much if you can help us at all." She dropped her head and spoke in a lower, almost forlorn voice, "I doubt if anyone or anything can help it."

"Mrs. Spencer," Joe spoke softly, picking up a pen from the desk and rolling in his hands, "perhaps you are right, but the very fact that you are here proves to me that you haven't completely given up. Isn't that right?" He gave her his best smile and she seemingly relaxed the smallest degree.

"I have tried all that I know to do. I work nights at the hospital, and I try to do all I can to keep things going."

"I understand you work at a psychiatric hospital near Bethany?"

"Yes, it's thirty four miles to my work each way."

"You work at night?"

"Yes, the eleven to seven shift."

"Jerry, I believe you told me that you were a teacher in Bethany? Am I correct?"

"Yes, pastor, I teach junior high school math."

"I believe you told me that you also worked at an additional job."

"Yes, I sell books, encyclopedae"

"Mrs. Spenser, please forget my prying into things that are none of my business, but I must get the entire picture. Jerry takes the children to school in the morning and then brings them home after school?"

"That's right," Laura replied, not liking the direction the conversation was taking.

"Then, Jerry sees to the children and their home work and chores and prepares the evening meal."

"Yes, Jerry is a good cook, better than me."

"After supper, he gets you up and you watch the children until he comes in from his second job so you can leave for work?"

"Yes, I am ready for work when he comes in around ten o'clock."

"By then, I imagine the children are in bed?"

"Yes. But sometimes Bobby, who is 15, stays up until Jerry comes home."

"Fine," Joe smiled again. "Then, the next morning, Jerry gets up and gets the breakfast and gets the children ready for school?"

"Yes, we usually wave at each other at the gate as they leave and I arrive."

And on Saturdays, do you work then?"

"Yes, I'm off Sundays and Mondays."

Joe decided to make a jab. "Do you contribute to the financial support of the family, Mrs. Spencer?"

"Absolutely not. I feel that it is a man's place to financially support his family."

"What do you use your income for?"

"It's none of your business, but I will say I see that the kids have a nice Christmas and that they get birthday presents.. I pay for my car and my clothes."

"Mrs Spencer," Joe was kind. "Most marriages break up over money matters. Tell me if I have gotten the wrong picture. Jerry not only supports the family financially, but he is raising not only his two children but yours also. With a set up like that, why do you want to change it by a separation or an divorce?"

"Since you are seemingly determined that you want to go into all the personal details of our life," her nostrils flared, and Joe saw the hatred in her eyes, "Jerry simply doesn't want to have sex with me anymore."

"Have you two talked about this matter?"

Jerry opened his mouth to answer, but Laura spoke first, her voice high and bitter. "No, I just moved into the guest room. He did not miss me for he has lots of young males for company."

"You are using your active imagination again, Laura," Jerry broke in. His face reddened, and Joe saw the rising anger. There was silence in the room for a few seconds.

"I try hard never to take sides in family disputes," Joe began, "but it appears that you sleep at different times. Wouldn't that be a factor?"

"No," she spat," he doesn't have to go out every night to work before I leave. We could have time to get together then." She was angry. "He has no time then for he has to rush out to be with his young male friends." She wanted to make sure that her point had not escaped Joe's attention.

"You say he meets these 'friends' each night while he is supposed to be working?"

"That's right!"

"Then if Joe found a way not to have to work at night, you believe he would return to your bed?"

"I have to have both incomes to keep the bills paid," Jerry broke in.

"Then it would be that the solution is simple. If Laura shared the expenses, there would be no need for a second job, is that right? Have you broached this solution to Laura, Jerry?"

"She doesn't want to talk about that."

"I feel that if a man can't support his family he isn't much of a man." Laura spat the words, her teeth clenched.

"Mrs. Spencer," Joe spoke soothingly, "do you have any other solution to this problem other than Jerry working at night?"

"That's his problem, not mine. He's the supposedly bread winner I just don't want him leaving the house at night."

"Then the way I see it is that you don't feel like contributing to the family support, and you don't want him leaving the house at night, then what is to be done?"

"That's his problem and he has been unable to come up with a solution, and that's why I want out."

"But what you are asking is an impossibility, Mrs. Spencer. Can't you see that?"

"No one ever said that life is easy, preacher." She smiled, her crooked, stained teeth making her face sardonic.

"Is there no common ground on which you two people can meet. Are you willing, Mrs. Spencer, to do anything reasonable to save this marriage?"

"I have told him and I have told him what to do and if he can't come up with a solution, then the break up is entirely his fault."

Joe sat there, a helplessness covering his entire being. He knew that it was useless to try to reason with this unhappy woman who permeated selfishness and for this man who evidently still loved his wife. He felt that Laura was mentally disturbed, and if he suggested professional therapy it would be ignored. He had the feeling that this woman had secrets that could not be fitted into her purse.

Joe felt a chill in the room. The silence was great as the couple waited seemingly for some brilliant solution from this preacher to this impossible problem. Joe felt helpless. He had always maintained that the life of any human could be defined as a series of changes. Change in the life and in the heart of each human being. He was positive that growth in any facet of a life was impossible unless change of some kind was present. Even a corpse had a semblance of life about it for it changed from day to day as long as flesh was present to go into decay.

As long as worms ate at the eye sockets to further the disintegration of the once living and breathing person.

This woman, he decided, was a walking disaster. Her mind was indeed set in concrete, even granite. How he prayed that something could be done He felt that no further words would help, and it was with sadness that he walked the couple out of the door. He noted that Jerry's shoulders sagged in capitulation and despondency. He found out later that the couple had divorced. A sad situation.

Joe had the belief that at least two distinct personalities lived in each individual: part was divine, a gift of God Himself; the other part, and usually the greater part, was animal. Joe, as a minister, fought to make the divine the greater part. That was his duty as he felt it. Many ministers and member of the laity honestly believed that the divine was the controlling factor: that it controlled most of the actions of church going people. Joe believed that those who said that were little more than sanctimonious hypocrites, afraid to face the truth. Joe felt that any man who consciously tries to stifle the divine within himself is fated to become one of the losers of the world.. He becomes a person dissatisfied with himself and could become fertile ground for a vicious criminal to growing to reality.

The really adjusted person, the one who plods day to day making a living, one who has in fact 'gotten it all together' has a degree of happiness and he does in fact realize that he has the divine spark within. He also realize that he also has a carnal nature and the devil is ever ready to cause it to explode. Such a person is most always ready to lend a helping hand to most people who call on him, even though he is letting his guard down for a time and is open for the unscrupulous to take advantage of him.

Such a person can really reach his fulfillment and can enjoy a nearness to God and His hopes for all mankind. It is easier for him to enjoy this than a person who who is selfish and self-centered and who is interested in the person wearing his shoes.

Joe long ago realized that one of the great tragedies of a man's life was when he truly realizes that he is a free agent, realizes his selfish yearnings, yet knowing of the divine spark within his being on a daily basis. Sometimes he depresses this spark to his sub-sconscious as a result of a tragedy in his life: he loses something. It might be the death of a friend or relative, it might be wealth or his health or even the loss of freedom to move in and out of society as he wishes.

Joe has been called on to make a weekly visit to the Jail in Bethany. He gave a short talk on his visit. He realized that he had a captive audience and attendance was mandatory at least bodily. He noted that some prisoners remained hidden in their cells and took no part in the meeting in the singing, in the discussions. Now and then someone was caught up in a faith trip and sincerely committed himself to a righteous life if ever he was permitted to breath free air again.

Joe did quite a lot of private counseling with prisoners. He had to be ever leery of a 'con-job'. He never expected to move a mountain of asocial behavior from a prisoner by a few sessions with a prisoner. Yet he had to make the effort. The most he could hope for was to remove a shovel or two from the mountain.

The paradoxical juxtaposition of the divine side of and the human (or carnal) side of a man possessed Joe as the days of his ministry sped by. Joe felt closer to God each day that he lived, and he never failed to credit God for the phenomenal success of Our Fathers House.

Joe was never really surprised when a person who he had believed to be a paragon of virtue turned out to have feet of clay after all. He worked with prisoners, ex prisoners, people down on their luck, with supposedly honest people, and he found one common skein in all: Underneath the facade each person wore, was a secret, sometimes unknown to the person himself if that were possible. Joe believed that it was possible for him to unlock this puzzle of man. As he sat and thought about all of this the phone rang and he lifted it to his ear.

"Our Fathers House," he answered.

"Brother Joe?"

"Speaking," Joe said.

"Pastor," a female voice said, "You don't know me, but last Saturday I was in the morning service, and your sermon moved me to a big decision in my life. I think it has helped me to do something."

"Do you mind giving me your name?"

"Linda Murchison."

"How may I help you?" Joe asked in a soft voice. Somehow, he felt fate was hovering about him.

"I feel that I must talk with you. It seems important to me. Actually, I somehow feel that it has a sense of urgency."

"Can you come to my office?"

"Yes, sir. I can. I could be there in ten minutes if you can see me then."

"Yes, I can see you now. Come to the office building in back of the church."

"Thank you, pastor. I will be there at once."

Linda Murchison walked across the parking lot to Joe's office. She walked with a natural swing of her hips. Her figure would draw the eyes of any mature male to it. Her smooth, wheat-colored hair was cut to shoulder length and it reflected the morning sun in waves. Her dress was chic and looked as if it was made solely for her., showing, if one looked closely, that much care had gone into selecting it. Today, she wore a mid-thigh length pink dress and a light weight purple sweater was worn unbuttoned. The violet of her wide eyes matched the hues of the sweater. She walked with a kind of hop that men found irresistible. She wore a trace of expensive perfume.

As Linda entered the office, Joe rose and greeted her and held the chair for her. He was conscious of her perfume and liked it. He saw that she wore little make-up.

"You made it quickly, Miss Murchison. It is Miss?" He smiled and settled back in his chair.

"It is Miss, and I wish you would call me Linda." Her smile showed sort of square even teeth, very white. Her mouth was soft with faintly red lips.

"You have a pleasant office here, Brother Joe. It fits you as if you belong here. Yes, I like it. A person could feel free in here."

"Thank you, Linda, I like it. All of my sermons are born here."

"I like to hear you preach, pastor."

"Thanks. I'm glad someone was listening. I sometimes believe that I am preaching to a lot of ears that do not hear."

"The sermon you preached a week ago, the one where the woman was taken in adultery. Preacher, that sermon changed my whole way of thinking." She dropped her head and was silent for a moment. She took a deep breath and leaned forward in her chair. "I am a woman of the streets, Pastor I have been practicing my trade for over ten years, since I was seventeen. I am from a large city, and it seemed the thing to do, go into that business. Pastor, I am ashamed to even talk about it, and not until that sermon did it dawn on me that I could ever forgiven. Your sermon pointed that out to me.

"I don't even know why I came to church that day, other than I had passed it often and its beauty and serenity seemed a magnet to me. It seemed when I got up last Saturday that I just had to go to your church. I found a pew about half way back and of all the sermons you chose to preach it was that one. It was as if someone had 'ratted' on me as a joke or something.

"I want to tell you that I went home and since then, I have had no customers. I just feel that I can never go back to that life again. The main thing I came for today is to find out if God can and will forgive me for all I have done. Can God show me how to straighten out my life? I don't mind telling you I wonder how I got the courage to come here."

"Linda," Joe began, "If a person is to be happy, he must first have a good opinion of himself. This will make him have courage, it well make him well-balanced and reasonable. It never fails to make a person constructive. If a person has a low self-esteem it could and often does make him a vengeful person. If one does not think well of himself he becomes sad and lost. I congratulate you on your courage. It is a giant step toward recovery.

"You must realize, Linda, that God is almighty and all powerful, yet there is something that He can not do: He can't break a promise. One promise he has made is that He will forgive sin, not only of Linda Murchison, but any person who comes and asks and has a contrite heart.

"You see, Linda, Man is basic evil. As the world goes on it seems that man is getting worse. Man's history is written in blood and present man was no better than their fathers or grandfathers, in fact, as I said, they seem to be worse. I compare sinful man today as tigers in the arenas when they threw Christians to the animals. The tigers waiting to be fed smelled the blood and saw the dying Christians and they got worse and worse.

"Sometimes a man falls so low that the only direction he can go is up. You have made the first step. You can believe on God, you might even hate Him, blaming Him for your present situation.. You might scream at him and demand things of Him. Actually, what else is there? An unknown land filled with horrible things leering at you and ever ready to suck the very blood from your body.

"I was afraid to call you this morning." She tried to smile.

"Good!. The Bible tells us that fear is the beginning of wisdom. You have indeed made a giant step though you will not realize it for some time yet, but realize it you will, believe me. I believe God puts the fear in our souls. Can you imagine being afraid of nothing? Man in his arrogance has stated that there is no God because you cannot prove His existence. The other side of the coin is that no man can prove that He does not exist either.

"You might be interested in a story I once read, I will put it in a future sermon, but I will try it out on you.

"It seemed that an atheist placed a full page ad in the local paper and it was a challenge to God to combat. He stated that the following day he would meet God outside the city on a small hill, and there he would do battle with God.

"Everyone was invited to the fight, admission free, and it would take place Saturday morning at nine a.m.." Joe saw that Linda sat on the edge of her chair in rapt attention.

"Anyway, this was an unusual thing and many people came. Many other atheists and others who were not sure of God's existence were there. Others came who were sincere believers. They all came. At the appointed time, the man yelled real loud: 'God, here I am, I am going to fight you!' Everyone was silent and nothing happened. Smiles covered many of the faces. They were enjoying this. Fodder for idle talk all over town.

"The man said that perhaps God was asleep, so he yelled, 'God, come down here and do battle with me. I can thrash you.' The man grinned and saw that the people were mostly on his side. He would show them He said, 'guess I had better talk louder,' his voice was louder. Then he said: 'I will give God one more chance. I will yell this time, and if he does not answer then, all of you good people will know that this God thing is a lot of silly stuff.' He braced his feet and in the loudest voice possible: 'Oh God, I challenge you to battle.' He threw back his head and opened his mouth wide to yell once more when a gnat flew into his throat and lodged in his wind pipe. In ten minutes or less he was dead.

"People who hear this story say it was an accident, a coincidence. I fully believe that it was not. God used that small insect to do His work. If this is indeed a true story, God made the gnat and He made it for one special purpose: to make man a liar."

"Brother Joe, I fully believe God sent me to your church, and I fully believe that He has a purpose for my life. I have had a hard life, pastor. I was sexually molested by my step-father when I was eight, yet I still feel that I am responsible for my sins. He said it was his way of showing me that he loved me, yet I can't put all the fault on him. After nine years, I found the courage to escape his brutality and strike out on my own. I guess you would say I fell out of the frying pan into the fire.

"When I left home I was picked up by a pimp who made my life even more miserable. But I began making money, lots of money, and when I had saved enough, I ran away again and came here. I bought a small duplex and rent one side to to a fellow traveler and live on the other side. I get enough rent so that I no longer have to practice my profession. But I have become to believe that most church goers are hypocrites. One of my main customers is a deacon in one of the churches down town."

"What is his name?"

"I think it better that I do not say. He is an old man."

"Linda," Joe leaned over the desk," most churches today, especially large churches are filled with many business and professional men who contribute heavily to the church The traditional preachers abstain from calling attention to the things these men do because they are fearful of losing their contributions. they cater to these people and they end their sermons at precisely noon and the people go home with no spiritual food. Most churches today have degenerated into nothing more than social clubs. The pastors have made mushroom beds out of their baptistries because they have no use for them. They dare not offend the least of the people. If a preacher pounds on the pulpit or removes his coat he is considered crude and they move to oust him as soon as possible.

"Even atheist go to church for they feel that if they are seen associating with the people in the church they can wear an aura of respectability and stability. Remember, Linda, stability is not faith. Stability can get run over by a truck of dogmas or whatever and vanish into thin air. Forgive me. I feel so strongly about what a real church should be that I get off the track at times.."

"I understand perfectly, pastor. I used to go to church and sit by my step-father and even he was called on to lead a prayer now and then and I began to wonder even then as a young girl. Were all church people like that? Did other girl's fathers do what mine did? Were all the other church people like that? Putting up a good appearance and hiding all the evil beneath a clean shirt. I do believe in God, Brother Joe."

"I believe you really do, Linda, and I also believe the road to your present has not been easy. You see, you, Linda, if you think of it, almost every progress of the human race has been accomplished by a revolt of some sort. You revolted against an abusive parent, you revolted against a cruel pimp, and now you are rebelling against your profession.

"The children of Israel revolted against the tyranny of Rameses of Egypt. The American Colonies revolted against Great Britain because of excessive taxes The Civil War came about because of slavery, the French revolted because of a political situation that favored the haves. The Russians even revolted and history books call it the rising up of the masses. In the 1300's, England went to far in their oppression of the poor with unreal taxes. Look at the 1950's in the United States. The blacks decided that they had had enough and the marches began and has not been totally resolved now. Women have revolted about being treated as second class people.

"Linda, even the Church has not escaped. Martin Luther led the way when he got tired of the Catholic Church telling him how and what to think. Some splinter groups have gone too far the other way. You see, Linda, I am considered a maverick because I am almost finatical on following the Bible as God reveals it to me.

"Linda, you say that you believe in God. I am sorry to tell you that that is not enough. The Bible says that even the Devil believes in the existence of God. The way it goes, a young person goes to Sabbath School and learns about God. He develops a 'knowing' knowledge of God. The next step is to develop this into a 'knowing of God in the forgiveness of sin'." Joe noticed that Linda had removed her sweater and had placed it on the back of her chair. He saw that she was a beautiful woman. His manhood could not help but notice that. Her face was a well-written page of the life she had led. Her eyes were her best feature, they still had a 'captured bird' look. He breathed a silent prayer that he might be able to help her reclaim her life.

"Linda, one of the best weapon that satan uses to further his kingdom is to get ordinary people to make something complicated about truths in the Bible that are actually real simple. Christ was a simple man who liked simple things. He detested the ostentatious of the church of his earthly time. He saw the leaders of the church flaunt their belief that they were so very righteous. They wore phylacteries, special braid on their togas, they stood on busy street corners and prayed out loud, their faces contorted as if they were suffering. Jesus scorned the traditional church and chose instead simple men such as fishermen and laborers. Soon He began formulating a new idea as to what the church should really be. Jesus once told Peter that he would build his church on the faith that Peter had expressed when asked how he felt about Jesus. I believe that that was why the officials of the traditional church hated Him so much.

"Jesus made fools out of learned doctors and lawyers, philosophers. He had a single, simple message based on the laws written in stone, the original ten commandments that came directly from God Himself. He did not preach killing and wars, leaving that to the little people of the world. Jesus opened the doors of Heaven to the common man, the little nobody next door. He preached the worth of the little guy. He preached the majesty of man's soul." Joe paused for a moment.

"Then pastor, you think that it is not too late for me to change my life into a life that God will be pleased with?" She smiled at him and relaxed, leaning against her sweater, her eyes fastened on Joe's eyes, her entire expression one of expectancy.

"Oh, Linda, believe me, I can assure you that it is not too late. I vow it with every fiber of my body. I will tell you that it will not be easy, but I feel you can and will do it. You have taken on a powerful enemy who does not play fair. He will use every kind of trick to make you think you are wasting your time. The devil will keep at you day and night, even in your dreams He will give you what looks like logical 'reasons' why you are fighting a losing battle. He will try to make you believe that my advise is 'stupid', He will have you actually believing that there is no way that you can win: that you are fighting a losing battle, and that you might as well surrender now."

"Pastor," Linda stood and began replacing her sweater, "I believe that I can do it. I would like to ask a favor." She stood and fluffed her hair and took her purse and hung it over her shoulder.

"I will if I can, Linda, try me." He smiled.

"You mentioned that I would have 'down' days, and I believe you. I would like to come in on such says for another conference, just to renew my courage."

"You call me at any time, Linda, I assure you that I will find time for us to talk away." He walked her to the door and said good bye as she left.

As Linda walked to the parking lot, she brushed beside a figure coming into the office. Joe was watching the tableux and as Bandy saw Linda he jerked his away not looking at him. Joe knew then.

CHAPTER TEN

Joe stood by the door as the old man entered, wonder what reason compelled this man to come alone to see him. Immediately his antennae vibrated warning Joe to be on the alert He closed the door and returned to his desk and looked at Bandy standing there, trying unsuccessfully to hide the hate hiding behind the cruel eyes. Joe invited Bandy to be seated and sat waiting for the deacon to make the first move. Joe suddenly remembered the Bandy of his youth, and how on numerous occasions he had deliberately baited the man into making a fool of himself. He breathed a silent prayer of forgiveness. Perhaps the situation at present was partially Joe's fault and it was for that that Joe asked forgiveness.

Joe saw that the man's face had a drawn, almost petrified look. His hair now was just a whisp, giving him the look of a diseased fox in the wild. He noticed that the ears still jutted forward giving the face, as before, the look of a pig. He felt a pang of sorrow for the man. This man had lived the last twenty years in an atmosphere of hatred. He had been defensive in every contact he had had with Joe all of Joe's adult life. Joe felt that the man's lack of self esteem had made the fertile ground in which the hatred had grown. It had even destroyed the man's pride and self-love.

Joe realized that for a man to feel inadequate, to bear the onus of it, he had to forever be on the look out for someone to blame. He had to make some excuse, some justification, for all that ailed him, all of his failures, for all his faults, even for his very sins.

Bandy put his hat on the edge of Joe's desk and ran a gnarled hand through his sparse hair. "I hope I didn't come at a bad time, Joe," He looked at a spot above Joe's head. "In fact," he sort of laughed, "in fact I was just driving by, and on an impulse turned on to your parking lot. I realized that I had wanted to talk with you in private for some time, so as long as I was here, why not now?"

"The time is fine, Mr. Bandy," Joe looked as his calendar, "I have no more appointments this morning. In fact, I have just completed one." Joe paused, licked his lips and wondered why this man who hated him more than any in the world could want to talk to him about.

"I know, Joe, that you know that I have been against all that you have started here in Bethany, and I have often wondered that if it would be possible for us to 'bury the hatchet' as it were." His small eyes reflected the poison within. Joe did not miss this, and a chill ran up his spine.

"In what way do you suggest that we 'bury the hatchet' Deacon?" Joe's eyes were like glass.

"Well, if you could ease up on a lot of these 'far out' beliefs that confuse the people."

"Do you have a particular one in mind, Mr. Bandy," Joe looked the man in the eyes.

"Yes. For example, stop this foolishness of meeting on Saturdays. You are a large church now and you don't need that gimmick any longer."

"You know my views on the Sabbath day, Deacon. You know that I will never cede that, and besides, if we met on Sundays what would it do to your own attendance. You would have to chose between Our Fathers House and your own church since I see you each sabbath in our church."

"And stop ostrasizing," Bandy went on ignoring the reply of Joe, "all the sacred celebrations such as Christmas and Easter, celebrations hundreds of years old."

Joe looked at the old man for a few seconds. He felt sorry once again for him. He noticed outside the window that the sun had come out from its hiding place It flooded the office with light.

"Sir," Joe turned the letter opener through his fingers, "I have repeatedly gone over this both from the pulpit and in the press. I see no reason for going over it again and again unless you request it. Deacon, I will never cede something that I honestly and deeply feel is the holy will of God. That is what I live for, Mr. Bandy. The will of God. I will live my life to its end for this. Each of us must live our life as best we can. Even a heroic life must end at some point, and all that is left is of this earthy body is a mound of damp earth. You see this has been a problem or rather a question asked by almost anyone who ever lived on earth. Why does a person keep on clinging to life seeing the many trials and pitfalls each step he takes? Unfortunately, most people leave the answer to that to the preachers, and sometimes I believe that preachers are filled with fear and are reluctant to voice an opinion on this deep subject.. Mr. Bandy, all my mature years have been devoted to the seeking of the truth as God my Father would have me understand it and give me the ability to interpret it to the members of my flock.

"Deacon, you seem to forget that this great nation was founded on the premise that each citizen has the right to be free. Free from government who dictates how and what we believe. If you will think back, Mr. Bandy, in all the years that we have known each other, I have never once criticized you in what you believed or did not believe. That is the way I feel that God wants His children to behave."

"Then I take it," Bandy stood up and took his hat in his hand, "you have no intention of changing even one thing?"

"I can do none other than to stand by my beliefs and convictions. I stand on them even to the death."

Bandy stalked out muttering under his breath. When he reached his car he muttered softly, "to the death? Buster, you don't know how much truth your fancy words mean."

Saturday dawned brisk and clear. Even the sounds of the traffic on the freeway seemed to be in harmony. Joe stood on the side walk in front of the church. He saw that the leaves from the trees were making shadows on the lawn. He shivered, though he was not cold. He supposed that most pastors were apprehensive each time before a service began. He could smell the odor of peach blossoms from a nearby orchard that abutted the food bank complex. Birds were rehearsing their melodies making sure that their songs were perfect. A few clouds rode across the blue sky, Joe took a deep breath and again thanked God for all the blessings.

He walked around toward the rear of the building and entered the auditorium by a side door.. He was always surprised at the size of the crowd. As he walked toward the dais, young children near the front waved to him. The massive organ was filling the air with soothing and reverent music. As he mounted the dais, the 100 voice chancel choir stood and sang the Doxology, and the hundreds of people stood and sang along reading the words from a giant 9x12 foot screen. Joe felt humble as always, praying for wisdom and ability to deliver the message he felt God wanted delivered.

Lee Roy Neal

Today he wore a black pen striped suit with a white shirt and a dark tie. His black shoes were polished to a gloss, His fingers were trimmed neatly, and as soon as the music portion of the service, he stepped behind the pulpit that he had made with his own hands. He supposed that this was the last thing he would make since as the days passed his time became more and more precious. Gary had already made the announcements and had taken the offering, and Joe stood and waited for the ushers to settle down.

"Today," Joe said quietly, the sensitive microphones picking up his voice and carrying it all over the auditorium and those meeting below on the lower auditorium. "Today, I am going to introduce you to the most dangerous word in human speech. Please turn to the second book in the Bible, Exodus. We will go to the eighth chapter and begin reading at the very first verse. I will as usual be reading from the paraphrased edition of the Living Bible.

"And the Lord said to Moses 'Go in again to Pharoah and tell him, Jehovah says Let my people go and worship me. If you refuse I will send out hordes of frogs from across your land from one border to another. The Nile River will swarm with them, and they will come out into your houses, even into your bedrooms and right into your beds! Every house in Egypt will be filled with them. They will fill your ovens and your kneading bowls, you and your people will be emersed in them.

"Then the Lord said to Moses: 'instruct Aaron to point his rod toward all the rivers, streams and ponds in Egypt, so there will be frogs in every corner of the land.' Aaron did and frogs covered the nation. But the magicians did the same thing with their secret arts, and they too caused frogs to come upon the land.

'Then Pharoah summoned Moses and begged:' Plead with your God to take the frogs away and I will let the people go to sacrifice to Him.'

'Be so kind to tell me when you want the frogs to go,' Moses said, 'and I will pray the frogs to go at the time you specify, everywhere except the river.'

'Do it tomorrow,' Pharoah said.

"I am sure that most of you know the story, but allow me to review it briefly The Children of Israel had been slaves in Egypt many years. God raised Moses to lead the children out of Egypt and back to the Holy land He had promised Abraham or Israel.

When Moses went to the King or Pharoah who history says was Rameses II, to let the people go. The Pharoah refused and God turned the water to blood. The king did not like that and told Moses to take the blood away and he would let them go.

"After the blood became water again the king changed his mind. It was at this point that God sent the second plague on Egypt. Now I like frog legs as much as the next person, but what happened to the Pharoah was ridiculous. The frogs were every where. You could get in bed and a green slimy frog crawled up in your face. You went to put a shoe on and a frog was inside. You r wife made some biscuits and the dough began jumping." Joe paused as the people laughed. "I say that it was awful. Imagine getting a cup of water and begin drinking and a big frog came toward your mouth.

"The king got the point and called for Moses and Aaron and told them that this time he was really serious. Just get rid of the frogs and I'll let the people go. Now look at what the Bibles says right here. When Moses asked the king when he wanted the frogs to go, the king said, Tomorrow.

"Ah, tomorrow. That's the word. The most dangerous word in the world and in human language. Isn't it really interesting and amazing at what the king answered. He didn't say right now! He said tomorrow. He liked frogs better than I do." Joe noticed that Bandy actually got close to a laugh. Pritchett actually laughed, wondering what point this upstart preacher would make. He had read that passage hundreds of times and just put it down to some more Hebrew history.

"I would like to name this sermon: Why Spend Another Night with the Frogs? Joe had moved to the side of the pulpit but now moved back to look at his notes.

"You know, a lot of people are like Pharoah. They want to spend one more night in their sins, meaning full well that tomorrow they would turn over that new leaf and begin living a good life. Tomorrow they would walk down that aisle and give their hearts to Jesus. Tomorrow would be the day! Yes, Tomorrow, the most dangerous word.

"The fable is told, or perhaps the story is true, that once Satan called a meeting of his leaders and, like corporations do today, wanted to toss around some ideas as to how to boost the company, how to get more into the Devil's domain. The meeting place was in satan's office in the midst of hell. About twenty imps attended, the leaders of the Demon world. Satan explained that figures were behind last year and he wanted some in-put on how to catch up.

"Several suggestions were made. One imp said 'I'll go up to earth and broadcast the lie that there never was a Jesus Christ.!'

"'Sit down, you dummy,' the Devil shouted. 'They wont fall for that anymore. There is too much historical evidence for people to fall for that.. They can open any encyclopedia and find a listing for Jesus Christ and find out he lived on earth. They find traces of Christ in a flower, a baby's smile. Archeologist have dug up positive proof of Christ's existence on the earth. The idea is stupid. Sit down!'

"After that, the other imps were reluctant to offer a suggestion, until at last one imp, smaller and uglier than the others timidly stood. 'Master,' he began, 'send me to earth and let me go up there and tell the people that there indeed was and is a Jesus Christ. I will tell them that Jesus lived and in the end gave his life for all lost sinners' The devil got a puzzled look on his face, but said nothing. 'I would tell all of those people that they had to accept Christ through a profession of trust and faith or they would come here, to Hell.' The Devil exploded. 'You are completely crazy. You need a transfer, for this heat seems to have gotten to your brain. The very idea' Satan was furious. 'Sit down you blithering idiot!' The imp did not sit. 'Hear me out, Master,' he said. 'Here is the hook. Tell them of God's saving grace and Christ's sacrifice, but tell them that they can do this tomorrow.' The devil smiled and procrastination sped forward to become Satan's best weapon for getting people into his kingdom.

"There's not a person here today who does not believe in the reality of Jesus Christ." Joe raised his voice, "There are few here that do not know of the atoning sacrifice Christ made. Moreover," he lowered his voice, "each of you know that you should walk that aisle and publicly confess Christ as Lord. You have fallen for the lie of the devil and have sunk back in complacency and told yourself that you will do it tomorrow or next week. He has filled your minds with excuses for not acting today, and my friend, he is planning on you waiting just one day too late.

"Today, I would like to go over some excuses that the devil had blinded you with. You smile and say, 'Brother Joe, I would act today, walk that aisle and confess my sins before men just as Christ commanded, but you see, I would have to change my life style. I have too much to give up to do that today.'

"Will you stand another story? It seems that in the days of ships with sails for transportation, a ship was enroute to the United States with a load of wild animals from the jungles to zoo. A large ape got out of its cage and was running amok on the ship, climbing the spars and tearing the sails. If a sailor got hold of the ape he would get an arm torn off for his effort. They had no weapons to shoot him and at last an old experienced sailor suggested that two men take a long iron rod and hold it near the ape. The captain did not know what else to do, so he gave the order. The ape, seeing the iron rod, grasped the rod in both hands as was his nature. Some men brought a large cage and the sailors held the rod with the ape clinging to it over the cage. All efforts to shake the ape into the cage failed, for the ape held on for dear life.

"Finally, the sailors took the rod with the ape clinging on it and tossed it over the side of the ship. The last anyone saw was the ape hanging on to the rod for dear life and he sank to his death below the waves.

"My friends," Joe slapped the pulpit, "as that ape held on to that iron rod, so you are holding on to your evil ways intending, seriously, to make that walk, tomorrow or next Sabbath or whatever.

"Someone says, 'Brother Joe, that's not my reason. I have a real one. I would walk that aisle right today, but I am afraid my friends will laugh at me' Beloved, listen closely, Your friends wont. They will rejoice They will be glad that you have found Jesus.

"Your salvation is a personal matter between you and God. If anyone is insensitive enough to laugh at you for bettering your life, for taking care of your future for millions and millions of years, then shun them, for they are no friends of yours. Pray for them that they might throw off the shackles of Satan.

"Someone says, 'that's not my reason for delaying, Brother Joe. I would come today, but I am afraid I can't live up to this Christian life. I'm almost certain that I will fall from the right path, so I will wait until I know I can make it and then, I will walk that aisle!'

"That is not a reason, my friend, it's an excuse!" Joe walked to the side and sort of leaned on the pulpit. "Yes, it's an excuse and not a very good one at that. Fear is a tried and true weapon that the Devil uses. Fear of the future or fear of what might happen.. If you never venture out on faith, then fear of what might happen will carry you straight into the Devil's waiting arms.

"Ready for another fable?" The audience murmured pleasantly. "This one is really way out, but it illustrates how stupid some people act regarding probable happenings. A Young man and woman were engaged to be married. They were at his mother's home and preparing the noon meal. The mother sent the young woman down into the basement to get an onion to use in a salad. When the girl got down there, she noticed a small hand axe hanging on the wall. She was terrified. She thought: 'what if when Frank and I marry and we have a little boy and he is sent down here to get an onion for the salad and what if that axe fell on his little head and killed him? She sat down and began crying. After a while the mother went down to the basement to find out the reason for the delay and when she found her daughter—to be weeping. When asked why the tears, she wailed 'oh what if when Frank and I marry and we have a little boy and he is sent down here to get an onion for the salad, and that axe falls on his head and kills him. Oh, I just can't bear it!' And the mother sits down and began weeping with the young girl.

"After a time, Frank, the husband to be, goes to the basement to find the reason for the delay and he finds the two women weeping, and when asked the mother cried: 'Oh Frank, what if when you are married and you have a little boy and he is sent down here to get an onion for the salad and that axe falls on his head and kills him' The young man looked at the woman and her daughter and calmly said 'You are both stupid women.' He took the axe from the wall and placed it on the floor and went back up the stairs.

"You laugh at that my friends and say that no one could be that stupid, but I tell you that if you fear what will happen the next minute or hour, you will accomplish very little in this life. May I skip a story this time and give a concrete example of what I am trying to do" He licked his lips and nodded to Gary and Mark, and they left the auditorium and returned with a long board, one on each end. The board was twenty feet long and two inches thick and eight inches wide.

They brought the board and placed it on the dais floor just to the right of the pulpit. Bandy and Pritchett leaned forward and wondered what in the world this idiot preacher was up to now. They had stopped long ago being surprised at the preacher. Joe walked to one end of the board and took his wallet and extracted a ten dollar bill.

"Imagine, I have money and the month is not quite gone!" Everyone laughed. Joe liked to have a relaxed audience. "I am going to place this bill on one end of its board like this." He placed it near the end of the board. "Now, I want to get a volunteer. Before you volunteer, listen at what you have to do. You are to start at the other end of the board and place your feet one in front of the other and walk to the end of the board without falling and then stoop and pick up the bill. If you can do that, it is yours to keep."

Several hands raised, and Joe chose a young man about twenty years old. He faced the audience with the man and explained the rules. The man said he understood, and carefully stood on the board and confidently walked to the end and stooped and picked up the bill. Joe asked for the audience to give him a hand.

"Now, sir," Joe again took his wallet and extracted a hundred dollar bill. "My, I must have someone else's pants on." The audience howled. Even Pritchett seemed happy. "Now, sir, would you like to try it once more, but this time, the reward is a hundred dollar bill." The man smiled and shouted 'sure!'

"This time," said Joe. I am going to place a paper weight on the bill in case some air blow it off before you get to the end."

"How could air blow it off?" the man asked.

"Because," Joe said, we are going to move the board. "He nodded to Gary and Mark and they signaled and two cables lowered from the high ceiling. The attached the board to the cables and hoisted the board at least fifty feet into the air.

A third cable came down with a chair attached.

Lee Roy Neal

"Now, sir," Joe smiled, "You see the necessity of the paper weight. "Please sit in the chair and when you get even with the board, step on the board and begin walking. It's the same board, the length is the same, and just do as before. Are you ready?

"If you think I will try that, you are crazy." He hurried to his seat.

"You see, my friends, the board is the same thing. The rules are the same, but another thing has been added: Fear. You see, my friends, fear is our daily companion. If before you started to church this morning you said you would not go for you might have a wreck, you would never have gotten here. If you fear the bath water in the shower will suddenly become scalding, you would never take a shower. We must learn to walk by faith." He smiled, ran his tongue over his lips. "Come on in, friends, the water's fine. The Chinese say that a journey of a thousand miles begins with a single step. You say that I make it so simple, and friends, it is simple. Jesus said we should come as a little child.

"I have a broken heart for the person who says that he knows the path to take. He knows Christ is waiting, and he knows and believes all that I have said here today, but I just will feel better tomorrow, I will be psyched up next week. My friend, if you feel the tug of the Holy Spirit today, better hit the aisle. You see, you can't say, I'll do it next week, or whatever. What if the Spirit doesn't come? You see, God has promised to draw you to him at least once. It might be the only time he will draw you. Let me quite this beautiful poem that says it better than I ever could:

NO OTHER DAY

The Spirit came to the innocent child
And pleaded in tenderest tones
"Dear little one, let me come into your heart
"And make it all mine own"
"Oh Spirit," the child cried, "I should obey
"But childhood was meant for fun and play:

Again
If Christ Came Again

The Spirit returned to the tall fair youth
And asked so tender and true,
"Make haste while God's grace shall last,
"Arise, God is calling you!"
"O Spirit," the boy cried, "I should obey,
"But the pleasures of youth now hold me in sway."

The Spirit came again, to the thin worn man
And pleaded as he'd done oft before:
"Make haste, the harvest is ending
"Take Christ! He's the same evermore!!"
"Dear Spirit," the man said, "I should obey,
"But I am too busy and tired to pray."

The old man now leans on a trembling staff
With a quivering and bitter sigh
"I've wasted a lifetime in sin and strife
"And now I am going to die.
"There's no other day. There's no other day!
"The Holy Spirit has gone to stay!"

Anonymous

"So, my dear unsaved friend, as the choir sings I gladly give you the opportunity to come in sincerity and accept Jesus as Lord of your life. I'm not asking you to join the church, that is a later decision which you can make and you are welcome here. Now as we sing, come on and make the decision of your whole life."

Gary said later that fifty-one people filled out decision cards and asked for church membership. As the people began coming down the aisle, many in tears, Bandy punched his pastor and said that Joe had planted these people as shills. Later he remarked that it was unreal. Fifty people in one service, when their church had baptised four people in over five years.

As the people returned to their pews, and the wheel chairs were rolled up on the stage. One blind man kept muttering, "I can't see, Help me, blessed Joe, Help me!" Joe laid hands on all the maimed and crippled and many shouted and left their chairs, and then only the blind man was left. Joe turned to the man and laid his hands on his eyes. Before Joe could finish the prayer, the man gave an evil grin and shouted, "I can see, I can see" And getting near the microphone and whispered, "Where do I get my fifty dollars?"

Many in the audience booed and jeered. Joe quickly lifted his hands for silence. Joe turned to the man and suddenly the man's eyes took on the characteristic look of the blind. He began screaming: "I can't see! I really can't see!" The stunned audience sat in silence, and Gary managed to get the man outside the door.

Later, the man confessed that Deacon Bandy had hired him to feign blindness in an effort to besmirch the name of Our Fathers House.

Joe felt that his enemies were abundant.

CHAPTER ELEVEN

Linda Murchison knocked on Joe's office door and entered almost immediately. Her face was flushed, for she had walked from her house, almost a mile. The early summer was acting as if it were mid summer. This was her second appointment and she felt awkward, even though the first meeting with Joe four months ago had been pleasant.

Today she wore a simple print dress that was a mixture of brown and yellow with a suspicion of green just for flavor. The skirt swept her knees and was pleated. Her blouse was a mauve, short sleeved and fitted loosely. A belt of knitted linen fitted around her slim waist. Open=toed flat heels encased her small feet. Her hair had grown since Joe had last seen her and if he remembered correctly, she had gained a few pounds. The blouse reflected the violet of her eyes. Joe saw at once that she seemed a different person. The hunted, furtive look was gone, replaced by one of serenity.

Joe got up as she entered and placed a chair near his desk. He smiled at her and almost once she relaxed, feeling pleased that he remembered her. It seemed that a fresh wind blew away the remaining cobwebs of her past.

"How have you been, Linda?" He settled back in his chair.

"Oh, Brother Joe, I'm doing super. I have a job in that sewing factory, the one that makes Cheer Leaders Uniforms. First off I want to tell you that I have enjoyed your services these past few months." She breathed deeply.

"I am pleased, Linda. You look as if you have been coping rather well."

"Financially, I am fine, pastor. You know that I own the duplex and rent out one side, and that pays the taxes and utilities, and all I need is money for my food and clothes. I tithe, and I still have money to put into a savings account."

"And your former life, do you miss it?"

"Sure, I miss it, but it is with pleasure. I am doing pretty well getting my life back as my own, but I still need a jump start now and then. That's why I called. I hope I am not taking too much of your time."

"Not at all, Linda. What seems to be the trouble? You look like a new person."

"Well, pastor, I still feel awful about my past"

"Linda, you must remember that God has not only the ability to forgive, but also to forget. Hold up your head and be not afraid to look anyone in the face. I believe that God does not want us to become some inane panty waist afraid to voice an opinion or unashamedly look anyone in the face.

"Do you remember when Jesus advised his apostles that if they did not have a sword to sell some clothing and get one. Yes, his men closest to him were armed. I don't mean this in your case. Just believe that you are forgiven and no one is better than you."

"I am so glad, Brother Joe. I do at times feel inferior. I do say that Our Fathers House is the most unusual church I have ever heard or read about. I have attended large churches before, but there it seems as if the poor pastor was afraid he might say something that would offend someone, especially some of the big supporters. You seem totally unafraid. You preach excitement. I like that. I like your whole outlook on things."

"Thanks. I try to remember what Jesus said in His Sermon on the Mount. He tried to tell the people to take care of today. He said 'think not on what you shall eat or wear or drink, don't worry about what will happen tomorrow. He means for us to prepare for tomorrow, but today is more important. I think that a person will be happiest if he lives while he can without looking back to the past, even a minute. Enjoy now and give thanks to God. Don't try to remember what you ate for supper last night or what dress you wore to church last Saturday. Do you see what I am trying to say, Linda. I have no quarrel for those who plan for tomorrow, but we should realize the frailty of life and make all plans tentative.

"I feel sorry for the rich man whose every thought is tomorrow. Don't spend a dollar today, save it for tomorrow. He will come to the end of his days and find that he has lost his whole life. Oh don't get me wrong. Plan for tomorrow; it will most likely come, but in case it does not, live and enjoy the jewel of today which is a gift from God.

You mentioned that I am different, Linda. I take that as a compliment, a great compliment.. I don't plan it, and I don't enjoy it but I am controversial. I happen to believe all that I read in the Bible, and that alone set me apart from most pastors.

"I was just reading in one of Hal Lindsey's book The Late Great Planet Earth where he mentions a survey made by Red Book Magazine. The survey was made in 1961 and it was done by a group of professional pollsters. It was a representative poll made in seminaries and in other Christian colleges. Remember, these people were studying for the ministry; were the future pastors of churches, Protestant Churches. The pollsters interviewed these future ministers and found that 56% rejected the virgin birth of Jesus. 71% did not believe in a life after death; and 98% did not believe in the physical return of Jesus to this earth. Think of that, Linda, 98% did not believe in the Second Coming of Christ! That study was made over twenty years ago, and I hate to speculate on what it would be today. If this is the thinking of the traditional clergy in whose hands rests the responsibility of getting the Truth to the people, it is no wonder that the traditional church today is little more than a social club or a weapon for Satan to give people a false sense of security.

"People such as yourself, Linda, hunger after God's truth and they see a church and go there and get nothing." He reached for his Bible. "I want to read you something that I read just this morning. It is in II Peter 2, 1 (NASB) listen:

"'But false prophets also rose among the people, just as there will also be false teachers among you, who will secretly introduce destructive heresies.'

"Linda, there are many churches, some very large churches, that have ministers standing behind pulpits, facing spiritually hungry people and they themselves do not believe in a personal God And the next step from there is for them not to believe in a personal devil. They, of course, are wrong on both counts, and it's things like that that Satan uses to cause doubts"

"I agree with you there, Brother Joe, for the woman who rents the other side of my duplex still practices her profession, and she never goes to church; yet she drives a new car, has fancy clothes and expensive jewelry while I go to Wal-mart or Sears for my things. I will admit that I get envious when I compare what she has with my possessions. It is at that time that the devil calls me a fool and I am proud to say that I spit in his face and let him know in no uncertain terms that I am happier now than I have ever been in all my life." She shifted in her chair.

"Linda," Joe had placed the Bible down and leaned forward a little, "the devil likes religion. He attends many churches every time the doors open. I am going to say something that it might be hard for some people to understand: It is actually dangerous for some people to go to church!" Linda jerked her head up suddenly, surprise in her eyes, and joy smiled and continued. "What I mean is this: The people go to church and instead of hearing God's word they are lulled into a false sense of security and are not directed to examine their lives. Many many walk an aisle without any knowledge of what they are doing. They have no one to help them look deep inside their hearts. They then think that they can leave the church and take their usual habits and go down the road with no change whatever. It's like taking the seasoning out of food. It is a bland and almost imitative of the real thing.

"If a person does not have a personal relationship with Christ, if he has no feeling of God's presence in his being, in his relationship with others in his daily life then you can believe that something is amiss. Because of the leadership in a lot of churches, and because of the absence of true teaching in a lot of churches, the churches are merely buildings with a cross out front and that is as near as they get to being the Bride of Christ as they will ever get.

"I was aghast when I read where one church gave green trading stamps for attendance at services, and the one that made me want to vomit was the one that had the offerings collected by bikini-clad young women. How the devil must have gloated and rejoiced in this. Am I getting through to you, Linda? I feel as if I am just making words."

"Yes, pastor, I understand perfectly. I am sure that it accounts for the doubts I have been having."

"Exactly!"

Again
If Christ Came Again

"When I get discouraged, it is simply Satan's way of making me believe I have made a mistake in this course for my life that I have taken. His way of trying to convince me that I have made a mistake.

"You have the point exactly, Linda. You don't need me."

There was silence in the room for a minute or so. Joe closed his eyes and leaned back in thought, or perhaps prayer. Linda waited patiently. Outside the window the sounds of water falling in the fountain. She saw two red birds playfully hopping in and out of the water. She heard the roar of the big trucks on the Interstate.

"Linda," Joe sat forward again, licking his dry lips, "I am a simple man. If I know nothing else in all this world, I know that God knows my heart and soul. He knows that my single purpose in life is to tell all mankind exactly what God's word says and means I criticize the traditional church in much the same manner that Christ did. God knows that when I began this ministry at the county fair grounds with no property and two helpers, Gary and Mark, that I never dreamed, nor did I strive for, of becoming pastor of this large and beautiful temple. It simply came, and I praise God daily for it. I criticize the traditional church, not in a braggadacio manner but in all humility.

"I can't help it, Linda, but I see the pastors of the traditional churches using clever, superficial words, painting verbal pictures of the 20th Century life, always placing emphasis on the material values and hardly, if ever, even mentioning the spiritual. They are simply neglecting the best part of man, his spirit. The only way that they can perpetuate themselves is to continue to create a market for the trash they peddle. They convince the poor people sitting in front of their ornate pulpits that their future existence is dung on a trash heap and that is all. They say nothing of eternal life with Christ.

"Linda," Joe continued, getting warmed up as if preparing a sermon, "You remember reading in school of the rise of the Nazi party under Adolph Hitler. This happened in the thirties. They took one small lie and forged it into an ever greater lie, inch by inch, until the German would believe anything they were told. As a tiny mustard seed can grow into a large plant, so can a small lie grow into an acceptable truth, which is no truth at all.

"God knows my heart and He knows that I am not saying that all churches today are fakes.. I am sure that God lives in a lot of them. I am different and can't help it and I am glad. In no way do I compare myself with the prophet Isaiah, but in the 20th.. chapter of his book he is trying to warn the people of coming disaster and their coming captivity.. He could not seem to get their attention. They went about their daily lives conducting 'business as usual'. They continued the marriages with the heathen, they continued the idol worship, and poor old Isaiah was considered a nut, a freak, someone to keep the small children away from him for he was a loony.

"Am I boring you?"

"In no way, pastor, please go on. What did old Isaiah do when the people would not listen?"

"He was discouraged, and prayed to God and when God answered, he could not believe that God was serious. He prayed again and came up with the same answer."

"And the answer was?"

"Well, God told Isaiah to remove all of his clothing, even his sandals, and walk around town stark naked and to do it for three whole years! To see some people today, especially at the beach, one would think their names were Isaiah and that they had a message from God. But in Isaiah' day, it was a shocker.

"I am different, I am controversial, and someday, perhaps, it will cost me my life. Nevertheless, Linda, I am determined to devote my life to preaching God's word as He reveals it to me. I must have been born with a bounding love for the underdog, the black sheep, the unfortunate, the dirty, the unsaved, the down-trodden. I am first of all a servant of God. God has blessed all of our efforts, look out there," he pointed out the window where school buildings were rising out of the earth like weeds, beyond that tiny cottages for the elderly were taking shape "Out there is a physical expression of God's love for His children.

"The schools of today are not educating the whole child. They are so frightened of the ACLU and other Godless organizations that they don't even dare to mention that they are Christian in any degree. In fact, they do all they can to be as non-Christian as is possible. They stand in horror if any mention of Jesus is made inside those atheistic walls. They receive the children as a wild animal with no religious training, and they keep them twelve years and belch them out as drug users and promiscuous sex advocates and they expect to see their product produce responsible, happy citizens.

"I do hope that the schools that Our Fathers House has will be more successful in producing responsible, happy citizens. At least that is my prayer. I trust that we will turn out people who are well adjusted not those of today's public schools who have trouble deciding what color condum to use or whether or to use one at all. I trust that the products of our school will have young people who have been exposed to the real teachings of Christ and who have been taught to think for themselves and to act for themselves and that they will be a happy group of citizens.

"The public schools of today have a track record of turning out a group of young people who are God-less, illiterate, unadjusted to life, and unhappy. I honestly believe that this is affront to God Himself.

"Linda," Joe suddenly sat up straight as if just coming back from somewhere, "forgive me. I have been thinking out loud and you did not come here to hear me rant and rave, but I am dead serious about this."

"It's fine, Brother Joe. Simply fine. I am so glad that you had me here to listen In fact, I thank you for letting me listen. I hope to hear a lot about these things in a future sermon. The world has need to hear these ideas."

"Perhaps God will let it be so."

"Brother Joe," Linda got up and began preparing to leave. I hope you will let me come back about once a week. I feel that you have let me share your thoughts with me, and I know I feel better than when I came. I realize now that the devil is forever on my case, and that I must pray constantly for God's help and guidance in putting Satan down and out." She turned and left the room and turning as she opened the door and said "goodbye."

Joe sat at his desk for some time, the thoughts splashing over his mind. He could not shake off a premonition that he was on the brink of something. Suddenly He began praying silently. He felt that it was God's will that man had the capacity and the will to decide his own fate. It had to be that way or man would be no more than a robot or a computer with buttons for someone to press to make him act. Joe knew that if he gave into his enemies and did as they wanted, most of his enemies would go away. He stirred in his chair and asked God's forgiveness of the very thought.

As he sat there and ran his thoughts to a communion with God he became possessed with a feeling of fear, a feeling of grief, he did not know what really happened. He compared it with the experience on the mountain top. He felt the room suddenly fill with a Presence. The fear was suddenly replaced with a warm joy. It had no end. It permeated every cell of his body. He suddenly felt that every question he had ever asked was brightly answered as if written on a large chalk board in flaming letters. Later, when he tried to explain the experience to Gary, he was unable to do so, He was positive that it was another 'mountain top' experience When he opened his eyes, he found that he was lying supime on the carpet in front of his desk, his arms and legs extended. He got to his knees and with tears copiously staining his face, he said "Speak to me God. Thy servant will hear. I am unworthy, but I am willing to do Your Will."

Suddenly, the Presence was gone, but Joe knew. He knew at last, and he also knew that he would never be the same ever again. It frightened him, and his heart pounded as if he had been running for miles. He remained on his knees.

"God, I hear your voice. I know your will, but I beg of you to change your mind. Please, Father, I have tried to be a good servant. I have tried with all my being to find and follow Your will. I have tried, Father, really tried, and now, as I understand your will, I find it hard to accept. Perhaps, God, I misunderstood. God, if there be any other way, show me. Help my faith, for I find it unbelievable that you will let this happen to me. I realize, Father, first of all that I am not worthy. I am not strong enough. I need strength that I do not have. I beg you, Father, find some other way. I am but a mere man, how can I summon strength for the road ahead? How can I bear this awful thing that is sure to come?"

Suddenly, Joe was ashamed. How often had he preached that God would strengthen the willing disciple? He stayed on his knees and some time later, a warm feeling came over his body. He honestly felt as if some huge, strong, loving arms embraced him. He was suddenly released from the fear. Though he did not have the strength for the coming events now, he had full faith that when the strength was needed it would be there. He felt free! Free to do God's will.

God had presided at his miraculous conception and his birth. God had been in charge in bringing him to Bethany. God had been in the driver's seat all along! God had given him his mind and his will. God had given him his thirst for knowledge. "I am His steward. He has intrusted all this to me. He has trusted me to forge ahead and not falter or look back. He has entrusted me with the message to all the wretched, the despairing, the down trodden flotsam of humanity on earth."

At last Joe stood up and again, as on the mountain, hours had passed. The sun was peeking in the western windows of his office. Already the canvas of the setting sun was stretched across the heavens, awaiting the paint brush of the Master Artist. He licked his lips, his heart pounded, he knew that he was filled with knowledge How was it possible that he had not known all along? Subliminally he had known all along exactly who he was. Yes, God, he breathed silently, I know, and Your Will is mine. I just pray that I am able to have enough strength. I feel unworthy, unworthy of this great commission. In his heart he felt a gratitude that God had revealed what was coming.

He left his office and headed for home. He knew that his mother would have the evening meal ready. He was wondering when or if he should reveal this latest to his mother.

CHAPTER TWELVE

Decon Bandy hurried toward the church where he was to meet several people of 'like mind and purpose' concerning Our Fathers House. A sudden flash of lightning lighted up the early spring sky followed almost simultaneously by a clap of thunder that rattled windows in buildings along the street and causing the deacon to jump into the air, his heart racing in a manner that his doctor had warned him about. A slight breeze was playing with the early leaves of the old elms along the street.

Bandy had had a fear of storms since he was three years old. Lightning had struck a tree across the street, and the air sort of sizzled causing his hair to stand up. The tree began burning and a foreign smell filled the air. Later, he convinced himself it was brim stone. Lightning flashed again and he had run into his house and into his room and hid under the bed.

Another flash and another clap sent the deacon into a run He had read someplace that the amount of time between the lightning and the thunder indicated the approximate distance where the lightning would strike. But who is counting he thought as he raced forward, ignoring his racing heart.

The wind picked up its speed and soon let the leaves know that play time had ended. The boughs of the trees bent causing the still burning street lights to play tag with the shadows in the street. The wind increased to a gale and as the deacon neared the church assaulted the walls of the church. The sky began to belch and drops as big as a walnut began to fall causing the scared man to go even faster. As he reached the door of the educational building, another flash of light and the dome of the courthouse was hit causing the clock to strick one clang like doom. If the door had not been made to open inward, he likely would have run through it.

As he entered the hallway, he stopped and slammed the door quickly. He did not want anyone to see his fright. He wiped his now almost bald head and wiped his hands on his trousers. He waited, catching his breath, calming his heart and entered the meeting room.

"Sorry, fellers,:" he tried to smile, "but that storm is getting nasty out there. I think the court house was hit. I did not wait to make sure. Hope those lightning rods do the job." He took his seat.

"Bandy," the pastor of a large church in a city some thirty miles away was all business, the weather held no interest to him. "this meeting that you have called had better be important. I have a lot of things to do., "I have a foursome at the Walton Country club at ten this morning." Others expressed displeasure and were anxious for the meeting to begin.

Bandy was chairman of a group of leaders from contingent church areas to discuss mutual problems and projects for mutual benefit. These projects were agreed on and then submitted to the concerned church bodies for definitive action.

"I am glad you all could come," Bandy began. "I know of your busy schedules, and I will be as brief as is possible. I would not have called this meeting, had I not thought that all of your feelings and opinions about Our Fathers House and its leaders coincided with mine. Joe has slashed and has hit all of our churches I firmly believe that he is a real threat to all of us, a threat to our very existence. If he is not stopped and soon, he might become unstoppable.

"I even went to see him last week in an effort to get some kind of compromise, and the man refused to even discuss it with me."

"I take it that you must have some plan in mind," Rev. Hal Porter of the Walton First Church said.

"I do indeed," Bandy was relaxed now, "I do indeed have a plan!" He looked around the room, "But before I say a word about the plan, I want vows of a code of silence about every word said in this room today. I'm talking serious business here."

The group nodded assent.

"When I left Joe last week, he said that nothing short of death would cause him to look back or change a single thing about his program. mainly to belittle and besmirch the churches that are dear to our hearts."

"What do you think he meant by 'short of death'?"

"I took him at his word." An intake of breath circled the table. "I don't think that anyone here would not agree that he must be stopped

Lee Roy Neal

in any way that is needed. I say any way, even if it means his extinction."

"Bandy," the chairman of deacons at County Line church spoke sternly, "Any way" Even murder?" He was trying to somehow get inside Brandy's brain, "do you aim to shoot him?"

"Of course I don't aim to shoot him. That would serve only to make him a hero and cause Our Fathers House to grow faster."

"But to plot a man's death, isn't that drastic?"

"It might be, but isn't it better for one man to die than for many? Wasn't that what the Pharisees said?" He shifted in his chair. "Would you have the progress made by the Christian Church the past 2000 years be wiped from the face of the earth?"

"What do you have in mind, Bandy," It was Hal Porter again. He did not like any of this, even though he hated Joe as much as the others.

"I want a war chest of $30,000 and with it I will see that Joe is disgraced, Our Fathers House is put to scorn, and the mighty Joe will be removed permanently from our midst." He looked around the table. I can guarantee the job, but it will take money and lots of it."

"I will do my part, but to kill a man, Bandy, I like that not one little bit..

"Who, beside yourself, said anything about killing him?"

"I am not clear on this. You said that Joe stated that nothing short of death would stop him, and you said you would get him removed from our midst, from the face of the earth. To me that means death."

"Trust me. I have it all figured out. I have the plan completed, down to the last detail. I assure you that our part in it will never be known. Never in a hundred million chances.."

"But how?"

"Brother Frank, do you really want to know?"

"Not me. I don't think anyone here wants to know. I know for sure I don't want to hear another thing about it. You will have my church's share and then I want no more meetings like this, nothing."

The money was quickly pledged, and arrangements were made for the cash to be in Bandy's hands within a month. Bandy was beside himself with joy. He at last was going to get the best of that upstart.

Again
If Christ Came Again

When Bandy left the church, he found that the storm had abated, and he smiled his crooked effort and took the calm weather as a sign that his success was certain. His plan was complete and had been for weeks. He had every facet in place in his mind, and he know who, what and were. The when would be a little tricky. He almost hummed a song as he walked home. The storm was gone and soon, the thorn in his side would be no more.

Where had this goal been born? Obviously in the very soul of the deacon. He had actually liked Joe as a young boy, but as the years passed and the confrontations grew, the affection had been changed to hate. What had inspired it? Had 'loss of face?' had Misery? Had stubbornness? He reasoned that his ego had been trampled, before witnesses, time and time again., but could that thing alone account for the venom of hate that permeated his body? He did not realize that the emptiness and despair in one man's soul could turn to hate for another being..

He must have realized that man himself is a beast.: dark of soul, of a filthy mind, dirty mouth, actually lower than a dog. Yet in spite of all that, he had the compassion of God who had actually robbed Heaven of His son to come to earth to actually die for this vile and unworthy creature.

Evil was like mistletoe that was a parasite and literally sucked the life out of a tree it happened to be clinging to. It had pretty berries and actually people liked the plant, especially at Christmas, and they thought it attractive. Yet, like most evil things, it was attractive yet deadly, for the berries were toxic.

If one really got down to it, there is not a day, an hour, not even a minute that God does not again rise from the dead in a figurative way. When the stone on some tomb is magically rolled away, God is resurrected each time a hurting human being finds solace and comfort. and looks forward to a really new day. God is risen again each time a soul is healed of the sickness of sin., each time sins are forgiven; each time a person finally says good-bye to drugs and illicit sex. Each person must face and accept the fact that each and every wasted life is the tomb in which God lurks and is patiently waiting for the resurrection so that the person might enjoy the life God mean for each person to enjoy.

How was it possible for Bandy not to understand Joe? It was a tragedy of no mean proportion. The tragedy of one of God's creations not having the ability to understand another of God's creations. Had Bandy ever tried to get inside Joe's thinking? For what reason had this hate lain festering and growing and eating at Bandy until at last, under the full control and guidance of Satan himself, it had sprung full grown. Even Bandy should have recognized the evil. Evil has a million eyes and hands and feet; has millions of excuses to exist and a billion ways to do the will of Satan in a person's life.

At this point, it was impossible for Bandy to turn back. The plot had been born in the very cess pool of Bandy's heart. Now, like Judas of old, he had reached out his hand and had embraced the evil plan of Satan. Bandy knew that all the others in that fatal meeting had embraced his plan of eliminating Joe and Our Fathers House. Evil men, supporting other evil men. As Bandy walked home, he knew not why, but from long ago, he remembered his high school English teacher making the class memorize a line from McBeth: "Bloody instructions which, when taught, return to plague the inventor."

Bandy reached his home and quickly entered his office. He would set the plan in motion, even now, before noon. It might take some time, even months, but in the end, Joe would vanish from sight.

+++++++

Joe and Gary and Mark were relaxed in Joe's office waiting for the other members of the team to come. Joe was silent, pensive. He was silently giving thanks to God for the phenomenal blessings of the past eighteen months. The main sanctuary had been completed in just a little over a year, the food bank was in place with almost evey major food chain donating food each week. James was the administrator of that phase of Our Fathers House and no one could have done a better job. It was super. He kept minute records in the computer of all food taken in, distributed and inventory.

The others arrived almost at the same time. Dennis, the attorney whose gift of land had given it the initial boost, he took care of all legal aspects of the church. James. the school teacher who had resigned to give full time to the work, and Phillip who had designed the magnificent building.

Thank you for coming," Joe began, leaning against his desk facing the others. I think that the time has arrived for us to complete the other steps of Our Fathers House.

"Phillip, I would like for you to complete the design on the Senior Citizen complex. We have those temporary houses there and you know what to do to incorporate them into the final plan. Also, we have out grown the present school building, and I would like to see a finalization of the school. You know what we should have: a school with a capacity of 1000 complete with full athletic facilities. If you guys will meet me here in the morning when it is light, we will all walk over the area and each have a prayerful input. Tonight, I just want to verbally lay the groundwork. As I go along, please feel free to make any input you feel led to make.

"I see a tract of homes, twenty to start with room to expand. I see the homes built in a horse shoe type oval each near enough to the other for companionship and safety, yet far enough away for a senior to have privacy. In the middle of the houses, will be a sort of day room where a commissary and a clinic with at least three hospital beds, a place for a doctor and nurse on 24 hour call. In this center place will be a place for meetings, and programs, and gatherings, all for Senior citizens. The small cottages would be one bedroom affairs with ramps for wheel chairs, and in each room of the cottage buttons that when pushed summoned help when needed. Each place will have a storage room and a small garden plot. Perhaps a sort of subway could run from the center to the Sanctuary for ease of getting to church. I want this center to be a haven of rest for our seniors."

"There should be a place for them to meet and play games and quilt and just visit," said Mark.

"You are reading my mind, Mark," Joe smiled.

"And the school with gyms, swimming pools, every educational device available. We should teach auto mechanics and other trades for those who do not enter college." James had a gleam in his eyes.

"Just one thing," Joe smiled. "Its March, and I would like for it all to be finished within one year."

"Why not open them next week, Joe?" Phillip joshed.

"If it could be done, I'm for it, but let's be practical. "James, I want you to head the school and let Mark take over the food ministry. James, we need to begin searching for Christian teachers who are of like mind with the tenets of Our Fathers House. Gary, you need to coordinate the two projects and work daily, almost hourly with Phillip.

"And Dennis,"

"I know, Joe, I know. Find the credit or money."

"You people don't need me," Joe laughed, "You each can read my mind."

"As a matter of fact, Joe," Dennis smiled. "we have almost 500,000 in cash in the bank, and our credit is almost without limit."

"Praise the Wonderful Name of Jesus," Joe almost shouted.

The following morning, the sun was riding majestically in the cloudless sky. Spring was making its early debut. Birds were singing and screeching and building nests. Butterflies fitted from early flower to flower, and even some early fruit had swelling branches heralding the blossoms of the fruit to be. Grasshoppers were busy going from tender blade of grass to another. The sky was so blue that it made one want to look through it to surprise God sitting on His throne.

The ever practical Mark and Gary had brought a supply of wooden stakes and hammers. At that moment, Joe was so filled with praise that he almost forgot his revelation of so short time ago, a revelation he had divulged to no one, not even Mary.

It was almost noon when they gathered in the church kitchen where a good meal had been prepared. Everyone seemed to relish this time when no problems were about to deter the forward thrust of Our Fathers House.

"Men," Joe began as he finished his meal, "I am so happy that the final phase of the church is on the way. We must never let down our guard, men. Never. Remember what Dante said: 'In the middle of our journey of life, I came to a dark wood.' Don't think for an instant that the Devil is going to play dead and roll over.

"Our best weapon to fight him with is a close daily walk with God, keeping in his will. Yet, God doesn't plan to hold your hand and do for you things that you must do for yourself. The main weapon when you are on your own, is knowledge. You all know how I

Again
If Christ Came Again

treasure knowledge. There is so much I want to tell you men, so very much. Someone has rightly said that knowledge is compared to a large river, like the Mississippi. It is too big, too enormous and vast for a man to drink even in a million lifetimes. We can, however, dip our finite cups into this great store of knowledge and we can be sated, but only for a time. All these words from the river, filtered through the eons of time, will satisfy you for a time, in other words, there is a limit. Yet there is one thing that has no limit, and that is a man's thoughts, Each man sets the limits of his own world of ideas.

Juvenal was wise when he said 'a sound mind in a sound body is a thing to pray for.' Psychiatrists are muddling in some things they know nothing about. God is the great psychiatrist, forget you not."

"Preacher," it was the sheriff's voice and Joe recognized it "There's a jumper on the water tower, will you come. I can have a car at your office in less than three minutes."

"I'll be waiting out front, sheriff."

By the time Joe had donned his coat and closed his office door, the familiar county car was pulling up. Joe got in and the deputy turned on his flashing lights and they sped off.

The water tower was located near the high school campus, and in the morning sun, graffeti stood out "Seniors, 88' was the newest. The school board had tried many things to stop the practice of some zealous senior doing the art work which could cause a fall to the death. When all else had failed, the board came up with a winner. It decreed that any class with a sign on the water tower would be forbidden to take a senior trip. 88 was the last year of the signs.

When the deputy and Joe neared the site, Joe found it hard to believe what he saw. People were rushing to the site, some dragging young children, one man was still wiping shaving cream from his face. People whose life were drab and uninteresting, were elated at this break in routine.

The deputy had to touch his siren before people left the street to let the car pass. A roar went up from the crowd of several hundred as they parked near the tower. Joe got out and look upwards. He saw a figure outlined against the silver paint of the tower. It looked young and was a man.

Lee Roy Neal

The deputy looked at the mob pressing against the foot of the tower and then upwards at the human being. The man stood outside the safety rail, his arms hooked around the rail and looking down at the ghoulish crowd below. The deputy yelled "move back, move back" but the crowd seemed deaf. "I hope if he jumps he takes a bunch of these idiots with him when he lands" he muttered under his breath.

Joe was disgusted at that moment with the human race. He thought of what he had read of public executions, in France, especially when people came with their picnic lunches and with small children getting as near the Guillotine as possible so that they could get a close-up view of a head being chopped from a human body.

Even in this country, in the early 1800's public executions were rampant. As hard as it was to believe, homeless children were hanged just for stealing food. Even then people came and watched and enjoyed. When public hangings were carried out by the sheriff's of each county, people made a day of celebration, bring small chiuldren to watched they were told was fun. Actually, Joe thought, what is so new about the violence on TV these days. It has only taken on a new form.

Another roar went up from the crowd as the man on the tower moved forward and unlocked one of his arms. One young man, gnawing at a chicken leg looked up and with greasy lips shouted "Jump!" Joe wanted to turn and leave, but the crowd had cut off all escape. A few dogs began barking, and now the crowd was taking up the chant "Jump! Jump! Jump!" He wanted to weep, but instead, he turned to the tower and placed his hands on the steel rungs of the ladder.

Joe began climbing the ladder on one of the legs of the tower, and as he rose, he wondered with a sad heart at how the Devil can cause otherwise decent people to become a mob. As Joe came into view of the crowd,the noise grew as if it was going to be a double feature. As Joe neared the figure, he saw that it was a young man about mid thirties. He was bare headed, his long blonde hair brushing his shoulders. His eyes did not have the look of a deranged person.

"Hi, feller," Joe said as he neared the top about ten feet away from the man. "I am a local minister, and I thought I would come up to see if I could help."

"If you come near me, preacher," I'll give that mob the show they came for"

"Let me get up inside the rail and I'll not come toward you." Joe looked down and estimated it must be over twelve stories above the ground.

Below the mob was getting restless. Gary had joined the gathering and when someone said that Joe had climbed the tower, he started to climb but the deputy stopped him. "No more up there, young feller" He stepped in front of Gary, "There's already two more than we need up there."

Gary saw the wind grab Joe's coat and saw Joe hold tighter to the safety rail. Joe had gotten within a few feet of the man and looked as if he were talking to him. The man lighted a cigarette, hanging by one hand to the thrill of the mob below. He nodded his head now and then and Joe held one hand high and the man again nodded.

"Get that preacher down, sheriff," a man shouted angrily. "If the man wants to jump let him jump. We're tired of waiting." Children began to fret, the crowd quieted down a little and still Joe and the man continued to talk. Gary got sick smelling the food being consumed about him. He wondered why people had to eat at a time like this. Even today people bring loads of food to a funeral. He just could not understand it. A dog ran between his legs, and two boys playing tag almost knocked him off his feet.

Joe suddenly turned and began climbing down the ladder. The tenseness of the crowd increased, and as Joe reached the bottom, the chant began again. He say Gary and said "Let's get out of here, Gary." As they walked away, Joe turned and looked up at the man he had just left and he waved a salute. The man saluted back. The crowd knew that the man would climb down and ruin all their fun. A few people jeered Joe as they went to Gary's car. As they reached the car, they heard an agonizing thump and screaming permeated the air.

"He jumped, Joe, he jumped!"

"I knew he would, Gary. I knew that he would."

As they went back to the church Joe told Gary about the man, the story that he had told Joe on the tower. He had been born to wealthy family. As a small child, he had his every want satisfied. As a boy he had traveled the world with his parents seeing every thing of interest on the face of the earth. He was married with one little boy. He was a doctor, the owner of a famous medical facility. Every minute of his life had been planned for him, and he was becoming famous as an organ transplant doctor. Life could offer no more, he had it all.

"But, Gary, to the world, he had it all. He was the envy of all he met. Yet, Gary, he told me that he had nothing. He had never met opposition in his entire life. If he wanted to be president of his Senior class in school, no one dared run against him. No struggle., No strife, no sweat, no worry about the outcome. of any facet of his existence. He had been everywhere, yet he had seen nothing. He had heard the greatest music on earth by the greatest artists on earth yet he might as well have been deaf for all that it meant.

"Gary, the man was a brilliant man. He knew he had had no fight, no denial, no strife. He had seen no glory. He was so bored with life that he decided that he could not bear it another day, he was through. He wanted to get rid of the boredom and the only way he knew was to go to sleep. The tragedy was not so much that he killed himself, the real tragedy that he had never learned to look around and see the majesty of God."

They reached the office, and as the two men sat, Gary saw that Joe's eyes were filled with tears. He did not know what to say.

"Joe," he began foolishly, "you don't have any cause to feel bad about that man taking his life."

"I am not weeping for a man who just took his life, I am crying for a man who never had a life. The man was a captive of wealth which is not always a blessing. His parents thought that they were being good to him, but in fact, they could be guilty of child abuse: giving the child everything but knowledge on how to live. Isaiah said 'My people are going into captivity because they have no knowledge'

"It is true today as well, The public schools are certainly and mercilessly preparing our youth for a life of captivity. The media are daily incessantly preparing our minds for a life of captivity. Gary, that is the most horrible captivity of all: the captivity of the human mind, the ability to reason or to think for yourself. Women starve themselves in order to look like some highly paid model. The very soul of mankind is being slowly squeezed into conformity much the way a sausage is squezed into a small bag. People who are human beings are slowly kept from the knowledge that would help them to remain human beings the way God meant for it to be. The knowledge of which Isaiah spoke, we refuse to see and accept, even if it is ever presented for learning."

CHAPTER THIRTEEN

The following morning, Linda Murchison was waiting outside Joe's office when he came to work. It was cold for March, and Joe knew that Linda was coming, but he had had to visit Mrs. Jefferies who was so ill that Joe had arranged to get her admitted to a hospital. He apologized for being late, and quickly unlocked the door and hung up her coat along with his. He saw that today she was dressed in brown. The skirt was full and had some sort of pleats he supposed. Very attractive. Yellow daffodils ran in irregular rows on the skirt, the green leaves making a trailing vine that all came together. Her blouse was of yellow silk and the patent brown belt encircled her thin waist. The blouse was tucked inside her skirt. She wore some brown pearls. Her hair was short, barely brushing her neck. She wore make-up so skillfully applied that it seemed she wore none. Yes, Joe thought as he took his seat, she is indeed a most beautiful young lady, and he quickly brushed the thought aside.

"Well, Linda," He began, "how is everything?"

"Fine, Brother Joe, but I am having a time getting rid of this cold." She sniffled.

"If I remember right" she said, "you had it two weeks ago when you were here last."

"Yes. I just hope that it doesn't turn into anything worse." She smiled.

"Well," he picked up a paper clip and began turning it between his fingers, "Aside from the cold, how are things going?"

"Fine, Brother Joe, but I keep having these thoughts, evil thoughts, and I can't seem to keep them away."

"Linda, all human beings, and I mean all human beings have the capacity to think evil thoughts. It is a burden that all human beings share. Evil, even evil thoughts, is a weakness. The devil knows this well, and he likes to get one of God's children to just think of something evil, and he takes it from there."

"But I feel so..so dirty when these thoughts pile in on me from out of nowhere."

"Sure you do, Linda, that is the touch of God, warning you to do your darndest to push them back in hell where they belong. That is the truth, and Linda, remember what Jesus said: 'The truth shall set you free.'"

"Brother Joe, I feel animosity toward that woman renting half of my house."

"Linda, you should not feel guilty of resenting the life style of that woman. You say you pray for her and that you invite her to church. You see, you found the truth. You found the way out of a life style that would surely lead to hell. You found the way, and you see her exceedingly prosperous and you think of your resentment, and it really isn't."

"Preacher, when I see old friends and know what they are, why is it that I feel depressed? Do I long for the old life and simply don't know it?"

"No, I do not think so. You see, Linda you are growing and you are having what I could call 'growing pains'. Truth is sometimes a hard task master, Remember, you must be strong. To face the unvarnished truth requires a lot of fortitude. I like to think of it as bravery. You see, Linda, not everyone is brave. Most people are fully satisfied to 'go with the flow' as the young people say. Go along with the crowd, don't rock the boat, don't upset the status quo. Never stand up and be counted That is the battle cry of most people today."

"I don't feel very brave. pastor."

"Besides my mother, I believe you are the bravest, most courageous woman I have ever known."

"I guess that proves that even preachers can sometimes be wrong." She smiled. and then was seized with a spasm of coughing. "I know I am not brave. I am a fearful woman. The past week I have really been down in the pits. I feel a premonition, as if I am on the edge of an abyss of some kind."

"Fear and bravery, Linda, are simply two sides of the same coin. Remember that a person can not ever be truly brave unless at first he is afraid."

"I used to be brave when my father was living. He knew what I was and yet I felt he loved me."

"Do you think that he would be disappointed in you today?"

"He would be proud! Do you think he is aware of my change, pastor?"

"You can be sure he knows, Linda. There is really no such thing as death. This is a scientific truth. Things and people never die. They simply change. If you burn a sheet of the newspaper, it still exists, it is just in another form. The seas ebb and flow and have been so doing for thousands of years, yet they are still there. Stars disappear only to reappear as a comet or some other form. Think for a moment: There is the same amount of water in the world today as when Adam walked the earth. Man cannot destroy matter. The water is used, runs back into the ocean and recycled to be used over and over.

"Linda, think for a moment how puzzling this is to a person who has never known God. A lost man's life must be so empty, so desolate, so fruitless without knowing a loving God. The lost see God as an illusion much the same as a magician might use. Never forget that the devil is ever at hand, and any small lapse and he goes into action. He will make you feel depressed, ready to listen to him.

"The only time that the devil lets a person alone, stops tempting him is when the devil has him exactly where he wants him. If he doesn't bother you, he has you where he wants you, but if he is ever sitting on your shoulder, fight him hard."

"I hate to keep bothering you, but believe me I need these pep talks. I am happy to see the length of time between them is growing. That's progress in my book." She stood.

"In mine too. I'm proud of you Linda. You always feel free to call me or come by any time, day or night." He helped her with her coat.

"I don't know how I can ever thank you enough." She quickly walked out closing the door softly behind her.

CHAPTER FOURTEEN

Joe could not remember snow coming this late in the year, yet there it was and just three days before the calendar said that Spring had arrived. He had called a meeting this morning of his staff, and had he known of the snow he would have canceled it. He was early as usual, for he liked these times alone. Of late he was really occupied with what was to come and what had already taken place. He knew what was coming, but he wondered how it would be precipitated. Common sense made him realize that Bandy would be in the thick of it. He knew too that he would not fight it, actually would be powerless to fight it.

As he waited, he thought of his relations with Bandy through the years. At first he liked the man. He liked to go to his house and cut his grass and then enjoy the cookies and milk. When had the change come about? When had the seed of the cancer of hate entered the deacon's being? Joe had read that most evil people were just surface people. They wore a facade of pretense. Deep emotion was not part of their life, they did not know how to have deep thoughts. Most such people were incapable of loving anyone. but themselves. Their malice finally destroyed them, but sad to say, they managed to destroy other people with them.

What a world we would have if God's love were not a part of it. How bleak, how hopeless, how very empty. Joe in reality felt great pity for the old deacon. Even now, he would help him if only it were possible. Joe shivered, and turned and gazed out through the snow at his mountain. He remembered his experience there, less than three years ago yet so much had happened it seemed much longer.

Even with the snow, Joe noticed that the peach tree just outside the window had begun to swell, announcing the life within regardless of this unusual weather. God's announcement to the world each spring "I Am God!"

Joe was suddenly filled with restlessness. He shivered feeling as if a cold wind was blowing across his grave. He threw the feeling off. He walked outside in the snow and watched the water flinging upwards and blending with the snow., He let the flakes make his dark hair white. He took several huge breaths, and licking his lips returned to the warmth of his office. He looked up when he heard cars on the parking lot outside. Time to get to work. His staff had arrived.

He had already made a pot of coffee and as the men came, he served each in his turn. He enjoyed this, even though Gary had balked once or twice.

"I am so glad that all of you could come. I have several things I must discuss with you." He took a sip of coffee and waited for the men to settle in.

"Phillip, everything out there looks simply great, I don't know how you managed, but here in less than a year it looks almost done.

"We are closing in, Joe. The weather has been almost ideal. We dried in all the construction before the first rains came, and this freaky weather today will have no effect on anything other than landscaping."

"James, will the school be ready this fall?"

"Sure thing, Joe, I have what looks like a good staff, and so far about 75% complete. Many of the teachers are finishing the current year in public schools. As you said, we will be able to handle three hundred students. You have taken the ball and have raced down the field with it. I do want you to speak to the faculty both privately and together sometimes before school.

"Mark, you know how I feel about the Senior Citizens. We have discussed this often but just to be sure, you know that we will require each of them to spend part of their retirement income for housing rent. This will give them a feeling of independence. Of course, no one is to be turned away if they have no funds. Even those can be given some kind of 'busy work' to make them have respect for themselves. They are happy if they pay their own way."

"Right, Joe. I love old folks. One day I hope to be one myself."

"And, Dennis," Joe smiled at the lawyer. "Any remarks on the finances?"

"No complaints, Joe. It is a miracle. Since we went public on the plans a few months ago, the donations have poured in. I find it hard to believe. You never ask for one dollar, yet the people continue to give. Nothing big, just drop by drop each week. I now think we can dedicate the new constructions debt-free."

Again
If Christ Came Again

"I have always thought and have tried to preach that a person, if he is right with God, will not withhold the money that is God's, churches do not need the bingo games or the garage sales or the pie suppers, carnivals and the like. God made one plan for financing His work, and man has never been able to improve on it. God is indeed good, and only with His help have we been able to come this far in a little less than three years.

"God will bless anyone who loves Him if that person will just give God a little bit of trust. A man must first have to have a good opinion of himself before he can trust God. I want each of you to remember and never never forget that God is in charge of Our Fathers House, and as long as He is kept in charge this work will prosper. If I were to drop out of sight tomorrow, this work will flourish and continue just so long as you continue in the way that I have tried to lead you, "I believe that each of you have asked me in private that you would like to be able to heal the sick. I say to you once again, you can! Christ promised that we could do all things He did, and even more. I say to you that if you really work at it, really pray and practice faith, you can be a channel through which God can heal the people.

"Paul was not just filling a page when he wrote, 'I can do all things through Christ who strengtheneth me.' He actually believed it"

"Joe," Gary was suddenly alarmed, "I have never heard you talk this way before. Is something the matter?" His face showed his great love for the minister.

"I do have some news for you, and it will sound as if I have lost my mind, but I do want each of you to hear me out. I am resigned to God's will for me.

"I will be going away from you in a few months." The gasp around the room was so loud that Joe waited until they settled down again. He waited patiently, hurting as these men were hurting. He licked his lips in the old familiar way and continued. "I am to be taken from you in a horrible manner. I don't know the details, but it is sure, for God has revealed it to me. I feel that Bandy will be the chief instigator of the plot."

"Bandy ought to be killed!" Gary blurted out.

"No, Gary, that is not the way." Joe looked deeply into Gary's eyes. "Bandy is just an instrument. I feel that God doesn't want us to fight this thing. Perhaps my departure will make Our Fathers House grow and grow so that it will be in all the states and over the world. God knows best. My death could really be the spark that set's the growth off."

"Your death?" Dennis was alert "You mean you are going, going to die?"

"That is right, Dennis. God has revealed this to me."

"You could have misunderstood God," Phillip said.

When Joe did not answer, silence invaded the room. Each man was trying unsuccessfully to fathom these words. Each man searched his own heart. Was this thing brought about because of something each had not done? Was there one single time when 100% effort had not been given? They looked anew at Joe whom each had followed, and whom each had given up his own personal life and had followed. They loved this man. They loved Our Fathers House. They had begin to relax, feeling that the hard times had passed and things would be better. Now, this bomb shell had exploded in their midst, and they were simply not able to cope.

"Men," Joe began calmly when the silence was unbearable, "I think you know that I have not preached a comfortable religion. I did not aim when I started to preach a religion that was like some dessert after a big meal. I admit to you that I have always felt sorry for Bandy. He is such a coward. Whatever he has cooked up it will be devious and under-handed. I can understand that I have never pretended to you that the way would be easy. Like the religion I have tried to bring to a needy people, it is not easy. The way before you will not be easy in any sense of the word. Your very soul will be tried in the fire. The media will have a field day. They will pounce on each of you for statements and they will dig at ever facet of your past lives. If you, in the eighth grade, passed someone in the hall and did not speak, they will find it and try to make something of it. I say to you, be prepared for the worst.

"I call on you to be prepared for a struggle against your very natures. You will come face to face with evil and it will be bad enough to scare you to death." Joe stood and began pacing, to and fro, to and fro. The men were silent. Mark looked as if he was about to weep. He was momentarily at a loss for words. He did not want to leave these men dangling.

"I am trying and failing miserably to get you men to have understanding hearts. You will receive it, but you must stay very near to God through constant prayer. You have to learn to lean. Lean on God's word.

"Gary," Joe took his seat once more, "I don't know when the axe will fall. But when it does, I want you to be in charge. Someone has to stand in the gap, and I think everyone here would agree to my choice. It might be a month, it might be a year, it might be within the next hour, but we must not be caught unprepared"

"But Joe," Gary voice raised, his heart pounding, "I can't take your place. I am nothing. I can do nothing."

"Gary, Gary," Joe smiled at the young man. "You will do fine. I am sure that each man here applauds my choice. Just as I have leaned heavily on each one of you, so must you lean heavily on each other. Lean on God, he is ever close when He is needed. You will each do great. My prayer is that in a very very few years, each of you will branch out and establish branches of Our Fathers House, using the mother Church as a base. Follow Christ's Command when He said "Go into all the world and preach the Gospel to every creature." I can meet death if I am assured that this first Our Fathers House will be the springboard wherein millions will be brought into the blessed will of the Father.

"When the time comes, and it will, when you each meet your own Bandy, do not flinch. Pay whatever price is necessary. Trust that daily you will lean on God for understanding, just like a small child. You see, He told us to do that. Be not frightened at the wind or a storm, worry and fret not, for God is surely there.

"Remember how Jesus, in the trying times He faced, he said simply 'Father' and immediately came the answer: 'Son'"

"Joe" Phillip spoke firmly, "What will Bandy do to you, will he simply shoot you?"

"No, Phillip," Joe pulled his lower lip between his teeth, "Bandy will do it covertly. I suspect he will frame me for something, and go on from there. Rest assured that the Devil will show him the way."

"It had better be good. I would like to see him drop dead."

"Dennis," Joe spoke softly, "put Satan behind you That is not the way Please realize that this could not be done except that God lets it be done. God is allowing it to happen.

"You men face trying times. So do I. We must not forget that tough times come to every man who lives without exception, but God manages to give us the strength to face each crisis Then we must know that we grow through the trials that we face and win. The pleasures that we enjoy are just 'between acts' intervals that hone us for the next jolt that comes our way.

"I realize that each one of you will be scared. You would be foolish not to be frightened. You will be assaulted. You will be tempted to abandon the cause and go back home as it were, but I know that each of you will weather the storm and stand fast. Try to forget me. If I thought that Our Fathers House would not continue, yes, even grow and grow, then I could not bear whatever lies ahead. If you let your guard down for one second, it could be fatal. I ask each of you to stand guard. I love you, men. I love your loyalty. God bless us one and all."

CHAPTER FIFTEEN

Joe was sitting outside his office enjoying the mid-morning sun. So far, July had been mild after the late spring. He had walked about the new construction alone, had walked into the senior citizen cottages he walked through each and every class room. He found everything perfect in his eyes. He walked back to the office and decided to bask in the sun a little longer. He took a seat on one of the carved stone benches. The water leaped high and changed into brilliant diamonds before falling back.

Joe looked about at the trim flower beds along one side of the cathedral. White daises with hearts of gold, Large grasshoppers, their yellow bodies shining as if shellacked, leaping and frolicking in the grass and flowers. A blue bird and her mate shrilled from the top of the tree nearby, every now and then diving to the ground like a dive bomber to snatch a hapless worm who only wanted to see the sun. A light wind from the east where the orchard was, permeated the air with the odor of ripening fruit. Joe thought of all the blessings that God gave to man and most of the time man never even noticed. It's a wonder God doesn't withhold some of these fringe benefits that man took for granted.

Today, Joe was in a reflective mood. He had resigned himself to his fate no matter what platter Bandy served it on. He hoped and felt that he was a careful custodian of the Word. He felt that the very fact that the traditional clergy had nothing to do with him. He still was vehement against those striped-trousered, frock tailed coat preachers who spent more time in building their images than furthering God's work. In stead of seeking God's will, they spent time in involving themselves in crusades that would bring publicity, crusades like social justice and the elimination of drugs in our schools. Such Pharasiac 'ministers' probably would not recognize the agonies that literally eat alive the spirit of a man. These people who were afraid to offend a large contributor in reality, when you came right down to the core of the matter, these 'preachers' had no time for God.

And our dear government. It had grown and grown until today it was like a mad bull let loose in a store selling cut glass and porcelain things. It was impossible to curb him without ruining the entire shop. He had read of a California boy who had made a discovery of how to run a car on water. The kid had devised a generator that split water into hydrogen and oxygen and used these gasses to run his car. He was the envy of all his classmates, and one by one he showed them his secret., He was advised to patent the process and go public with the sales. The kid had barely started when the government agents called on him and told him to cease and desist. When the kid asked why, they explained that whole countries would collapse if their income from oil was cut off. The boy defied the agents and was subsequently framed for murder and was sentenced to prison for life with no possibility of parole.

When someone found a possible cure for cancer, the government would not let it on the market until expensive tests after tests after test were done, causing the inventors to abandon the projects. No wonder when someone discovered something, they were hated, persecuted, ostricized and if licensed had it taken away just because they dared to be different or take some approach to a problem not taken before. Joe knew it was dangerous for a man to think, for once thoughts came, solutions raised their heads and trouble came. Wasn't that the crux of his present problems? God made all the animals and things in the world who never gave Him any problems, and last of all He made man and that appeared to be a mistake.

The traditional church was a trap that had begin in the third century. Man had been like a sheep, doing what the one in front did. When someone came along and pointed to the errors they followed, falling into the trap of their own making, they stayed there. All they had to do was to unset the trap and they were afraid to do this.

These people say they are 'conservative' and will not rock the boat, and they are lying to themselves and the sad thing about it, like the unfortunate man on the tower, they miss having a life at all.

Joe was so overcome that he went into his office and locked the door. He silenced the phone and fell on his knees, his hands resting on the seat of his chair.

"Father," he began. "You know that I have tried to stay in your will. I am resigned to the fact that I must be sacrificed. I am willing, and ask You for the needed strength for the ordeal ahead. I even yet, plead with you to have mercy, that you devise some other way, but Thy will, not mine be done." He was silent for a moment, he could feel the loud beating of his heart, was it an anticipatory wait? No sound was present. Even the traffic on the freeway was absent. Joe knew that oft times God answers prayers with silence.

"I have tried to do your will as I understood it," he continued. "I have preached the things that I felt you wanted preached, I realize, that being human, I have fallen short of your will for me, I ask forgiveness. I have tried to show You to the people I have strived to show the dignity to man, your creation I ask again that you change your mind." He was silent. Joe realized that a simple truth that escapes most people: God travels on His own schedule, and in his own way. "But Father, You know my heart, and I am ready to follow your will.

"Father, I thank you for the ones you have give to me to work and carry on Your work. For Gary, lead him as you have led me as he carries on. And for Mark, who is so young. Give him the wisdom that only years of living can bring about. And Father, Bless Dennis. It was your touching of his heart that brought the impetus to Our Fathers House. Give him courage in the days ahead. And bless James, lead him in training young minds in Your way and will. Father, you know that all mankind is basically evil and dark of soul and selfish and drawn to the ways of this world. Man is carnal in his thoughts and resents anything God-like. Help James to lead the young minds entrusted to him, lead them to Your way for their lives.

"Father, I thank you for Phillip. Help him to design and build even larger buildings for Our Fathers House. Give him inspiration and courage.

"Father, please Father," Joe's voice rose. I don't ask that you take these men from this arena, but I ask you to bolster them in the moments of trial, for trials strengthens them. I am ready and willing to face tomorrow. You know that I am submissive to your will. I do ask for physical and mental strength and for fortitude to be a good example of a child of yours."

Joe knelt for some minutes, he stood and replaced the phone and was sitting down when it rang.

Our Fathers House, this is the pastor."

"Brother Joe," he was cut off, "This is.." he heard a gasp and then an intake of breath, "Lin..da. Please come." The phone went dead. Joe jiggled the receiver a few times then hung it back.

CHAPTER SIXTEEN

Joe reached Linda's house in less than ten minutes. He slid his car to a stop and quickly ran up the steps and rang the bell. When no one answered, he turned the doorknob and, feeling that Linda was in some sort of trouble, walked into the room.

"Is anybody home?" He called loudly He heard a groan from the other room, and quickly crossed the living room. He pushed open the door to the bedroom. Linda was lying on the bed and moans were coming from her swollen lips. Joe quickly reached her and she opened her eyes in recognition.

"What's the trouble, Linda?" He noticed a glass of water on the stand by the bed.. He tried to get her to drink it since it seemed that her throat was in need of moisture. She shook her head at the glass.

"N..nn..no" He saw that she had been savagely choked.

"Who did this, Linda?" His voice was near panic.

"B..Ba..Bam" And she died without saying anything else.

Joe frantically reached for the phone to get 911 help but the phone was dead. He quickly ran from the room and saying to no one, 'I'll go get a doctor." He reached the front porch and raced toward his car just as a city police car came to a stop behind his car.

"Thank God," Joe gasped, running to the car, "Get a doctor at once. The woman in that house is either dead or dying."

The policeman called for help on his radio, and then told Joe that he should come back inside the house with him. They found Linda apparently dead, and the officer reported on his portable phone.

"I am at the Murchesen woman's house at 312 Dallas Street. We have here what appears to be a homicide. I request a back-up."

Joe never remembered much after that. The 'back-up' was the sheriff, and he immediately placed Joe under arrest. He placed cuffs on him and pulled a laminated card from his pocket and droned:

"You have the right to remain silent and not make any statement at all. Any statement that you make at all will be taken down and may be used against you at your trial. Any statement you make can and will be used as evidence against you,. You have the right to have a lawyer present to advise you prior and during questioning. If you are unable to hire a lawyer, one will be appointed for you prior to questioning. You have the right to terminate the questioning at any time. Do you understand these rights as I have read them to you?"

"I understand," Joe said. He would be glad when this nightmare was over and he would find himself in his own bed.

"They shoved Joe down the walk and threw him into the back seat of the squad car and it rolled away with lights flashing and siren blasting the air. He was placed in a cell and was not allowed to make a phone call. He looked around the cell and recoiled at the filthy oily mattress and the stinking toilet with no commode seat. The only place to sit was on the filthy mattress which was on a cot looking thing swinging from the wall.

"The cell had a lattice front of quarter inch steel with small squares about two inches square. Little light came into the cell. Down the hall he could hear the police radio making sounds as officers over the county checked in. Several times people came by his cell and gaped. Once he heard one visitor remark:

"It just goes to show you. Preachers are the worst of the lot., the biggest law-breakers of all. Look at that Bakker fellow, abusing that girl in that motel room, and that high-stepping Swaggart guy and now, it has come to Bethany. The pastor of the largest church in the state and now charged with murder, no less. I hope that the needle they use on him is dull, very dull."

Many came to look and to jeer. Joe did not answer any of them. He had gotten tired, he had to sit on the filthy bed. He hoped that someone told Dennis and he would come. He could get him released.

The following morning, Dennis had not come. He was thirsty and no one had offered him a drink. He asked to make a phone call and was told to shut up. He asked for some water to drink and he was threatened with bodily harm. He had been unable to sleep and everything was in a whirl; for he could understand nothing of what was happening. Questions crowded his mind. How had the policeman come so promptly as he was leaving for help? What had Linda been trying to say just as she died? Why had they arrested him? He was running for help. Is that a crime?

Why wouldn't they let him call Dennis? He knew that Mary must be frantic when he had not come home. Why wouldn't they give him a drink of water? Why withhold food from him?

He heard a commotion in the corridor and then Dennis' voice. Soon Dennis was let into his cell.

"Why didn't they let you make a phone call?"

"I asked them and they told me to shut up."

"Brother Joe," Dennis was still flushed from anger, "I don't know what this is all about, but there is no power on earth or in hell itself that will make be believe you are guilty of murder. The judge will not set bail so we have to go from square one. Believe me, Brother Joe, they will not get away with this." He left in a hurry and Joe could hear his loud voice outside. He had not been gone long when they brought him food and water and some clean sheets.

Joe was alone with his thoughts. Back in his mind he knew that his testing time had come. In a way, Joe was glad to be alone and not have to share the cell. He had always believed that the best thing that could happen to man was now and then to be totally alone. He felt that he had always know it, but volunteer aloneness is not the same as compulsory aloneness. Voluntarily aloneness was a time to eat when you wanted, to sleep when you wanted, to cry when you liked. He felt that he could spend these lone hours praying and planning and resting.

He felt helpless realizing that he knew nothing of what was happening. He knew that man in all his wisdom did not have answers to questions of life. Man still did not have a cure for the common cold, yet he had been able to walk on the surface of the moon. He couldn't even answer a simple question as to why cement got hard. He knew only that it did, not why. Electricians still did not know what electricity was. "God help me," Joe cried.

CHAPTER SEVENTEEN

The town slept. Joe stood at the window of his cell and looked out into the night. He could not sleep. He saw the dark streets stretching out into the darkness, streets that he had walked as a boy and as a free man. A light wind woke the leaves up and he heard the rustle outside the cell. There was a sense of peace everywhere except in his heart. Outside was space and control, moist coolness and lots of time. He wished that he could sleep He thought of Mary and remembered when they let her come for a visit. She vowed her loyalty and told him over and over that he could not even think of doing a murder. He thought of his home now, the immaculate kitchen he had not really seen before He remembered the simmering blue enameled coffee pot. He could even remember his favorite cup, the saucer, and the silver spoon. He must try to get some sleep, for the day was nearing, the day of his trial just hours away.

It was a beautiful day when it finally arrived, June 6th. 1988 The whole town of Bethany was alive with the fresh scent of late spring flowers and trees and plants. The smell of freshly cut grass mingled with the exhaust fumes. The morning sun was being reflected from the top of Joe's mountain, and the traffic on the freeway was in full swing oblivious of the tragedy about to unfold in the county courthouse.

There was a feeling of excitement everywhere. All the parking places were filled, and many had had to park blocks away on the fair grounds. and it was not eight a.m. yet. Several people were sweeping in front of their stores, their brooms raising small clouds of dust in the clear air. In the stately elms on the courthouse lawn were playing host to dozens of nest—building birds.

The sky was a sort of cobalt blue, and now and then a crow would sail into the still air. High, high above, an unseen jet was leaving white threads in the blue of the sky.

High above Joe, on the third floor, Daniel Harris had come early to his office. He had one of the fancy courthouse offices, and he enjoyed the time he spent there. He came early today just to go over his notes just once more. This case would propel him into the race for the Attorney Generals race next year.

Harris was a smallish man with almost red hair that, at thirty-seven was beginning patches of pink scalp beneath it. He had a head much too large for his body making him look top heavy. His hands were what one could call grasping. His nose was much too large for his face and was pushed a little to one side of his freckled face, the result of membership on his high school boxing team. His lips were thin and from between them huge yellow teeth were trying to escape. His breath was almost always foul, causing people to stand back from him when talking. His ears were plastered to his head making him have a slight hearing problem. People who knew him spoke in a slightly louder voice when addressing him. Since winning the office of County attorney three years ago, he had let his diet slip and he was now slightly overweight. His copper colored fingers testified to his over a pack a day cigarette habit. Harris was a ambitious man and a born politician. He seemed to know exactly what cases would further his political career.

Daniel Harris had one formidable opponent standing between himself and the nomination of his party for state attorney general, and he instantly knew that this murder trial was the key to the nomination. Win it, you're nominated, lose it and you're out. Harris knew Joe and had once attended one of his services, and he had wished that the defendant other than this man, but he was never one to look a gift horse in the mouth. He felt that he had a no-lose case on his hands. Deacon Bandy was going 'gung ho' for a conviction, and he had managed to get the county commissioners to require tickets to the trial, and Bandy had managed to corner all of them and passed them out to his friends and associates. He had control over who came to the trial. He did not want a bunch of Joe's friend to be there to start anything. Each recipient of the tickets must be a pro-Bandy person. How Bandy had figured out this was a mystery. He was pleased that the crowds that had attended the two weeks of jury selection had with few exceptions were out for Joe's blood.. Harris took one last drag on his cigarette and headed down the stairs to the court room.

Harris entered the room and was pleased that the entire section between the spectator section and the jury box had been reserved for the press, and all the twenty chairs were filled and seven reporters stood.

He saw that Bandy sat right on the front row of the spectator section directly behind the prosecution table. Harris shivered a bit as he saw the self satisfied smirk on his evil face. He would not have been so happy if he had ever been exposed to and had remembered the writings of Omar Khayam who wrote:

> *The morning finger writes, and having writ*
> *Moves on. Not all your piety or wit*
> *Can lure it back, to cancel half a line*
> *Nor all your tears wash out a single word of it.*

It was likely that Bandy had never heard of the Arabian tent maker whose verses were so applicable of today's world.

Promptly at ten o'clock, Judge Seth Thomas entered the room with his black robes flowing in the breeze. The court bailiff screamed: "All rise!"

The judge adjusted his big frame in his high backed chair, wiggled a bit and nodded to the court clerk who stood and read the case at hand.

"You may begin, Mr. Harris."

Daniel Harris calmly walked to the jury rail and smiled slightly before he began his opening remarks.

"Ladies and gentlemen, you know why you are here, but it is appropriate to clarify the situation in case some point is not absolutely clear." He cleared his throat and walked to the side so that the media would get a good view. "We are here to try the defendant on a charge of first degree murder. We will show you beyond any doubt whatsoever that the defendant was in the home of the deceased at the time of her death. He was apprehended in front of her house as he was fleeing the scene. We will prove that he had sufficient motive for wanting her dead. I will be brief throughout this trial and so will my opening statement. You will hear and see the evidence, and you will be compelled by such evidence to bring in a verdict of Guilty of murder in the first degree. Thank you." He walked back to his seat smiling slightly at the media.

Again
If Christ Came Again

The Judge nodded to Dennis Shepherd who stood and walked to the jury rail.

"Ladies and gentlemen," he began, "according to the district attorney, we might as well let you retire and bring in your verdict of guilty." He looked into each pair of eyes, trying to fathom the thoughts. He was dressed in a conservative gray suit with a blue shirt and tan tie. He had pleaded with Joe to let him hire a famous trial lawyer as capable as Marvin Beli or other famous men. Joe wanted no part of it. He said over and over that he would not fight the charges that it was the will of God that things go as planned. Not one dollar of God's money would be wasted on a defense. "But, my friends," he continued, "things are not as simple or as 'cut and dried' as you have heard the district attorney say and that he would like for you to believe. The fly in the ointment is this:" He paused again and then raised his voice slightly. "The defendant is not guilty! I ask that you keep your hearts and minds open until the last bit of evidence has been presented." He turned and went back to the defense table and took his seat beside Joe.

"Call your first witness, Mr. Harris," the judge barked.

"Thank you, your Honor. My first witness is Sheriff Alex Dixon."

The sheriff walked to the stand and calmly took his place and was sworn. He took his seat and crossed his legs. He wore typical western clothes and his ruddy face be spoke many hours in the open.

"Please state your name and occupation, please."

"You know me, Dan."

"For the record, sheriff, please, for the record."

"My name is Alex Dixon, and I am the duly elected sheriff of Bethany county."

"Sheriff, do you happen to remember what you were doing in the morning of March 6th this year?"

"Sure, I was passing the house of the deceased. I had been out to the lake to check on some stolen cars."

"Please, Sheriff, keep your answers plain and simple. We do not need to know where you had been, just where you were."

"I was passing in front of the dead girl's house when I spotted the defendant," He pointed to Joe. He had been watching a lot of TV trials, "that's him there,. And he was running full tilt out of the girl's house."

"Are you sure he was running, Sheriff?" Harris put a lot of stress on the word running.

"Yep, he was running and fast. You would think he was trying to break the four minute mile."

"Tell the court what you did then."

"I recognized him as the preacher at that big Glass church on the freeway so I stopped him."

"Where you alone, sheriff?"

"Nah, my deputy was with me."

"You stopped the defendant as he was fleeing the scene.."

"Objection!" Shouted Dennis, "the word fleeing denotes guilt"

"Sustained," said the judge.

"You stopped the defendant who was running out of the deceased's house?"

The sheriff nodded, then said "Yes"

"What, if anything, did the defendant say?"

"He said that he wanted a doctor, that a woman in the house needed one bad."

"Sheriff, what did you do then?"

"I kept the defendant by the car and sent the deputy into the house. Almost at once he came running out saying that there was a dead girl in there. I used my radio and called for an ambulance to be dispatched pronto. I then placed the defendant under arrest." He smiled his satisfaction.

"Your witness, counselor" Harris sat down with a flourish.

"No questions, Your honor," Dennis wanted to tear the stupid sheriff's testimony to bits, but Joe had tugged at his sleeve as he started to rise.

"Your honor," Harris smiled. This was going to be easier than he thought. "I will now prove the Corpus Delecti. I call the county coroner, Andrew Sipes."

Andy Sipes looked as if he were crawling to the stand. He was stooped and he held his head down and he was sworn and then managed to seat himself in the witness stand. He managed to raise his head and seemed to be staring past Harris and had his eyes fixed on the twenty foot ceiling of the courtroom near the back as if the gold leaf trim he saw there held his interest. Bandy leaned forward, licking his lips.

"Please state your name and occupation."

"My name is Andrew Sipes and I am the Coroner of Bethany County."

"In the course of your duties as Coroner of this County, did you on March 6 last have occasion to examine a body?"

"Yes sir. I was called by the sheriff and asked to pronounce the body of a young lady."

"Do you remember the name of the young lady"

Sipes took a small well worn notebook from his coat pocket and turned a few pages. "It was Linda Murchison."

"After you pronounced her dead at the scene, what did you do?"

"I called for a wagon and had the body moved to the morgue."

"What happened then.?"

"I made a detailed examination"

"Were you alone?"

"No, the sheriff and his deputy came along too."

"After you examined her, what conclusion did you reach?"

"All the vital organs were negative. She had died from strangulation."

"Did you perform an autopsy?

"Yes, sir, I did. later that day."

"Will you tell the jury the result of your findings?"

Bandy leaned forward. If that shrimp failed him now, there was nothing that he could do, but the little man followed through beautifully.

Sipes consulted his little book, his white hands trembling slightly. "The body was that of a white female about twenty five years old. Death had been caused by strangulation. Livid marks about the throat and larnyx showed that she had been choked so hard that no air could get to her lungs."

"Mr. Sipes, could the air have been cut off by something like a cord?"

"No, sir, a rope or cord would have made a narrow marks. Those marks were wide, like those made by a man's hands."

Lee Roy Neal

"Objection!" Dennis was on his feet. "This calls for a conclusion of the witness."

"Over ruled." The judge used his gavel.

"Go on Mr. Sipes" Harris smiled at the press.

"Well, the woman had been choked to death. It was as plain as day."

"From the condition of the internal organism could you determine the approximate time of death?"

"Yes,sir. She died at approximately 3:00 p.m. June 6/"

"This was not a death from natural causes?"

"Absolutely not. The woman was choked to death. And such a pretty little thing."

"Mr. Sipes," Harris waited for silence in the court room. "What else did the autopsy show?"

"The young lady was about six weeks pregnant.." Bedlam ensued, and no amount of pounding on the bench could quiet it down until it ran its course. Finally Judge Thomas rose and roared, 'Silence!" The crowd subsided into silence. The judge sat back down. The judge was known for clearing a court room on many occasions.

"There is no doubt, Mr. Sipes. Linda Murcheson was six week pregnant? I understand that she was not married."

"She was pregnant, and being pregnant and having no husband is not unusual in this day and age, Mr. Harris. You know that. Why I remember when I was a young boy…"

"That is all, Harris interrupted. "Your witness, counselor" He smiled as he took his chair.

"Mr. Sipes," Dennis had ignored the pull on his coat by Joe. "What are your qualifications for being coroner of this county?"

"I am a graduate of the Southwestern Medical School."

"And, sir, are you an experienced pathologist?"

"I have had over thirty years experience" He smiled, showing his missing teeth.

"And is there absolutely any doubt at all as to the pregnancy of the deceased?"

"I object of your trying to cast aspersions on my veracity."

Again
If Christ Came Again

"Never mind your veracity, Mr. Sipes, just answer my question." Bandy suddenly felt a surge of blood in his ears.. He breathed easy when Sipes spoke again.

"Linda Murcheson, the deceased, was six weeks pregnant at the time of her death."

"Did you get a second opinion, say an assistant, or a doctor here in town?"

"Your Honor," Harris was on his feet. "I have remained silent for a s long as I am able to. This whole line of questions is ridiculous."

"I agree, the judge said, "Mr. Shepherd, I think you have exhausted this line of questioning. Get on with it."

"No more questions, your Honor." Dennis sat down. His face showed his helplessness. Joe on one side offering absolutely no defense and he felt powerless. He did not believe for a moment that Linda was pregnant. He suddenly felt a chill permeate his body. He felt Joe was right some time ago when he said that Bandy would frame him. How could one man hate another so much? Was it natural instinct that caused one man to want to destroy a fellow human being? He knew no other explanation for it.

Dennis's face showed his complete dejection. Of course Linda had not been pregnant. It was plot in the cess pool of the sick mind of Deacon Bandy. It was regrettable, Dennis mused, that some people were meaner and were more evil in their religiosity than others were mean and evil in their atheisitic lives. To try to cipher Bandy's mind, using logic of any degree would simply be an exercise in futility. Dennis simply refused to accept the inevitable. He could feel the evil fouling the air around Bandy. A sudden cold came over Dennis chilling his very bones. He looked at the smirking deacon. He could almost feel the evil in the room. Here was evil from the very hands of Satan. Evil had an infinite number of eyes and brains and hearts to do its will. Dennis also knew that evil men were most loyal to other evil men, and an evil man had to find a scape goat, someone to blame for their own short comings, and tragically, Bandy had chosen Joe.

Dennis wondered if there was some way of getting inside Bandy's skull and brain. He quickly purged the thought, for he realized than Bandy was, at this point, unreachable: like a prairie fire racing uncointrolled across the wild expanse of Kansas, a fire that devoured all in its path, and no amount of food sated the vorascious appetite of the flames.

Helplessly, Dennis wondered what the world would be like if everyone was like Bandy. What, he thought, if only a majority, say 51% of all people were like the evil deacon. There would likely be no songs, no art, no light, no music. Even colors would be unknown. No charity, no pity, no gentle people, nothing good would exist. The whole world would be one of friendlessness, lonliness, pain. No one would be able to enjoy the innocence of a new baby or the bashfulness of a new bride. There would be no friendly or caring neighbors. Dennis sighed. I would not like to live in a world populated by people like Bandy. He came to the present again as Harris rose to his feet.

"Your Honor, I call my next witness, Mr. Halbert King to take the stand."

Halbert King was a medium tall man in his early thirties. He had what many would call a 'fetching' smile This often caused many a young female heart to skip a beat. His smile was so brilliant, his eyes so sparkling that one failed to notice that he had an oversized nose that took over more than its share of his face. He was slim and neat and when he raised his hand to be sworn, his manicure showed. He gave every evidence that here was a meticulous man who gave every attention to details.

"Please state your name and occupation."

"Halbert King. I am an investigator for the district attorney's office of this county."

"In March of this year, can you tell the jury if you had a special assignment?"

"I did. I was to go to the home of Linda Murcheson, the deceased in this hearing. I was told to make a thorough inspection of the murder scene."

"Tell this court what, if anything you found in the source of your investigation that might, in your opinion, be pertinent to this case."

"I found the defendant's fingerprints on the front door, on the telephone instrument, and on a drinking glass by the bed."

"What you are saying, in essence, Daniel smiled at the jury, "what you are telling this jury is that without a doubt, the defendant had been inside the house of the deceased, Linda Murchison."

"Without a doubt."

"Your witness, Mr. Shephard, and Daniel Harris strode to his seat at the prosecution table, a sardonic smile on his face.

Again Dennis shook off Joe's hand and walked over to the witness stand. He paused for an instant and then in a calm voice: "Can you swear that because the defendant's prints were in the house of the deceased, can you swear that the placements of those prints point to the guilt of the defendant?"

"No," King said, "I can't swear that the placement of the defendant's fingerprints point to his guilt, but, I can't swear that those prints point to his innocence either."

"Mr. King," Dennis raised his voice, "can you swear that the prints you found inside that house were made on the day that Linda Murcheson died?"

"I don't know when the prints were made, but I can swear that there were no other prints superimposed over those of the deceased."

"And what can you infer from this?"

"I'm not being paid to infer anything. I am paid a salary to collect evidence and then let the evidence speak for itself."

"Then, is it fair to ask or state that you have no opinion whatever as to the guilt or innocence of the defendant here today?"

"None whatsoever, counselor, none whatsoever." Dennis sat down, dejection coloring his entire body.

Daniel Harris rose and spoke confidently. "I now call…"

"Mr. Harris, Just a minute," the judge interrupted him, "the hour grows late, and I will adjourn this court until ten tomorrow morning." He hit the desk with his gavel.

The bailiff shouted: "All rise!"

In a few minutes, Joe and Dennis were seated in the witness room off the main courtroom.

"Joe," Dennis began, looking carefully into the eyes of his pastor and friend. "You are tying my hands and closing the door on your defense by the minute." His voice showed the strain "I thought that you told me that Linda was clean, had left her profession and was living a Christian life. How do you account for her being six weeks pregnant?"

"Dennis," Joe saw the hurt in his friend's eyes. He licked his lips and was silent for an instant holding his upper lip between his teeth. "I have the feeling that you wish that you had never heard of me."

"No way, Joe, no way. Never let me hear you say that to me again." Dennis voice showed his anger. He calmed and Joe saw a lone tear feel its way down his friend's cheek. "Joe, I never lived until I met you and you showed me how to have a life."

"Dennis, thank you for those words They are indeed a ray of sunshine in my dreary world. They make me know that I have not lived in vain. I often wonder why a man has to complicate his life and the lives of almost everyone he meets and touches, causing both to wollow in a quagmire like that used by pigs. You never see a dog acting like that. Dogs are simple. They have an unwavering trust and loyalty, and are ready to take what ever comes as a result of their own actions. As for your question: there is no way on earth that Linda could have been pregnant. No one could fool me that much."

"I thought so. It is all a Bandy plot. He left no stone unturned. Wonder what he has on the coroner?"

"I am saying again, Dennis, this is part of my fate. I explained that I must be sacrificed, for the sake of God's Kingdom. Try to understand and become reconciled to it. Our Father's House will grow because of this. How, I do not know, but trust me on this Dennis, it will grow. You have to be patient and you will see. Remember your favorite song you often request that we sing in church?

We are often tossed and driven
On the restless sea of time
Somber skies and howling tempests
Offt succeed a bright sunshine
In the land of perfect day
When the mists have rolled away,
We will understand it better by and by.

Again
If Christ Came Again

*Trials darken on every hand
And we cannot understand
All the ways that God would leads us
To that blessed promised land
But he guides us with His eye
And we'll follow til we die,
We will understand it better, bye and bye.*

"You see, Dennis, that song was written over 100 years ago by a man named Charles Tindley. It says so much about the Christian faith. I do not understand, but as long as I trust the 'why' to God, everything will turn out all right.

"Please, my dear friend Dennis, Try to get the picture: God lives! He is not dead nor does He sleep. Man needs his God. If God did not exist, man would have invented one. You see, the very nature of man, like nature, abhors emptiness, a vacuum, a nothingness. When a young mother cries at the loss of her baby, and when a man bemoans the fact that he has lost his fortune or his family or his health, religion of some kind is the answer to peace That is the reason that the little African mother throws her baby in the river in an effort to appease the river god. A man has to have a God. His God might be money or fame, but he has to believe in something. The worst thing that can happen to man is to find himself in possession of unbelief. Dennis," Joe put his hand on his friend's shoulder. "Try not to worry and let us leave all of this mess in the capable hands of our Heavenly Father."

CHAPTER EIGHTEEN

MAY presented the citizens of Bethany another gorgeous day, for white clouds floated like paper boats in a blue sea high above. It was early, but already people were in line getting ready to rush to a front seat in the courtroom where the sensational trial was unfolding. Each clutched a coveted ticket which was scrutinized carefully before the holder was passed through the door.

The air was permeated with the odor of fresh blooming roses and ther red and white Crepe Myrtle that huddled near the courthouse walls. The soft apple-green of a weeping willow danced lightly in the pleasant breeze. Traffic around the town square was extremely heavy and the sounding of horns and the slamming of doors filled the crisp air. Nearby large trucks were grinding gears after having being stopped by the traffic light on Hiway 19 which intersected the nearby Interstate less than a mile away.

As the deputy sheriff brought the manacled Joe into the courtroom he saw that even the standing room space was depleted. Joe was so chained that he had to make a sort of skip to get to the seat at the defense table. Dennis again looked at his pastor and his friend and he felt a fresh anger as he remembered his futile efforts to have the manacles removed from Joe since he posed no escape risk. Bandy and the sheriff thought it would be more impressive to bring this dangerous criminal, into the public view in manacles showing the desire of the sheriff to protect the public. It simply looked good to the voters and satiated their lust for the sensational.

Dennis had slept little last night and every inch of his being reflected this. After the talk with Joe yesterday, Dennis was on the verge of giving up, but in the deep of the night he resolved to again continue the fight though the specter of losing reared its head higher and higher. Joe was innocent, no doubt of that. Joe was innocent. It was as if Joe had had a revelation of his fate by God Himself. Had not Joe himself said so in so many words if one read through the haze or between the lines.

Where was God in all of this travail? Why didn't Joe call on God for help? Could he, like Jesus, call ten thousand angels? Could not

Again
If Christ Came Again

God suddenly strike Bandy dead and thus frighten the rest of the blood-thirsty populace to tuck tail and run?

What goes on, Dennis asked himself in the middle of the long and sleepless night. Was it a battle between God's omnipotence and his gift of man's free will that the struggle lay? Was this the main conflict? Was the struggle more subtle yet? Did it involve the very nature of God Himself? Why did God allow evil to exist? Why didn't he simply say a word and cause the devil to disappear? Simple: God wanted no robots, for that was what the result would be. Man had to have the right to make a choice, and he had to have the gift of struggle, the desire to attain the plateau of being in the will of God, and this could not be if there were no Devil. God could bind a soul to His will, but then the soul would be without the freedom of choice.

Joe had chosen the role of martyr. Joe was acting as if..as if..he, like Christ, must die for Bandy's sins. It was insane, Dennis had rolled and tossed and struggled most of the night. He refused to entertain the thought. Joe was an enigma to be sure. He had powers like no other in Dennis's experience.Everything he touched in the name of Diety prospered. A person could be healed over long distance. He had absolutely no interest in money for himself. He owned no property. He gave his salary away. Dennis remembered his college days when, for a time he had become an agnostic and then had slipped into atheism. He had even joined a club that evolved into a church of Satan where he had dropped out and had run away and back into his Christian beliefs.

One tenet of the wierd church of Satan was the Devil's Creed. It was so subtle, so dangerous he tried to erase it from his memory forever:

> Do you believe in God?
> Do you believe in His omnipotence
> Do you believe in his omniscience?

If the inductee looked puzzled, the explanation of the word was given: His total knowledge of both past and future.

Do you believe that all man has freedom of will?
Do you believe in punishment for sin, including going to hell?
Do you believe in his Satanic Majesty, the Devil?

Dennis had gone back to his dorm and pondered the subtility of this credo. He went over each item in the manifest. There was not a single thing there that any curate in the world would not subscribe to. Not one, and yet, it was part of the initiation into the church of the enemy of God. Yet, taken as a whole, Dennis sat up in his bed that night. Taken as a whole: Satan's fire coupled with God's mercy..God's omnipotence contrasted with man's freedom of choice. Couldn't God, being all powerful, make a man do his will? Even without free choice? Then it came to Dennis, the young college student: God can, even if he knew the end of the road, refrained from coercing a person into doing His will. The whole thing boiled down to this: It was not the all power of God and the free will of God that the battle raged. It was on another plane: It boiled down to the very nature of God Himself.

Dennis looked at Joe afresh. He had a serene look that involved his whole being. Dennis knew then, that nothing he could say would throw Joe off the tract he was on: the tract to the needle in the execution chamber.

Somehow, Joe felt a sense of relief as he listened to the routine of "all rise" and all the rest.

"I call my next witness, Melody Bell."

Melody Bell was in her mid-twenties, and she could prove it by her birth certificate, but she had the face of one of forty years. Her once beautiful hair had been dyed and singed so often that it had died with a dull brassy look. Each strand looked stiff like a part of a wire. It did not look like a wig, for no sensible woman would wear a wig that looked like that. Her complexion was coarse and deep pores were visible even without looking closely. Even heavy pan makeup could not hide the ravages of a mis-spent life.

Today, for her appearance in court, she wore a simple white dress and she was uncomfortable in it. She was more used to her daily uniform: the briefest of mini-skirts. Her eyes were cruel and cold and one look revealed her real profession. Dennis watched her carefully and wondered how such a person could come to this state in life. Surely at one time she had been a beautiful young innocent girl. For a certainty her mother had not raised her to be a whore. He supposed that no man really sought the intrinsic evil that daily touched his life. Yet had not the Jews held that man was intrinsically evil from his birth? And that man was an evil being all the days of his life? He had read that all ideas were born in a man's brain, then couldn't the corollary be also true, that all evil originated in the brain?

At one point in Melody's life she had stopped being an innocent lovable child, and through the years had evolved into what sat there in the witness chair today. She lifted her hand to be sworn and the diamonds on her well kept fingers flashed rays of fire all over the room. She listened and carefully followed the words of the baliff and giving a final clack on her gum said I do. She crossed her legs much to the delight of the young reporters nearest the chair. Many men in the room slid lower in their seats in hopes of not being identified as one of her regulars, should she happen to fasten her eyes at the wrong moment.

"Please state your name and occupation" Harris said.

"Huh?"

Harris reddened. "Please state your name and occupation."

"My name is Melody Bell and I am an entertainer."

A titter spread over the room and the judge used his gavel.

"Where do you live?"

"I live in Bethany. I shared a duplex with Linda."

"Were you at home the day Linda was murdered?"

"Objection!" Dennis said.

"Mr. Harris," the judge was angry. You know better than that."

"Sorry, your Honor. Where you at home the day Linda died?"

"Sure, I was home all day." She clacked her gum again.

"Did you happen to see anyone over on Linda's side of the house on March 6th of this year, especially after noon?"

"Yeah, only one person came to her house that day."

"Did you know the person?"

"Yeah, everyone knows him. It was the person sitting at that table. The preacher in the big church."

"Melody", Harris stepped closer to the witness and lowered his voice somewhat. 'I want you to think carefully before you answer my next question." He wished that she would stop that infernal gum chewing. Why hadn't he warned her to leave the gum at home? "How long was the defendant in Linda's house?"

"He was in there long enough."

"Long enough for what? No, no, don't answer that question."

The room erupted and the judge pounded the desk.

"Objection!" Dennis was on his feet, his face red in anger.

"I withdraw the question, your Honor."

"Strike the question," the judge barked.

"Melody," Harris continued after the room was quiet. "Did you hear any loud voices coming from the room that day?"

"I heard an argument. He was telling her that he would not marry her., He said she could have an abortion." The judge pounded the desk and stood and threatened to clear the room before the bedlam subsided. Melody was thinking of the stack of crisp hundred dollar bills hidden in her home. She knew the poor fool was a goner anyway, so what did it hurt. She dreaded when the deacon came back for a visit in her bed, but she could take a vacation.

"You are sure, Melody. You could hear?"

"The walls in that dump are so thin you can hear the toilet flush next door. I heard plain as day."

"Besides voices, did you hear anything else?"

"Yeah," she chewed again. "I heard Linda crying and I heard a scuffle. Once I heard her cry:'stop it'"

"Anything else, Melody?"

"I heard a sort of gurgle, and then things was quiet, and then I heard running out the front door."

"That is all, Miss Bell. Yours Mr. Shepherd."

Harris smiled, a grin of victory on his face."

"Miss Bell," Dennis was so angry he could hardly speak, his lips were white. He managed to keep his control. "You said that your occupation was entertainer. Please explain to the jury what you meant by that.

"Objection! Objection!" Harris shouted. "What this lady meant and how she entertains has no bearing on this case. It's a blatant attempt by this man to badger the witness."

"Sustained. Mr. Shepherd, you know better than that."

"Miss Bell," Dennis was still angry. "Do you know what perjury is?"

"Sure I do. Do you take me for a dummy?"

"I don't take you for anything, Miss Bell. I wanted only to make sure you knew what perjury is and that committing it could mean a trip to prison."

"Objection." Harris was on his feet. "Counsel is threatening the witness."

"Sustained., Mr. Shepherd, I shall not warn you again. I am on the verge of fining you for contempt of this court."

"Dennis turned again to the gum chewing witness. "Miss Bell, I am interested in knowing why you were so interested in what went on next door?"

"Linda and I were friends. We watched out for each other."

"And you just happened to be looking out the window at the exact time the defendant supposedly entered the room, and you just happened to be listening to each word that was said."

"You got it buster. Linda and I watched out for each other. I cared a lot for Linda."

"Is it possible, Miss Bell, that you could have been mistaken as to what was said that day? I know that you said the walls were thin, but to hear every word..that's hard to believe."

"Believe it or not. I heard every word, and I hope that that man pays for killing my best friend." The gun was chewed faster than ever, the cold eyes flashed. Dennis knew it was useless. Bandy had done his job well. He sat down.

"Your honor," Harris stood. "This is the state's case. The state rests."

The courtroom became noisy. No one had expected so short a prosecution case. He must be really confident, Dennis thought.

"Your Honor," Dennis stood. "The defense requests a recess before putting on its case."

"I'll allow thirty minutes." He rapped the gavel.

Joe and Dennis were soon seated in the witness room. Joe was calm and serene and all of his sympathy went out to this true and dedicated friend.

"Dennis," Joe's voice was soft. "try to relax, Take it easy. I have told you how this whole thing would end. Go with the flow, my dearest friend."

"It's almost impossible to do, Joe. What a liar that woman is. Wonder what it cost Bandy? Anyway, Joe, I want to discuss your testimony before we go back in there."

"Don't put me on the stand, Dennis."

"Joe," his voice had traces of panic. "You're all I have. I can call no witnesses at all because I have none. I have to call you. All I have are character witnesses. I have to call you, Joe to refute all the lies that are piled up in there."

"Dennis, I don't want you to put on any defense"

"Joe, you are risking your life. It's the same as suicide."

"Not in this case, Dennis, not in this case. Believe me. We all must learn to live in our own skin. We each must resign each self to the will of God. Why is it so hard for you to accept this, Joe?"

"Because I love Our Father's House, and because I love you. And if we lose this case it will all go down. I am afraid."

"No, Dennis, because of this, Our Fathers House will grow and grow. Trust me in this.

"And these are your final words.. Joe?"

"That is so, my dearest friend, Dennis."

"You do know that Bandy killed Linda and framed you for it, don't you?"

"Yes, Dennis, I know. She told me just as she died. I know and I forgive the deacon for it. I pity him for he will have to answer to God for what he did."

"I am helpless, Joe. All we can expect now is a miracle."

They returned to the court room and when all was quiet the judge spoke: "You may begin now, Counselor."

"If it please the court, your Honor. We will present no defense The defense rests."

Reporters stumbled over each other as they raced for telephones. The crowd applauded and Harris sat with a sardonic grin on his face.

In all of his experience and reading he had never heard of a defendant in a capitol murder case not making any kind of fight. The man was committing suicide.

"Mr. Harris," The judge had finally restored order. "You may make your summation to the jury."

This was Daniel Harris's finest hour. He had written and rewritten his closing statement, for he was the star of the show, and he had to be ready for it. He was certain of the nomination now. Victory was his, and he was right proud. He sauntered over to the rail before the jury box and leaned on it slightly, looking into each and every face. He tried to get the expression on his face and in his voice denoting 'I am your friend" or 'trust me and believe me'. He cleared his voice and in a loud voice began:

"Ladies and gentlemen of the jury, I realize that the past days have been trying days for each of you. It costs a person to do his civic duty for his country. May I say that in my opinion, you have paid the cost with flying colors. On behalf of the people of Bethany County I wish to thank you.

"It is sad to have to participate in a murder case, and it is doubly sad when it is a neighbor before the bar. And to make it even harder, the defendant is a man of the cloth. Yet, here we all are, here in one room, brought together by fate and circumstances make a judgment Not a simple judgment as you make on what to fix for supper tonight, but a judgment that concerns life and death.

"I don't believe that there is a one of us here today who would not rather be somewhere else, even in a hospital, anywhere but right here. But, we are here and we have to face the task before us.

"No one has asked the defendant to be born into this world, or ask that we ourselves be born, but we all have been born and now our lives touch each other tragically." Harris swallowed and then continued.

Bandy sat still trying to give a non-challant look but had failed miserably. The utter joy in his cold eyes was liken from the deepest pits of hell. He simply could not take his eyes from the faces of the jury. Dennis looked at the man who had perpetrated this entire farce. He could hardly stand the sight of this miserable man whose dead hair was almost gone and his sallow skin was ugly and flabby. His wide nostrils looked permanently distended, his eyes were cold and held an evil expression.

"But, Ladies and Gentlemen," Harris had resumed his speech. "We are here and we must do our sworn civic duty A life has been taken, not just any life but a human life. You realize that of all the things God created, man was the crowning jewel. In creation, he spoke everything into being in creating them except man. When He made man, words would not do, He made man in His own image out of clay, and He breathed into the lifeless nostrils and the clay became a living soul. To God, Man was special, made in His own image and He caused him to come alive by using His own divine breath, "Now, one of God's children has been ruthlessly murdered Her beautiful young life has suddenly ended, gone like a puff of smoke. I will briefly review what you have heard these past days:

"Liinda Murcheson was murdered by choking. Someone with strong hands did this horrible deed. The defendant has strong hands made so by years of working in wood. Testimony has placed the defendant in the murder room. His fingerprints place him there and the next door neighbor placed him there on the day Linda died. He was apprehended fleeing the scene of carnage.

"The defendant had, not only the opportunity to kill, but," he turned and pointed a finger at Joe and raised his voice, "he not only had opportunity but a reason to take the life of Linda Murcheson. He had a reason, ladies and gentlemen: he had gotten her pregnant and had refused to marry her. He was afraid she would tell the world what he had done.

"Yes, the pastor of one of the largest churches in this country was afraid that he would follow the fate of Jimmy Bakker and Jimmy Swaggart, so in panic, he did what he thought was the only thing left for him to do. He silenced Linda Murchison in a way that would silence her forever: he murdered her.

"And," he grabbed the rail before him with both hands and lowered his voice. "In case you have not thought of it, this fiend murdered an unborn child when he murdered Linda Murchison. He murdered his own flesh and blood as well." Harris stopped talking and he took a large handkerchief from his pocket and wiped non existent tears from his eyes. Dennis noted that today was the only day

Harris had sported a handkerchief in his pocket during the trial. How convenient.

"Excuse me, ladies and gentlemen. I love children with all my heart, and my wife and I have tried for years to have children with no success, and when I think of that man murdering a helpless child, I get chills all over my body.

"I will not prolong this, friends,. The judge will give you your instructions at the proper time. I know that you will do your duty with brave and unselfish hearts and afterwards you can say to Linda." he looks upwards "Linda, and her precious little baby 'Linda, it's all right, my dear, It's all right, little mother. We caught your murderer and will make him pay' If you will do that, you will have no trouble in bring in a verdict of murder in the first degree, I thank you." He sat down amid a silence in the large court room. He took a drink of water and mopped his face. The room continued in silence, and had not the judge been so strict, surely applause would have broken out with people standing in ovation.

Dennis stood slowly, every eye in the room on him. He carefully evened the sheets on the desk before him and waited for suspense to build. The afternoon sun came in the tall windows and miraculously a bright halo spotlighted Joe and Dennis. The silence everywhere was phenomenal. Bandy dropped his head and couldn't look. He trembled as if God Himself had placed His hand on his shoulder, he actually expected to be exterminated on the spot. Just as suddenly as it had appeared, a cloud erased the halo, and Dennis walked to the jury box. He looked at the men and women and spoke softly.

"Ladies and gentlemen, from listening to the district attorney one would think that nothing more is needed to be said. You have your orders, and shouldn't even have to leave the jury box that you can, as in many of a western movie where the men simply whispered to one another render a verdict. All the i's are dotted and the t's are crossed." He turned to Harris who still wore the smug look of victory. "I congratulate you, Mr. Harris, on a beautiful speech." He turned back to the jury and in a firm voice spoke: "Unfortunately, nothing in the speech is true." Dennis raised his voice: "That man is innocent!"

He moved a little closer to the rail and almost whispered::"That man is innocent. Look at him. He does not have the ability to commit murder. He can't even kill a chicken. His hands are made for helping, not hurting.

"The law says that if you have the slightest doubt of that man's guilt, even the faintest little bit, the law says that you must acquit him. The Bible that that man lives by says: 'Come, let us reason together' so, ladies and gentlemen, let's reason together. Look at that man sitting there. Look beyond those manacles and chains, can you find the least sign of criminality in his whole being, his eyes, his mouth, anything? You were told to look at his hands, please look again. Those hands are kind, those hands have made many pieces of fine furniture, perhaps in some of your very houses, they make beauty, are incapable of inflicting harm to anyone or anything. Look at him again. I beg you to. Can you see anything there but love, can you detect anything else but God-like qualities?

"Let's begin there. I have the utmost contempt for anyone who is not his own master and in control of his own mind, So, right now, forget everything you have heard and think with me. Back up a bit to your own childhood when you yourself possessed a childlike faith, the kind that Jesus said that we should all have.

"What are we doing here? Do each of us hear and see the same things? Why is it that I find no fault in this man? Oh, I know that I have known him closely for almost three years, and I hear him preach each week, yet, I find no fault in this man who will takes his salary and gives it to the poor and needy. He drives himself and neglects his own health and comfort and ease to go into the highways and hedges and minister to those who hurt. he cares nothing about your belief or credo. He sees only the need and the pain.. He has been a channel through which God has healed hundreds, perhaps thousands of sick and maimed, deaf and blind. Most of these people have been like the ten lepers in the Bible whom Christ healed and only 10% returned to give thanks. Many in this room today have been healed at this man's hands, yet many are here today to see you commit murder by finding this innocent man guilty.

"Joe loves Bethany, and believe it or not, he knew years ago that if he stayed here, disaster would overtake him at the hands of a Son of Satan." He paused and looked Bandy full in the face. "He knew this and yet he stayed to meet his fate. He has an uncanny ability to see inside a person, to see under the facade a person hides behind. Joe knows most of the secrets of this town, and yet, in the years that I have known him, I have yet to hear him lift his voice in condemnation against any man or woman." He paused as if remembering, and he let his voice fall a little lower.

"I have seen him take a dirty, filthy, stinking piece of human flotsam in his arms and lift him to the heights God meant for His children to attain and set him on his feet again to 'go and sin no more' with some of Joe's personal money in his pocket. Look at him now, Ladies and Gentlemen, that man has been betrayed by the very people he longed to help, the very ones he tried to steer towards a fuller life.

"Do you want to know exactly why that man sits there in chains?" He turned and faced the audience and raised his voice. "Think, each of you, all of you here in this place where justice is supposed to be meted to one and all, Why is that man there wearing his chain in humility. Why is he here? Well, my fellow citizens, I am about to tell you." Bandy's heart raised in panic.

"That man is there because," he lowered his voice and no one dared to breathe. "that man dared to be different. Yes, you heard me right. He dared to be different." He faced the jury once more. "Did you hear me? He dared to be different. He dared to march to a different drummer. If he had gone along, followed the crowd, headed a church that met on Sundays, asked no questions, rocked not the boat of conformity, dared not ruffle the waters of complacency, stayed in the ruts of the traditional church, he would not be sitting there in chains on trial for his very life. He would be pastor of a little church with less than a hundred members and be would not be here for you to pass judgment on.

"History is rife of stories of people who dared to be different, who dared to get out of the well worn ruts of traditionalism. Did you know that throughout human history, it has been the 'different' who have been the humanitarians, the torch-bearers not only of new programs and ideas, but also of understanding and love and sympathy. If our society really and truly wants to make progress, if true liberty is the goal of every man and woman, then society must turn to these 'oddballs. We cannot afford to stifle their voices crying in the wilderness.

"I would like to call your attention to a famous 'odd-ball' who lived in the 1400's. He had gone to school and had been taught by learned men that the earth was flat. That was nothing new, everyone knew that. But do you know what? Young Christopher Columbus was 'different'. He was the 'odd-ball' of his day. He said that he thought that the earth was a sphere, round, and if he could get the money, he would prove it. People would meet him on the street and move aside so as not to become contaminated by the crazy man. No one would advance the money, except, a Queen named Isabela, Queen Isabela. She hocked the crown jewels and financed Columbus's idea. Even when proceedings were eminent to 'put him away' he sailed away and all the brilliant philosophers and others went to the dock to watch him sail over the edge and drop off into nothingness. There went the Queen's jewels and man thought that she would be a good replacement in the booby hatch. When Columbus returned after returning from the East after he had sailed west, he made a monkey out of each of his critics. You know, he had to leave his native country for fear of the mobs who wanted to kill him for proving them wrong.

"And another 'odd-ball' comes to mind. For years school kids had been thought that the sun rises in the east and sets in the west. many here today would not argue with that fact. But one smart kid dared to think for himself. He dared to be different. He laughed at the Greek Mythology story that the son of Appolo drove a chariot across the heavens in the back of which was the sun. He had read that once Appolo got careless and drove the chariot too close to Africa and turned the skin of people there black. and so on. He did not believe it.

"But the young man, Gallelo, showed his 'difference' by stating that the sun did not move at all. The earth rotated around the sun. The educators of that day, mainly the churches, would have none of that. Why the church had taught for centuries that the sun moved, and here was a Joe, I mean Gallelio who was 'different'. The leaders of the church called the young man in and in fatherly tones showed him the error of his ways. When the young man refused to stand before a church tribunal, a jury, if you pleased and recant and admit the error of his thinking, When he refused to conform, he was tortured in the most inhumane ways, he was tortured beyond human endurance until he did recant.

"Mahatma Ghandi often said that the reason he could never become a Christian was that most Christians that he had met had just enough Christianity to make them miserable, just enough Christianity to inoculate them finding the real thing Christianity really represents. He often said that he never sought redemption from the consequences of sin, but redemption from sin itself.

"Jesus was most emphatic when he said: 'Woe unto you, lawyers, for you have taken away the keys to knowledge ye entered not therein yourselves, but them that were entering, ye hindered.' Jesus never minced words. He drove the money changers and merchants from the Temple. You know, I find this very interesting: if Jesus did not approve of the things going on in the church of His day, how do you think he would feel about the modern traditional church of today?

"I will hazard a guess: Jesus is just as unhappy today over the merchandising of men's souls as he was then.

"El Morya wrote long ago that if a messenger to you was an ant, heed him. Never make the mistake of thinking that the messenger's beneath you. If a person looks upon a person as 'beneath' him whether educationally, morally, or economically, he is in danger. Often God sends a messenger to us to test our humility.

"Such a messenger sits there in chains waiting for your verdict. His life rests in your hands.

"Recall, if you will, the Scriptural story of a man named Naaman, the captain of the host of the king of Syria. Elisha pointed out the captain's snobbishness quickly when the captain's donkey spoke.

"Yes, if the messenger to you is a flea or an ant, heed it. It could very well be your response to the message counts in Heaven. Do not ignore the messenger. If the messenger repeats things you already know, perhaps you got the wrong message.

"Because of the preconceived ideas of the Jews as to the social standing the coming Messiah would have, because of these notions, the Jews lost out on the most important thing ever to come their way. Remember where the three Kings sought the new born king? They did not look for it in Herod's palace.

"As a whole, mankind, today,,makes it almost impossible for God to save them. The traditional church member today is so accustomed to turning over the responsibility for worship to preachers and deacons and elders that they are living in total ignorance. Instead of receiving the message from God directly, they have been lulled into letting the preacher do all the thinking for them and are living in total ignorance of the will of God for their lives.

"Joe is different in that he preferred to teach the people into receiving the real message of God, the real teachings of Jesus. He tried to show us how to lay aside our favorite concepts with which our whole being has been clothed. Joe tried to rid us of the dust of tradition. Jesus exemplified this when He laid aside his cloak and washed the dusty feet of His disciples.

"Today's disciple must realize that if his feet are to be washed, he must do it himself. He knew that this is vital if each of us were to become clean and clear-headed. He taught that each of us must walk in the steps of the Master. Joe's crime was that he tried to teach the Christian of today to stand outside the frozen orthodoxy of the traditional church, because he knew that there was no room there for inferior self-correction. Yes, Joe is different. Joe is an 'odd-ball', and that's the reason he sits here today in chains.

"The knowledge of the truth and right, and the mental strength to follow that right should be the ultimate goal of education. Joe again attacked a sacred cow. He was different. Bring out the torture instruments, the boat is rocking. Joe believes that each child must be exposed to the Bible and the teachings of Christ. Today's children get little or no Christianity exposure at home and none in school. Today's school heads are running scared, for expensive lawsuits make them fearful of even silent prayer in schools. Look at an average school-aged child today. He gets no religious training at home, none in the schools, and if he happens to attend a traditional church with a friend, some preacher scares the living daylights out of him by telling him he has one foot in hell and the other on a banana peeling. The traditional church teaches that God will forgive sin yet place emphasis on don't do this and don't do that thus leading to impossible living.

"The question of morals including sex, the questions of one's relationship to to his peers or to society as a whole, the relationship of society to an individual are all questions of such tremendous importance that it is dangerous to leave these to tradition. Yes, Joe is different in educational beliefs.

"Ladies and gentlemen," Dennis was tiring, "I am not here to give you a lecture on education, but I do want you to see the real person sitting here in those chains. I imagine that most of you realize that education in this country is in awful trouble. Something is badly wrong when a young girl can't have her ears pierced without parental consent, yet that same girl can have an abortion without consent or knowledge of her parents. In Russia today, Bibles are freely and openly distributed to school kids, but in our beloved United States, it is illegal to give a Bible to a student, yet condoms are shoved into the hands of children. Some in a choice of colors.

"Eighty per cent of our high school students get drunk once a week Yes, we are in trouble, and the traditional church has failed the people by keeping silent and doing nothing as all of our life is drained from us. Mustn't rock the boat. Mustn't call attention to yourself. The defendant sitting there bucked the system and on every hand exposed the danger to us and as a reward he sits there with his life in your hands.

"Ladies and gentlemen, I have talked overly long, but my heart is breaking. I have tried to convince you that the world needs this man. I beg you not to deprive the world of all the good he has left in him. Don't remove him from our lives. Like Jesus, 'he openeth not his mouth' in his defense He is angry with me for even making this plea to you on his behalf. In closing, I ask only that when you retire to that room there and in the sanctity of that room, I ask that each of you ask yourself the question: what evil could this man possibly do? What real, honest-to-goodness-proof has been offered here today? If, by chance, you are on speaking terms with God above, ask Him how you should vote today. I thank you." Dennis went and took his place beside Joe and put his head on his arms and wept copiously.

CHAPTER NINETEEN

CNN News seemed to make the biggest splash over the airways and in the pages of the newspapers of America. The newspaper headlines were as high as three inches in some publications and almost without exception, used the trial in Bethany as the lead story.

Our Fathers House Minister Convicted!

The pastor of one of the largest church in the nation was convicted yesterday of Capitol Murder. The trial had been held in the Bethany County Courthouse with the jury setting the punishment as death by lethal injection. The case had attracted national and international attention because of the many extraordinary things connected with it.

For example: admission to the court room was by ticket only and these could be obtained only through the office of the sheriff's office, and as a result, none of the pastor's followers had been able to get a ticket. Only those friendly to the prosecution were allowed in the courtroom. The prosecution put the defendant at the murder scene, and gave a motive the desire of the pastor to keep her quiet about her pregnancy.. The other very unusual thing about the trial was that the defendant refused to allow any defense whatsoever.

The pastor was defended by one of the key men in the church, Mr. Dennis Stephens. Stephens made a most eloquent appeal to the jury that left many in the courtroom in tears.

When the verdict was brought in the crowd cheered so loudly and paraded about the courtroom that veteran jurist, Seth Thomas cleared the courtroom for fear of the defendant's life, for many spectators slapped the pastor before the room was cleared.

The pastor was well known for his ability to heal the sick and for giving sight to the blind. He was controversial in that he held his church services on Saturdays which he claimed was the true sabbath, and because he refused to celebrate Christmas and Easter saying that Jesus had not been born on December 25 and that Easter was a pagan holiday in celebration of the heathen god Ishtar.

In less than three years the pastor and his flock had erected a multimillion dollar plant and had just completed a church school with a capacity of almost 1000 students. Included in the plant were 27 homes for senior citizens called Senior Citizen Haven.

Spokesmen for the church were aghast at what had happened, and assistant pastor, Gary Kilpatrick said that the work would continue as it was the expressed will of the convicted pastor that it do so.

The convicted man has asked that no appeal be made, but state law requires that every death sentence case be automatically appealed to the State Supreme Court. This is just another example of the blurring of the lines between church and state in America. The Jim Bakker affair rocked the nation a short time ago, and this was followed closely by the Jimmy Swaggart affair of his being found in a motel room with a prostitute. This latest sensation has caused a nation to pause and wonder when these events in the religious community will end.

This writer could be called one of the vast 'unchurched' people in the country today. He personally darkens the door of a church and feels that the church is one of the institutions in America should disappear from the face of the earth. He went on to express his knowledge of the Bible by citing the last book in the Bible, Revelation where the church is mentioned thirty times in the first five chapters where John, the Revelator, describes the Tribulation, a time when untold agony will cover the earth. Thereafter, John does not mention the church at all. This writer asked a well known theologian why the church was not mentioned during the agony period, and he explained that the church had already gone home to be with God.

Most people want to see the church stick around saying it is good to see the spires piercing the blue of the sky, but how much more can people stand? How many more of the Bakkers and the Swaggarts and the like will it take until something is done about it?. If the sentence of the convicted pastor is upheld, the man will be executed early next year."

Lee Roy Neal

The TV and news stories went into great detail. Many pictures of Our Fathers House flashed across the screens of the world. Interviews with Mary and Joe's brothers and sister were done to the point of nausea.

Deacon Bandy should have felt elated, and he did, to a degree. He had feasted on his hatred for Joe for years, and now that he was legally rid of the focus of his venom and would soon be rid of his presence, he felt a sort of let-down, and this he could not understand. He simply would get on with the rest of his life.

Bandy was the personification of hate, not passionate, not ardent, for it was not an emotional hate. His hate could be likened to the hate of a doctor for germs or disease and illness: a hate like that of a raccoon's hate for a dog; like the hate of a minister for sin. Bandy's hate was an action hate: a hate that tends to destroy everything in sight and it was this hate, born in the bowels of hell itself that was the instrument of Joe's coming death.

And Bandy had thoughts of his own death and often asked himself for a definition of Death, and found no easy definition. He knew of no simile for the word. He thought of one definition: "death is the absence of life' but that did not define death, it merely stated what death was not.Christians maintain that death in the designated moment (assigned by God) is birth. Sure, birth to eternal life, but what about premature death such as Joe's in a few months? What about abortion? In one sense, Joe's coming demise was an abortion. Is any kind of life to be preferred to no life at all?

So, Deacon Bandy hated Joe. Why? Usually, when one person hates another it is for a reason: because he is different, being not like or what the hater is. Actually, too be hated by one such as Bandy should be a compliment for who would like to be like a walking personification of hate such as he? In reality, any person who is one whom everybody likes, everyone, without exception, never made a mark in the world; never made a ripple on the waters of life. Did not Jesus say somewhere that if the world loves a person, that person was no part of Him? Gospel writer wrote that 'he who is loved by the people of the world or he who loves the things of the world, is God's enemy.

If one is to truly believe what the Scriptures teach, Bandy's day was coming, for Jesus, Himself, said: "Be sure your sins will find you out."

The morning following the verdict the sheriff in his freshly starched uniform got into his washed and waxed squad car backed up to the jail entrance of the Bethany jail, and with Joe, still in cuffs and leg irons shoved him into the back of a vehicle designed to transport prisoners to the State penitentary. The back compartment of the vehicle was separated from the driver's seat by a heavy steel grill. The back doors could not be opened from inside the prisoner compartment. Before the door was closed, Joe looked out on the lawn and noted that the wind was making music in the giant oak tree near the building. He smiled at leaves playing jump rope on the gentle fingers of the wind. He sat on the hard seat as the vehicle sped away with sirens screaming and bells clanging, and the blue and red lights flashing.

The trip to the prison was about four hours driving away, and the sheriff and his deputy were thinking of the one sumptuous meal they would have before returning to Bethany, all on the county of course. As the vehicle drove toward the highway, Joe closed his eyes to the familiar scenes of his youth and his adult life that had been filled with happiness. He saw the steel gates of the doctor's estate where the insane woman had been healed. He saw the school building where he had spent many happy hours. He tried to draw a full breath, but his arms had been lashed to his body and he could hardly move his hands because of the steel bands. He suddenly realized that he had a monstrous pain in his temples. His apprehension and the pain quickened at the same time, and he felt that he had to use the bathroom, but he knew that his request would be met with stony silence, so he controlled the urge.

Suddenly he was filled with terror; more than any he could ever remember. 'How much more, Father,' he silently prayed, 'how much more?' One horrible word kept protruding into his thoughts, and he fervently pushed it aside. Dennis wanted to appeal beyond the state courts, and he was tempted to agree, but he pushed the ugly thought away and realized that he must 'drink of this cup' and he wanted to get it over with. One question hovered over all of his thoughts as he

Lee Roy Neal

sped out toward his final destiny. did he fear death? He had to admit that he would have to be insane if he did not fear death. Jesus had been quoted by Socrates when he said that death was simply a sleep. So, the average man asks himself, why fear death? If there was an after life, then it was all the better.

Joe knew that he must be brave, but somehow he did not feel brave. Didn't Jesus, Himself, in the garden ask God to take the coming death away? His exact words were 'let this cup pass from me'. If Joe showed any weakness during the coming ordeal the world would point to his weakness to the detriment of Our Fathers House. He resolved to remain calm and trust in God to supply the needed strength to do so.

Joe actual found himself sleepy and went to sleep. He woke up when the vehicle stopped. He looked up and saw the walls of the prison ahead.

CHAPTER TWENTY

The Death House was, as one would expect, a sad and foreboring place, just seeing it from the outside. The main building was constructed of red fieldstone, and it had been there almost a hundred years and it looked it. The main building was surrounded by a twenty foot high wall made of huge granite blocks, and the top of the high wall was crowned by coils of sharp barbed wire. In each cornor of the wall rose watch towers that went ten feet higher than the wall. The towers were open on four sides, and in each tower a man stood with a high powered rifle in his hands. The tower was manned twenty-fours each day. If a prisoner somehow managed to get over the wall, he would not take many steps until one of the rifles killed him, for the blast from a single bullet from these guns could neasily remove a man's head. In addition, atop of each tower was a huge search light that spanned the area during the hours of darkness, These lights revolved automatically, but could also be concentrated on any suspicious spot.

That late May day the weather was threatening with the low flying clouds dark and somber, for not a ray of sunshine was seen that day at the prison. The surface wind raised small clouds of dust around the wheels of the vehicle as the sheriff stopped the car. A guard walked from the gate house to the car and after identification was assure, the gates swung open and the vehicle entered. The sheriff and his deputy were always glad to be going out of these gates, for the atmossphere inside tended to make one's flesh clammy, for they could not help but realize that most people who entered those gates never emerged alive. Joe heard the gates close behind the car with a thud of finality. Suddenly, he remembered a verse from his English class in his senior year at Bethany High School. The teacher had passed out the verse, written in German, and had offered extra credit to any student who memorized it.

Lee Roy Neal

> *"Wer niesein Brot mit Triinen sass*
> *Wer nie die kummervollen Nicht*
> *Auf seinem Bette weinend sass*
> *Der kennt euch nicht, ihr himmlischen Micht."*

Joe had had an exceptional teacher in that senior year, and Joe was challenged, not that he had needed the extra credit, but that he longed to find what those foreign words meant, and part of the credit was to find the translationl He found it the first try in a volume of Great Books of the Western World.

> *"He who never ate his bread in tears*
> *Who never sat weeping on his bed*
> *Through long nights of anguish,*
> *He knows You not, You heavenly Power."*

Joe felt that those words had special meaning for him at that time, and most of the 250 mile ride to the prison he prayed. Being separated from the two men in the front of the car by a heavy mesh barrier that precluded any conversatiuon between the front and back of the car.

The vehicle approached the huge red building and stopped before an entrance door. As Joe emerged from the car, still chained and cuffed, he noticed a second building about 300 feet away from the main building. He learned later that this was the building where the executions took place. Joe surmised as much when he first saw it. It reeked of death itself. It was a low squat building constructed of the same red material, and the whole thing had a permeation of finality. Inside the death house was a holding cell. Here the condemned was taken 24 hours prior to the date with death. Here he was allowed only a visit from the clergy all other visits would take place in the larger building.

Between Joe's prayers enroute to the death house, Joe oft remembered a section of the Lord's prayer that went: "Forgive us our trespasses." He often wondered if perhaps that portion had been translated incorrectly. Should it not have been translated: "Smite us for our sins and iniquities". He had prayed and prayed to God to let this cup pass, that he might wake up and find that it was a horrible dream. He tried and tried to fathom what good his death would be for Our Fathers House. He felt that the disgrace of his ignominious arrest and convention and execution would hurt the work. Joe knew he was innocent, and he was aware that God knew it too. He knew that Bandy was the mighty force behind it all. Why, God? Why? He prayed in vain. It was as if God had turned away and was not interested in any way.

Joe was turned over to the officials inside, the sheriff receiving a paper stating that 'one live body had been received.' Not a person, a live body. Joe felt the irony of the whole thing. Joe had learned along ago that God never duplicated one of his creations. No two anything was exactly alike, no two snowflakes, no two leaves. No other person was like Joe, for he was a unique creation. Joe wondered and was thankful that there was none other like Bandy.

Prison clothing were issued after Joe had been mugged and fingerprinted. All the clothing, including underwear was dyed a bright red, actually a flourscent red, for the color of blood? He was then taken to a cell block in the heart of the building. This was the real death row. Prisoners who had a set date for execution were placed in cells in the order of their date with the needle. By accident or design, a prisoner enroute to the small squat building outside had to pass each cell to add to the pain of those left behind.

The cells were separated from each other by a cement block wall so the prisoners could not see each other. Each cell was eight feet square. One can imagine the size if two sheets of 4x8 feet plywood were placed on the ground side by side. A cot was hung from the wall and a thin mattress pad covered the springs and a sheet and blanket and pillow completed the bed. A comode without a seat and a small lavatory completed the furnishings. Prisoners wrote or read from the cot. The door had no lock and were opened and closed by an electric switch in the front offce. Prisoners could talk to each other but never face to face. They were allowed to play games such as checkers and chess, by reaching outside the cell to a board placed on the floor.

Joe was given the number WM-2285 with the WM meaning white male. In the office each name was listed with the date set for execution. There were 285 inmates on Death Row when Joe arrived and this matched the number he wore on his clothing. He learned that some of the inmates had been there for fifteen years and even more as their appeals moved slowly through the courts giving an inmate a sort of a sense of safety believing that he would never be executed. Many there were cling to life through some technical absudity.

Thew law seemed always to favor the felon. For one example: A man had wanted to divorce his wife in order to marry his mistress, but the wife refused, and the man had no legitimate grounds that would stand up in a court case. The husband knew that his wife could not swim, so he feigned reconcilliation and took his wife on a picnic-fishing outing. He got her in a boat in a deep body of water called a gravel pit. It was so named for it was the hole left after gravel had been taken away. The man deliberately capsized the boat and his wife drowned, He was convicted and sentenced to death, but the appeals court threw out the conviction saying that the original indictment had failed to say what liquid the woman had been drowned in. People talked of this for days and wondered what liquid would be out in a hole in an open field? Beer, perhaps?

Another case, equally as absurd was the case of a wealthy lady in a nice car driving from Oklahoma City to Dallas, gave a ride to two young men hitchhiking along the road. As they neared Dallas, they told her to stop at a small road saying that they lived just down the way. They pulled her from the car and stomped her to death and drove off in the car, They were aprehenned and convicted and sentenced to death and the case was overturned because the original indictment had notn specified what the men had stomped the woman to death with.

To try to fathom the evil in men such as these and Deacon Bandy, one had to try to understand the inherent evil in all men. Christianity taught that all evil came from one source: Adam, the first man for he was the beginning of all sin on earth, sin that began in the garden long ago. Joe had often preached that if the true church was to survive in this century then all must be taught that evil men are clever with a main goal of being able to survive, and most of them do survive and they abound everywhere. However, he said, each evil person has within his being a time clock that is ever ticking toward self-destruction.

It is imperative that all people who sincerely try to follow the teachings of the true church must know that a 'smoking gun' is ever pointing at the very heart of Christianity. Often within the traditional church lurks the vital germ that could grow and wipe man from the face of the earth. This evil swaggers with its many faces in the daylight hours, but at midnight, when one's guard is down or when he is asleep, this evil strikes at the very vitals of God's people.

Crime is the enemy, he often preached, crime that is condoned by society either willfully or by not taking a firm stand when found. Abortion which is another name for legalized murder has killed more people in the past twenty years than were killed in all the wars this nation has waged in its history. For every two people who enter an abortion clinic, only one comes out alive. Where were God's soldiers when this dastardly evil was legalized? They were not protesting in the streets for sure. When, at long last, people woke up to the evil among them, it was then too late. The roots had grown deeply.

Criminals flaunt the law, and if they are convicted for some heneous crime, they laugh knowing that the chance they will actually be executed are remote.

One, when a blind man ran into aa wall, he explained that he had found the end of the world. The courts of today, legalized by law abiding people have erected such a wall that could very well herald the end of the world.

Joe had not been in his cell one full day when he learned that the 'death watch' was in effect. A prisoner was to be executed that very night. Although all prisoners in that building were under a sentence of death, none expected ever to be executed. The scourage of America, the ACLU had a representative present each and every day looking for some flaw, some inane thing, such as what liquid the woman drowned in or with what did the men stomp the woman to death.

But on this night, a prisoner who had been on death row for twelve years was scheduled to take that 'last walk'. This man who had been convicted by a jury of his peers had been fed and clothed at a cost of $100 per day for all those days, had been kept in style with free medical care and air conditioning and entertainment and after appeal after appeal (paid for by the tax payers) had finally come to the end of the trail. He was scheduled for the long sleep.

The man who was the star of the proceedings was known as Luke the Kook. He had been given that name because he had feigned insanity from the day he had been arrested, He was talking a lot tonight, even laughing how he had used the insanity ruse to great effect. Each person allowed him to talk about anything, and while no one could see the fear in his eyes, he could not hide the fear in his voice. He had had his last meal, and he had made his will. The beneficiciaries had been his felow inmates. To one he left his TV, to another his small space heater, and to another he had left his collection of Playboy magazines.

Luke had witnessed many people leave that cell block during his twelve year tenure. He knew the routine well as did every other resident. But today, it was his turn, and his voice showed his panic. Today, the entourage would stop at his cell and open his door. When the door slid open they would be there ready for him. He didn't want to die. Hadn't he said many times that he was sorry for killing that little giirl who was only five and who, had he let her live, would be a senior in high school today?

Before, when it was someone else's turn, Luke had gotten a vicarious mosochistic thrill in seeing others disappear from their midst, taken away never to return. He never believed that he would be the star of the proceedings. Yet, tonight, it was different. The bells were tolling his name. perhaps, he thought wildly, perhaps if he stayed way back in his cell, they would forget about him.

"Maybe," his voice sounded hollow and made Joe feel pity, "maybe they will forget about me and not come." He gave forth a hollow giggle that caused each inmate to feel a chill, for each man was not 100% sure that one day he would be in Luke's shoes.

"Nah," someone shouted. "They always come. They never fail. They tie a red string around their finger so that they can't forget to come." Again someone gave forth an hollow laugh. Each man's thoughts were, as always, putting himself in Luke's position.

The main door opened and each man held his breath. A few subdued voices and then the marching feet coming ever nearer to that last cell in the row. Closer, and ever incessantly closer.

"Here they come,Luke!" one sadist cried gleefully. They didn't forget. This is your night. You are the star tonight, Luke!" He clapped his hands for a short space of time.

The death procession stopped before Luke's cell and the door slid open. Luke retreated the few steps to the far end of the cell. The man who all evening had been a chatterbox was suddenly struck dumb. His vocal chords froze, his jaws clamped together as if he were already a corpse whose body was cold. He was filled with the greatest fright he had ever before known.

"It's time, Luke," the warden spoke softly.

"I don't wanna die." Luke yelled and every man heard the terror.

"You have to go, Luke." The warden could not help but feel pity, even though he remembered the murder and rape of an innocent child.

"But I dowanna die."

At a nod from the warden two guards entered the cell and took Luke by his arms and propelled him to the hallway. Luke's feet and legs refuse to bear his weight, and the two guards lifted him along the aisle. As he passed each cell, the men saw that Luke's neck was a rubbery mass as if it had been broken. His eyes were open and filled with fright. Some prisoners turned their back to the scene knowing that some day they were scheduled to be in Luke's place. Joe was on his knees by his cot and he was praying for the condemned man.

The procession stops at a small room next to the office where Luke was changed into other clothes. An hour before Luke had been showered and now he was being dressed in his shroud with loose sleeves and legs and where, after the execution, he could be quickly placed in a coffin that waited near the room of death.

The men moved out the door and along the walk to the death house. The minister led the way reciting David's Psalm: "The Lord is my Shepherd, I shall not want..."

The night before had belonged to the man who was to die this night. He had been allowed to choose the food for his last meal. He selected the programs for the TV set in the hallway. He was given a Bible if he asked for it. He was given a new set of playing cards if he wanted to play solitaire all night. He was allowed to go to the Crow's Nest to have a last visit with family and friends, and he could call on the phone anyone he wanted to talk to. It was indeed his night.

But now, the last the men saw of Luke was his lifeless body being carried down the hall toward his destiny. Toward oblivion.

CHAPTER TWENTY-ONE

The Crow's Nest was a room built atop the Death Row building. It was built so that a condemned man would have a private place to make a final visit to anyone he cared to be with. Usually the visitors were family. Some of the men never took advantage of the Crow's Nest because they had no friends and no family they wanted to contact. This place was indeed a humanitarian act on the part of the state.

'Luke had not taken advantage of the place, for he had no friends and he never mentioned family. As he was propelled toward the squat house of death, he seemed unaware of what was happening. It could have been nature's way of helping him to cope. The guards could not miss the sight of the short squat building just a few yards away. They hated this part of their job and each guard had to take his turn. They hated to enter the place for any reason, saying it felt as if it were filled with departed spirits. many laughed at their fellow guards' suspicions saying that it was only a combination of stone and mortar and wood and steel. But many believed that the building had taken on a life of its own and had clothed itself in terror, for many men had died within its walls and no end to the dying was in sight.

The building at one time housed an electric chair, but now a more humane method of execution was in place. Some had wanted to replace the chair with the gas chamber, but the needle finally was chosen. Most penal authorities chose lethal injection for they said that it was painless, but no one had ever returned to give proof of the fact, The procedure was rather simple, on the face of it.

The condemned was placed on a gurney and six broad straps were securely fasten around his body and secured to the gurney. When they were tightened, no movement was possible except for the head of the victim. This had been the results of many executions when the condemned would sometimes move and pull the needles from the body.

The chemicals were basically the same in all states, but some small variation could be found. First, a standard saline solution was administered in the right arm. Next a large dose of Sodium

Thiaphenethol was administered. All the while, the condemned is in full view of the witnesses, but the person administering the chemicals was in the next room hidden from view. The Thiaphenethol is a sort of 'don't care' drug similar to that given in hospitals before surgery. Next a solution of Pidulan is shot through the tube leading to the body. This is simply a muscle relaxant. Finally a solution of Potassium Chloride is sent down the conduit, and as this enters the blood stream it causes the heart to stop beating. It usually takes less than six minutes to complete the execution.

Witnesses usually stand in a small room adjacent to the death chamber and watch through a large plate glass window, The witness room is about fifteen feet square, Witnesses entering the room see that a curtain is drawn across the window, and after the gurney with the condemned is in place and all of the tubes are exact, the curtain is drawn No recording devices of any kind are allowed.

When the curtain is opened revealing the scene showing a man lying on a table with tubes leaving his body and disappearing through an appeture in the wall. The warden steps forward and reads the death warrant, His voice is heard through a michrophone overhead. The warrant had been written by the judge who presided over the trial of the prisoner. Sometimes these words are those of a judge who has died, especially if the appeals have taken years. Next the warden asks the condemned if he has any last words,. He is given permission to speak. Some speak, some do not say anything. The warden then announces that the sentence will be carried out. The chemicals begin flowing, and all watch a fellow human being change worlds. In a few minutes, a doctor enters the room with the ever present stethoscope around his head. He places the mike on the person's chest in several places, Next he takes a small pen light and raises each of the eyelids. "I now pronounce this man dead." and it is over.

Luke the Kook fought the procedure each and every step of the way. He fought when the straps were tightened and only his head moved from side to side with spittle coming forth sometimes spewing into the air. He was doing this when the curtain opened. Some of the witnesses closed their eyes. Luke gave no evidence of hearing the words of the warden and stayed mute when asked if he had any last words. The chemicals began flowing and the head stopped moving and soon Luke lay dead having paid with his life for the life of the little girl.

Back on death row all was silent. The TV was blank and no radio blared into the air. Each man was busy with his own thoughts and they did not make for pleasant company. Joe could not see any of the faces, but he imagined that each man was going each step with Luke. He was sure that each man asked a common question: 'Am I the next one?' He was sure that each man was praying in his own fashion praying that their lawyer would step up work on the appeal.

Less than three weeks from Joe's date of execution, he had the use of the Crows Nest. It was his first trip to the top of the building. He saw that all four walls were of plate glass. Every movement in the room could be seen by the guards on the towers, but they could not hear any words spoken there. Comfortable chairs were scattered all about in a vain effort to make the place seem 'homey'. A large table occupied the center of the room where conferences could be held. Many last wills had been composed there.

Joe had not been in the room long when Dennis, Gary, and Mark came in. Joe noted from the expression on each face that each of the men was living his moment of truth. He saw how they tried, but failed, to hide their feelings of sorrow. Joe had directed that this would be the last visit he would have from anyone. He explained that he needed to be alone during his last days.

After he had greeted each of them and each man had said the things in his own mind and heart, Joe took charge. He stood and walked around the room as he spoke.

"Friends," he began, licking his lips in the old familiar fashion, I don't think I need to tell you that I am innocent of the crime of murder. You also know that I feel that Our Fathers House will grow tremendously after I am gone. I honestly see it growing into a world wide church. I also know that I was placed here on Death Row by the Traditional Church, or members of it. My crime has been that In was rocking the boat, because I did not travel in the ruts made for hundreds of years by people who know little or nothing of God's will. I could never be pastor of a people who demanded that I make them comfortable in their religion., a sort of a reward after a week of hard work.

Again
If Christ Came Again

"I really felt sorry for the phariasees who led the mob to the crucifixion of Jesus. They were so weak. Bandy is the perfect example of the Twentieth Century Phariasee. He is a coward. I would have been a coward myself if I preached only what the people wanted to hear. They wanted to be soothed into a complacency that required no action on their part. Gary, I ask that you preach that religion is a call to arms to fight Satan and all of his army and all the evil that they represent. I just want each of you to know what my crime was and it was to preach the truth. Bandy and all of his imps used this to put me here.

"You know," and Joe stopped pacing for an instant, He sat at the table and the three men leaned forward. Joe's voice was lower. "You know, I feel sorry for Bandy, I feel compassion for him."

"I don't feel any compassion for him,," Gary blurted out.

"Gary," Joe placed his hand on his friend's arm. "You are like Peter who, when they came to arrest Jesus, drew his sword and cut off the ear of a nearby man. "try to get the bitterness out of your heart and try to as the kids say today, 'go with the flow'.

"You have a tremendous job before you. All of you do. Into your capable hands I throw the torch to carry on the work of Our Fathers House, which we have built together We each believe that this is indeed Christ's church, His bride as it were.

"One can march in parades,, attend patriotic meetings, even enlist in the army, but most of this will be of little value. The real fight, God's fight, is in the battlefield but is instead in the schools and on the streets and even in our homes.

"My beloved friends, early in the battle ahead you must know that our greatest enemy is the media. Please understand when I say that there are thousands of good people in the media, but each must adhere to the dictates of their bosses or else their livelihood will vanish. Remember how fast they pounced on the Jim Bakker and Jimmy Swaggert stories. It seems that they take a great glee in expounding the fall of a man of the cloth. The media as a whole acts as if their aim is to kill the church in America and they are to lead America into being a godless nation.

"Remember that they work in a subtle manner They had much to do with removing prayer from our schools as if they were fearful that some praying child might find God. They have the leaders of the public schools running scared. No, Gary, pray to God to rid you of this hatred for Bandy. Leave him in the hands of God, for God will take care of Bandy and his ilk.

"Gary, preach that religion is not a clock wound once a week. Show them that true religion is not shown by a sober expression. Teach them instead that religion is a cloak to wear with pride each and every day. Show them that religion is a brightly colored bridge between man and God. Don't be afraid to depict Jesus as a happy man who wanted happiness for His followers. Jesus laughed, he enjoyed fishing, He even drank some of that wine at that wedding in Cana., Show Jesus laughing with the little children.

"Gary, above all, be true to yourself. Be in constant prayer that each of you stay in the blessed will of God. Each of you be just, and you will pay for it when some other Bandy attacks you. The world is not ready for a truly just man, for it fears him, and the average man, knowing his own limitations, just can't understand a man who is just and good. That's the reason that the world is an armed camp against them. That's why the good and the just are the targets of the evil of the world. Remember that good men are always being assassinated or murdered or crucified or driven into the arms of poverty.

"Dennis," Joe turned and spoke directly to his friend. "Our Fathers House would not be where it is today except for you The school would not be a reality except for you financial and legal expertise. I ask that you continue your faithfulness to the work which we all believe to be God's true church."

"Joe,' Dennis actually blushed. "I can't see that I did all that much. Somehow, when I first met you, I felt that you were on the right track. All I did was climb on board the band wagon. I will, of course, continue as always and try as best I can to follow the will of God. Gary and Mark have done as much or more than I have. I feel that Bandy will expect Our Fathers House to go down and end up on the auction block now that you have been removed from the helm. I speak for Gary and Mark and promise you that that day will never come."

"Mark," Joe now gave his attention to the youngest member of his team, "You may not realize it now, but the children who attend our school are in reality a vanguard of many many different Our Fathers Houses."

"I realize that Joe, but often I feel so unworthy and helpless."

"To me these are the signs of a true calling. You will be sensational."

The room was silent for an instant, and Gary broke the silence after a time.

"Joe, we have done something that we hope will meet with your approval. It is a most ticklish matter, but one that has to be broached. We three feel that we have to discuss this with you before...before.." He could not say the words.

"Let me, Gary," Dennis broke in, "We have selected a place on the church property to take your body.

We felt that a nice memorial would be good. We hope you don't mind." He took a deep breath and held it until Joe spoke.

"Beloved," Joe began, "The time has come when I must reveal something to you. I have to tell you something before I leave you. I, myself, did not know this until three years ago." He paused, licked his lips and then continued. "I was born without an earthly father. My earthly life has paralleled that of Jesus in many uncanny ways. I have been very close to my Heavenly Father all of my life, even as a young boy. I have followed the teachings of God to the best of my ability. I believe that this is the reason Our Fathers House has been so successful."

The expressions on the three faces were incredible.

"Joe," Gary said, "that is all the more reason that we should let Dennis file an appeal, get a stay of execution. We can't let this horrible thing happen."

"God allowed it to happen once before," Joe smiled, and each person in the room seemed at a loss for words. Joe stood and walked toward one of the windows and stepped upon a sort of stage that was there. It had been a place where guards used to stand, but complaints of lack of privacy, removed the guards.

Joe stood on the platform and looked down at each of his friends. Nothing was said, but the men could not take their eyes from Joe's face. Later, they tried to explain what happened, but Joe's face began to glow. There was simply no other word for it, his face glowed as if a light within illuminated it. As they watched, the glow spread to Joe's hair and the tips of each hair seemed to resemble a fireworks sparkler. Next his red prison uniform seemed to be shining so brilliantly that it hurt their eyes.

Not a word was spoken but all three men fell on their knees and put their faces to the floor. Outside the guards saw the light and thought that the Nest was on fire, yet they could see no movement or flames, only the brightest light they had ever seen. Later, each was sure that they heard a voice as plain as day: "This is my beloved Son in Whom I am well pleased."

The next thing the men knew was that Joe was shaking them gently telling them that it was time to go. The leave taking came and went before another question could be asked. Each man was filled with sorrow, with perplexity. They made their final farewells and returned to their car realizing their helplessness over the events beyond their understanding.

They spoke little on the return trip to Bethany. Each man was bearing his own sorrow silently…a sorrow that was in reality a private hell for each of them.

CHAPTER TWENTY-TWO

Deacon Bandy seemed to be the happiest man in Bethany the day he opened his post office box and saw that he had received an Official letter from the State. He could feel his blood pressure rising as he savagely ripped open the envelope. He almost tore it trying to get the page unfolded. He read the typed words rapidly and emitted a loud "All Right!" causing other postal patrons to look at him carefully.

"I still have a little pull in high places," he spoke aloud but to no one in particular. He waved the letter in the air, an evil look covering his entire face. "I have permission to witness the execution of that sex fiend preacher." People back away, saying nothing, and one man, the owner of the Western Auto store surmised that at last the old man had become certifiable. As the deacon left the post office, people shook their heads in dismay.

Early Summer was Bandy's favorite time of the year. It was a time when the crops were at long last free from a killing frost and the year had settled down to passing without passion. He took steps much lighter than usual as he walked from the post office to his home on Buffalo Street less than four blocks away.

The morning sun had already finished showcasing the reds and the pinks on the canvas sky and was blending them into a pure blue of the sky. Ground covers mostly of English Ivy lined the walks, and late tulips were waving their heads in beauty. Cannas were bursting out of their confinement and one yard was completely covered in Shasta daisies. Leaves in the trees were turning a darker green, and some early peach tree buds were showing lots of pink. Birds in the trees had almost finished building their nests. God was again showing His handiwork to heedless man.

Bandy reached his house and since his wife was still sleeping got a cup of coffee and walked around the back yard. In some unexplained fashion, his thoughts returned to the teen-aged Joe working behind a mower, a happy smile covering his bronzed face. He saw him at the table sinking perfect white teeth into a cookie. A left over leaf and the wind were playing tag along a flower bed. Bandy seemingly caught himself and shook his evil head and forced his mind to return to the present. He patted his shirt pocket to reassure himself that the letter was had not been a dream. To one passing by, the deacon looked over ninety years old, yet he had just turned seventy-two. He wore a rumpled suit today an his tie had a gravy stain, but he could not decern it for the cataracts now rendered him near blind. Even the rumpled suit needed a visit to the cleaners. He wore raunchy clothes in a sub-sconscious way to convey to the holier than thou denizens of Bethany that he didn't give a snap of what they thought of him nor what was said about him.

His beady eyes were almost slanted closed, and his jowls drooped pulling the edges of his mouth down so that he was always wearing a frown. His head was completely devoid of hair and his skin was the color of wet concrete. His red veined ears still had a porcine look with a slight forward slant, and his nose was even larger than in the days of his youth. His drooping cheeks were well lined with hideous gullies. Above his white eyebrows were deep parallel furrows. He had a plainly visible 'turkey neck' these days. He took another sip of the hot coffee and returned to the house and taking the letter from his pocket, he laid it on the bar, He set the coffee cup aside and took his glasses, for he wanted to savor the glee once again.

The letter was an answer to his request to the state that he be allowed to witness the execution which was now only three days away. "Wow!" he said aloud. His arch enemy would be dead this time next week and all Bandy troubles would be at an end. He left the letter where his wife would be sure to see it and walked to his store. He was the only employee now for his business had shrunk to almost nothing. As usual, he walked with his head down as if looking for a lost coin, and since Joe's conviction, even those whose friendship he had valued seemed to shun him. He was ashamed to look a fellow citizen in the eye for fear they could read the black secrets of his heart.

He stood in the idle store and once again tried to analyze his relationship to Joe. He had long ago come to the conclusion that his amonosity had had its beginning when the boy had unconsciously attacked some of his cherished beliefs and tenets long ago when Joe had been little more than a lad. Bandy had never realized that all men, all sensible men, often questioned anything that touched their lives. Had not Christ posed a question while on the hated Cross?

Unthinking faith, Joe had once said in one of his sermons, is in reality no faith at all. Was not Job filled with questions amid his lamentations while lying in a pile of ashes? Most members of the traditional church simply refuse to think, leaving it to the man behind the lectern. No questions, no meditation, swallow whatever was said with or without a grain of salt. And for goodness' sake, never ask a question for your ignorance might show.

The Christian Church almost collapsed 1700 years ago. It had become stagnant, fruitless and was close to death and disappearance. At that time, the church was a laity based organization. Then the power of directing the church was turned over to the clergy. Where the church had been a laiety-driven organization it then became a professional-driven thing. The average "Christian" got into the habit of paying their preachers to do their thinking.

In the Twentieth Century the effect was very plain: Six days to follow Mamon and kick up the heels and do 'whatever felt good' and then to the church to wear the mask of piety to salve the conscience, the 'still wee voice' for that session last Tuesday with that other man's wife in that other man's bed no less. Go hear a canned sermon that had absolutely nothing to do with inspiration. Put in a few coins if your sins had been more than usual. Buy a window or a pew in the new building and fondly look at it each week and tell yourself what a good person you are, the brass plate telling one and all of your generosity.

In the average traditional church today, the Holy Spirit is allowed little or no power. If a person shouts 'Amen!' a mite too vociferously, he, more than likely, will be tapped on the shoulder by an usher and told that this is a worship service. The programs of the church and its activity or like planned by a few 'leaders' of the organization and then usually in secret. The layman is bound and gagged and told not to do the dangerous exercise of thinking or else. If some foolish layman dares to offer an idea or opinion alien to the thoughts of the 'establishment', he is quickly forbidden to speak or teach or preach in the church. In many cases, even able teachers, professionally trained, living exemplary lives, are ostricized and silenced and giving to understand in subtle ways that the only contribution they are expected to make was money.

For example, if a layman, having experienced and survived the worst week of his life enters the church in an effort to find solace finds that there is no time to help him lick his wounds, finds that there is no time for him, no time to get a pat on the shoulder from a fellow layman or anyone in authority. Time was precious and must be spent in 'worshipping'. It is pathetic that the staid, traditional beliefs of the traditional scream out, 'don't fold, spindle or mutilate' me.

Where, please tell, in the traditional worship service does the Commands of God given a chance to flourish? When is there time or a sermon that would provoke a listener to good works? To confess your sins to someone? To comfort a fellow brother or sister? To 'bear another's burden'? To teach the Word to others on Sunday mornings? The Sunday morning meeting is the only time that the church comes together, and it is rare if not impossible to find a body with a plan or a desire to teach the people to follow the commands laid down by God.

Imagine a person failing to exercise his divine gift of thinking. Some people even treat the act of thinking as a sin. 'Listen to the preacher,bub, he knows what is good for you.' Surely Satan get's his greatest thrill out of seeing the way church services are conducted today. God does not desire or want 'namby-pamby' Christians. Proof of this can be found in Revelation when God said he would 'spew them out of his mouth'. God has no use for a weak slave. He ordained for his Chosen to make an overt fight against evil. Perhaps that is why he allows the Devil to roam the earth 'seeking all whom he may devour'.

The evening before his scheduled execution, Joe had been unable to go to sleep. He lay on his bunk, and as per his request, no radio or TV blasted the silence. All at once, an alien feeling permeated his entire body. He found it hard to draw a full breath of air. He felt a vapor in the air as if his lungs stopped taking in the vapor. His temples began to throb. The agony in his mind and body worsened. He had a sudden urge to urinate and went quickly to the toilet and did so. For the first time in his memory he actually felt terror. He gasped for air with his heart throbbing. He closed his eyes and simply said one word, "Father." Almost simultaneously he felt in his ears the simple answer: "Son."

Suddenly his heart leaped, and he was filled with the most happiness and a sense of total understanding. He had thought that he understood it all before, but now, it was if he had suddenly been permitted to get inside the very mind of God Himself. All of the questions were answered, and all the unknowns were revealed to his complete satisfaction. He lay there and was filled with rapture and love for the Father. It was as if God had pulled aside the curtain of the future and had allowed him a long and loving look.

Joe got from the cot and fell to his knees. He had a profound urge to worship God. He wanted to shout his praises for God's goodness. If Joe had told anyone of his true feelings at that moment he was sure that the execution would be postpones for he would be rated as insane and thus not subject for execution.

Suddenly, it was gone. The spirit, the feeling, the passion. All that was left was a serene feeling and a clear understand that all was well and that God was in complete charge. He was happy! He lay down and fell into a peaceful sleep much like a baby in its mother's arms.

Joe's keepers were all convinced that Joe was a good man and had no business of being there. In no way, they had often discussed among themselves, that he was a criminal, for they knew a criminal when he was in their charge, and Joe was a man apart, not one of those usual denizon of their care.

The thing that had started this feeling among the guards had happened shortly after Joe's arrival at Death Row. One of the prisoners had had a severe asthma attack and was unable to breathe. His rales and screams frightened all of the other inmates. As the man was loaded on a gurney enroute to the hospital, Joe realized that the man would not survive the trip. As they came in front of Joe's cell, he asked for permission to lay his hand on the dying man. Already the sick man was purple and the chest had stopped moving. The men moved the gurney near Joe's cell and Joe reached through the bars and gently laid his hand on the dying man's head. The wet head was turning from side to side and fright pained the man's features. Joe said in a calm voice: "In the name of Jesus, my sick brother, Be Healed!" Instantly, the color returned to the man's face and he sat up on the stretcher and smiled as he began taking in huge draughts of air.

"I'm okay! I can breathe," he shouted The medic made a quick examination and shook his head and the prisoner was taken back to his cell.

Afterwards, the guards found themselves stopping by Joe's cell to talk The men confessed their worries on almost every subject imagining from Aids to losing their jobs.

"I believe that it is natural for a man to fear," he had once told a guard, "Even a small baby has a fear of falling. Only a faith in God can deliver a person from from his fears. David always remembered in his Psalms what God had done in the past, and that gave freedom from fear, for he knew that God had delivered him from harm in the past and He would do so in the future. Once," Joe continued when speaking to a man who had come to him and spoke of his young son who was to undergo surgery the following morning, "I found a small bird that had fallen from its nest. I picked him up and fixed its little wing and even built a small cage for him. I fed it worms and would often talk to it. You know, that little thing never did lose its fear of me. When it was well, I let it loose and it flew away in fright.

"That bird is like many Christians today. They never realize that in rescuing that bird, I was like our Heavenly Father. I offered love and safety for the bird, even gave it a name. I cared for it just like God cares for His people today. Today, people shun God and the Bible, and their ignorance is pathetic. A recent survey showed up the ignorance of the average American regarding the Bible. Ten per cent of those surveyed thought that Joan of Arc was the wife of Noah, and that thirty-eight per cent believed that the Old and New Testaments were written immediately after Jesus died. God extends His hand to people in trouble today, people such as yourself filled with fear for the safety of your child facing the operation tomorrow. Usually man shuns the helping hand proffered and backs away just as the bird did.

"Man backs away from the offered hand of the Heavenly Father acting in much the same way as did the stupid little bird." Joe smiled as he saw the lines of worry leave the guard's face. "You know, I feel that man with all of his intelligence is more stupid than the bird for man was given the greater gift of reason where the bird had none."

That last day of earthly life of Joe was uneventful. He had no possessions to leave to the other inmates. Before he had left Bethany, he had made a will leaving all of his earthly possessions (which were meager) to Mary. He ordered a simple meal, and the guards marveled at his demeanor, his calmness, as if he knew something others did not know.

He remained in his cell and quietly lay on his bunk, and when the time came, the warden came to his cell and found Joe on his knees praying. Joe said nothing when the warden announced that it was time. He stood and walked with the entourage to the office where he calmly donned the execution clothes In the death house, Joe quietly climbed on the gurney and closed his eyes as the straps were put in placed and tightened. He winced a little when the needles were placed in his arms. The drugs were administered soon after the warden read the death sentence orders. Joe was asked if he had any last words. He remained mute. At a nod from the warden the chemicals began in the IV's: sodium pentothal to induce unconsciousness; pancuronium bromide to halt respiration; potassium chloride to stop the heartbeat.

The last of Joe's cell mates had seen of their friend was when the gurney was pushed toward the green door, its rubber wheels making slight squeaks on the tiled floor. The green door opened automatically and then closed when the party had cleared it. It closed with a sort of finality.

The End
or
The Beginning?

Printed in the United States
707900002B